PR Women with Influence

Carolyn Bronstein, DePaul University, *Series Editor*

VOLUME 6

The AEJMC—Peter Lang Scholarsourcing Series
is part of the Peter Lang Media and Communication list.
Every volume is peer reviewed and meets
the highest quality standards for content and production.

PETER LANG
New York • Bern • Berlin
Brussels • Vienna • Oxford • Warsaw

Juan Meng and Marlene S. Neill

PR Women with Influence

Breaking Through the Ethical and Leadership Challenges

PETER LANG
New York • Bern • Berlin
Brussels • Vienna • Oxford • Warsaw

Library of Congress Cataloging-in-Publication Data

Names: Meng, Juan, author. | Neill, Marlene S., author.
Title: PR women with influence: breaking through the ethical and
leadership challenges / Juan Meng, Marlene S. Neill.
Description: New York: Peter Lang, 2021.
Series: AEJMC—Peter Lang scholarsourcing series; Volume 6
ISSN 2373-6976 (print) | ISSN 2373-6984 (online)
Includes bibliographical references and index.
Identifiers: LCCN 2020036073 (print) | LCCN 2020036074 (ebook)
ISBN 978-1-4331-6514-6 (hardback) | ISBN 978-1-4331-6510-8 (paperback)
ISBN 978-1-4331-6511-5 (ebook pdf) | ISBN 978-1-4331-6512-2 (epub)
ISBN 978-1-4331-6513-9 (mobi)
Subjects: LCSH: Women public relations personnel. | Public relations. |
Women executives. | Leadership in women. | Sex discrimination against women.
Classification: LCC HD59 .M3848 2020 (print) | LCC HD59 (ebook) |
DDC 659.2082—dc23
LC record available at https://lccn.loc.gov/2020036073
LC ebook record available at https://lccn.loc.gov/2020036074
DOI 10.3726/b15025

Bibliographic information published by **Die Deutsche Nationalbibliothek.**
Die Deutsche Nationalbibliothek lists this publication in the "Deutsche
Nationalbibliografie"; detailed bibliographic data are available
on the Internet at http://dnb.d-nb.de/.

© 2021 Peter Lang Publishing, Inc., New York
29 Broadway, 18th floor, New York, NY 10006
www.peterlang.com

We would like to dedicate this book to our families, Angelina, Po-Lin, and Terry, for their unwavering support, encouragement and love.

Table of Contents

List of Figures   ix
List of Tables   xi
Foreword   xiii
Preface   xv
Acknowledgments   xix

Section I In Search of PR Women with Influence: Definition, Meaning and the
    Unbalanced Leadership Scene
Chapter One: Introduction: Why Study PR Women with Influence   3
Chapter Two: Research Design and Methods: How We Approach This Subject   25

Section II A Grand Landscaping: National Survey Results on PR Women's
    Leadership and Ethical Challenges
Chapter Three: Situational Barriers to PR Women's Leadership Advancement   41
Chapter Four: Ethical Leadership and the Meaning of Building Influence to
    Women in PR   63
Chapter Five: PR Women's Leadership Development and Participation
    Opportunities   85

Chapter Six: Balancing Professional and Family Responsibilities: The Roles of
  Instrumental Support and Mentoring   107

Section III Deep Conversations: Insights and Lessons from Current Women
  Leaders in PR
Chapter Seven: How Women in PR Define and Achieve Influence   129
Chapter Eight: How Women in PR Approach Ethics Counsel   157
Chapter Nine: Support Network: Work-Family Integration and the Influence
  of Mentors for Women in PR   173

Section IV Synthesis and Summary: Building a Constructive Path to Drive Change
Chapter Ten: Building an Ecosystem: A Constructive Path to Leadership for
  Women in PR   197

Index   213

Figures

Chapter Three

Figure 3.1. Leaders' vs. non-leaders' perceptions on situational barriers   49

Figure 3.2. The impact of situational barriers on women's leadership advancement in public relations   52

Figure 3.3. Top issues causing the underrepresentation of PR women in leadership   54

Figure 3.4. Professionals' projection of issues to be improved in next three years   57

Chapter Four

Figure 4.1. Using strategies to build and expand influence when providing leadership and ethics counseling   71

Figure 4.2. Readiness for providing leadership and ethics counseling by race (in percentages)   74

Figure 4.3. Do top communication leaders demonstrate ethical behaviors? Opinions of surveyed female professionals (in percentages)   77

Figure 4.4. Perceptual gaps on ethical leadership along the hierarchy reporting line   78

Figure 4.5. Assessment of principled behaviors of ethical leadership by race   80

Chapter Five

Figure 5.1. Resources for leadership development supported by
organization as observed by female professionals (in percentages) 89

Figure 5.2. Resources for leadership development as perceived by different
ethnic groups (agreement in percentages)   90

Figure 5.3. Resources for leadership development as perceived by age (in
percentages)   91

Figure 5.4. Leadership participation opportunities as observed by
respondents (in percentages)   93

Figure 5.5. Leadership participation opportunities by race (agreement in
percentages)   95

Figure 5.6. Organizations' efforts in supporting women's leadership
advancement: in the past and in the future (mean scores as
rated by different ethnic groups)   96

Figure 5.7. Performance of top communication leaders: evaluations on
key dimensions (in percentages)   99

Figure 5.8. Evaluation on top communication executives' leadership
performance as reported by different ethnic groups   101

Chapter Six

Figure 6.1. The impact of work-life conflict as perceived by female
professionals (in percentages)   110

Figure 6.2. The impact of work-life conflict as perceived by different age
groups   110

Figure 6.3. The impact of work-life conflict as perceived by different
ethnic groups   112

Figure 6.4. The impact of work-life conflict compared by leadership status 113

Figure 6.5. The impact of work-life conflict compared by organizational
type   114

Figure 6.6. Coping strategies to manage work-family conflict, from most
preferred to least preferred (in percentages)   116

Figure 6.7. Numbers of mentors in professional career reported by female
professionals (in percentages)   120

Figure 6.8. The dynamics of mentors' gender changes as the number of
mentors increases (in percentages)   121

Tables

Chapter Two

Table 2.1. Demographic profiles of interviewed female executives 30
Table 2.2. Primary areas of job responsibilities in communication 32
Table 2.3. Respondents' ethnicity 33
Table 2.4. Respondents' tenure in current organization 33
Table 2.5. Reporting level and ethnicity 34
Table 2.6. Respondents' education levels 34
Table 2.7. Salary range by organizational type 35
Table 2.8. Salary range by hierarchical reporting level 36
Table 2.9. Scope of leadership roles and functions 37

Chapter Three

Table 3.1. Organizational type vs. gender of direct supervisor/manager. 43
Table 3.2. Organizational type vs. gender of the highest ranked
            communication leader. 44
Table 3.3. Assessment on situational barriers and their influence on
            women's advancement. 46

Chapter Four

Table 4.1. Defining the meaning of having influence: Perspectives from women in PR. 66

Table 4.2. Women of color define the meaning of having influence with strong opinions 68

Table 4.3. Assessment of principled behaviors of ethical leadership as demonstrated by the highest ranked communication leader. 76

Chapter Five

Table 5.1. Performance of top communication executives: evaluations on key dimensions 98

Chapter Seven

Table 7.1. Preferred influence strategies 134

Chapter Eight

Table 8.1. Preferred influence strategies for ethics counsel 168

Foreword

A book of this caliber, on one of the most important topics in public relations, is long overdue. For decades scholars have been writing about the disparity in gender and racial representations in public relations leadership. The field heavily employs women, but they tend to be in technical roles. Leadership positions are reserved for men. White men in public relations often ride a "glass elevator," a term coined by Christine Williams (1992), as they quickly ascend to the top, passing many deserving women along the way. It is a phenomenon that happens most often in professions favored by women, and public relations is no exception.

Today the public relations industry is at a crossroads with enormous pressure to adapt to society's rapid move toward diversity. The field must find balance in its gender and racial diversity at all levels of the industry. And, further, it needs to create a culture that mentors and educates women who move into leadership. This book offers a roadmap to help agencies, corporations and other entities address the disparity in leadership and build strong female leaders who can manage through complexities.

Through its 51 interviews and large-scale survey of public relations professional women, this book offers the most thoroughly researched discussion of the intersection of gender and race in public relations leadership. Authors Meng and Neill draw insights from their multi-method research approach on female leaders and the challenges they face. The book uncovers the struggles and successes of women in leadership, and it offers strategies to help women build influence and leverage skills for success in their roles. Female professionals will find the insights in this book valuable as they face ethical and leadership challenges in today's workplace.

One of the most important contributions of this book is the list of recommendations that the book makes for organizations to improve their leadership pipeline for women. Following the suggestions in this book will help companies and agencies create a workplace environment that cultivates strong female leaders.

Whether you are a public relations scholar, educator, practitioner or student, this book will challenge your thinking about the profession, and it will help you understand how together we must move forward with an eye toward leadership development for diverse professionals.

Strong leadership is critical to any organization and any profession. As former practitioners in the field, we have witnessed much of what the book describes first-hand. And, we are thrilled to support the work of Meng and Neill. The Arthur W. Page Center and The Plank Center are proud to co-sponsor this research.

Denise Sevick Bortree, Ph.D.
Director,
The Arthur W. Page Center for Integrity in Public Communication
Penn State University

Karla K. Gower, Ph.D.
Director
The Plank Center for Leadership in Public Relations
The University of Alabama

Reference

Williams, C. L. (1992). The glass escalator: Hidden advantages for men in the "female" professions. *Social Problems, 39*(3), 253–267.

Preface

The inspiration for *PR Women with Influence* came to us in the fall of 2017 at the PRSA International Conference in Boston. At that time a substantial amount of research had already been published criticizing the public relations profession for lacking racial diversity and inclusion, skewed gender representation at top leadership, persistent pay gap between men and women, whites and nonwhites, and frequent ethical transgressions that undermine ethical public relations practice. The wide variety of topics in which these studies were conducted inspired us to develop a project with the objective of bridging the current ethical and leadership challenges facing the women in public relations and the most urgent need to diversify the profession. In essence, by turning our focus on women in public relations and examining the ethical and leadership challenges they are facing, our purpose is to stimulate scholarly research from the perspectives of ethics and leadership development that supports public relations education, advances theory building in public relations literature, stimulates change, informs practice, and transforms the profession to be more diverse, equal and inclusive.

Career advancement and leadership development continue to be challenging for women in public relations over the decades, but what better way to overcome the barriers than to learn from the experiences of women who have identified the obstacles and found ways to overcome them. With this in mind, we grounded this book in rich empirical evidence gained through two phases of research conducted

in the field: original survey and interview research with women in mid-management and senior-level positions in public relations and communication. Although
the text presents and analyzes a wide range of topics and issues related to women
and ethics and leadership practice in public relations, every attempt has been
made to present our research in a clear, concise and comprehensive approach.
Several unique contributions were made throughout the production of the book.

First, this book examines the joint topic of ethics counseling and leadership
challenges that women in public relations have to manage in order to empower
themselves and their followers to achieve leadership and carry out ethical responsibilities. Secondly, research presented in this book does not only enrich the body
of knowledge in women and leadership in public relations, but also provides
research-based insights for understanding identity- and gender-based leadership
development skills and ethics counseling strategies. Lastly, we dedicated research
efforts to examine the additional challenges faced by women of color in actual
practice.

Through these unique contributions, this book presents a current and compelling picture of women in leadership in public relations and ethics by providing
a reflection and discussion on the following topics:

- Situational barriers to women's leadership advancement in public relations;
- The meaning of building influence to women in public relations;
- The strategies to set out principles that uphold the core values of ethical
  leadership;
- Women's leadership development and participation opportunities in public
  relations;
- The crucial supporting roles of mentoring and sponsorship in leadership
  advancement;
- The support network for balancing work-family integration; and
- The participation and support of a multitude of sectors in building a con-
  structive leadership path for women in public relations

By building upon thoughtful responses and rich insights from current female
professionals in real-life situations, this book provides an in-depth presentation
of ethics and leadership theories in public relations and communication management. Together, these insights build a roadmap for younger generations
and women of color who aspire to enrich their leadership capacity along their
career path.

This book also provides unique contributions to public relations education as
it is appropriate for advanced undergraduate and graduate courses in public relations, strategic communication, ethics, communication and business management,

leadership theories, diversity, equity and inclusion to facilitate critical thinking and special topic discussion. There is a dearth of books specifically addressing the joint topics of ethics counseling and leadership focusing specifically on the experiences of women, despite the fact that women represent the majority of professionals working in public relations. Such need is addressed in the Commission on Public Relations Education 2017 Report on Undergraduate Education. Therefore, this book is particularly well suited as a supplementary text within public relations curricula, both within this country and globally. This book also would be useful as a text in student activities, continuing education, professional learning and training, and special workshops and certificate programs on women, ethics counseling, and leadership development in public relations and communication management.

Acknowledgments

We would like to thank the many organizations and individuals who helped us carry out this research project and produce this book. Foremost, we are especially grateful to The Arthur W. Page Center for Integrity in Public Communication at the Penn State University and The Plank Center for Leadership in Public Relations at the University of Alabama for sponsoring and funding the research project. Both Centers were excited about the project from our initial discussion of it.

We want to thank the women executives and practitioners in the field of public relations and communication who set aside time to be interviewed and surveyed for this study. Their experiences, thoughtful responses, and rich insights illuminate this book.

We would like to acknowledge all of the diligent and talented people who are part of the AEJMC—Peter Lang Scholarsourcing Series, Volume 6. As always, special thanks goes to Carolyn Bronstein, the Series Editor, and the members of the Series Editorial Board, including Carolyn Kitch, Radhika Parameswaran, Gregory Pitts, Katie R. Place, and Meghan Sanders, for their guidance, comprehensive reviews, valuable critiques, and encouragement throughout this process. Erika Hendrix, the former Acquisitions Editor for Media, Communication, and Performing Arts at Peter Lang, worked with us closely to ensure the successful transition of this project from the editorial committee to the production. Their time, energy, and oversight contributed significantly to the quality of the Series and ensured its success.

For their very capable and efficient work during the production phase, we would like to thank the following individuals: Jacqueline Pavlovic, manager of the Peter Lang's U.S. production, Ashita Shah, editorial assistant, Sarath Kumar, the Production Editor from Newgen KnowledgeWorks, and the rest of the production team.

Similar to the women in our study, we have benefitted from the counsel of mentors such as Dr. Bruce K. Berger, Dr. Bryan H. Reber, Dr. Mia Moody-Ramirez, and Dr. Minette Drumwright for their unwavering academic support. Finally, we would like to thank our spouses, Po-Lin and Terry, for their patience and perseverance with this 3-year project. Without the support of these individuals, the completion of the book would not have been possible.

—Juan Meng
Marlene S. Neill

In Search of PR Women with Influence

Definition, Meaning and the Unbalanced Leadership Scene

This is the introduction section of the book, which provides background and a framework leading our research project.

Chapter One reviews literature regarding different perspectives of leadership research in public relations and introduces the leadership framework on which this book is based with an emphasis on the gender inequality in leadership positions for women in public relations. By doing so, we present the five leading research questions that guided our study and research design. Chapter Two continues with a detailed explanation of our research design. The interview and online survey methods are documented in this chapter. The demographic profiles of the female communication professionals who participated in our interviews and survey are presented in Chapter Two as well.

CHAPTER ONE

Introduction: Why Study PR Women with Influence

According to a Pew Research Center survey on women and leadership in 2015, most Americans find women indistinguishable from men on key leadership traits such as intelligence and capacity for innovation. Some continued and recently updated corporate research also finds that women in leadership positions were perceived "just as—if not more—competent as their male counterparts" (Zenger & Folkman, 2019, June 25). In addition, many agree that women are stronger (or scored at a statistically significant higher level) than men on a wide variety of leadership competencies, ranging from taking initiative, practicing self-development, being compassionate, displaying high integrity and honesty, inspiring and motivating others, building relationships, to well organized and structured at work (Women and Leadership, 2015; Zenger & Folkman, 2019).

However, this general agreement on leadership competencies at the perceptual level does not change the unbalanced scene between men and women in leadership roles, as well as the percentage of women sitting in the corporate boardroom in the U.S. and globally. The efforts on filling the leadership pipeline did not take care of the problem itself. A number of industry reports make clear that women still face the reality of underrepresentation in leadership positions across various industries. Zenger and Folkman's (2012) longitudinal research on men and women leaders in the workplace has found that the majority of leaders (64%) are still men. Moreover, the higher the level along the hierarchical reporting line, the more men there are (Zenger & Folkman, 2012). Zenger and Folkman's 2019 study reveals that only 4.9% of *Fortune 500* CEOs and 2% of *S&P 500* CEOs are women. They further claim that the numbers of women residing at the top leadership level are declining globally and the gap widens for women of color.

PR Women in Leadership

The public relations profession has been criticized for lacking racial diversity and inclusion. At the same time, the gender representation in the industry remains skewed at the top leadership level. The *PRovoke* published an article in 2015 addressed that while women make up 70% of the PR workforce in the U.S., they only hold about 30% of the top positions in the industry (Shah, 2015). According to the U.S. Bureau of Labor Statistics, women make up 71.4% of those employed in the public relations industry in 2019. The ethnic makeup of the public relations industry in the U.S. is 89.8% whites, 8.0% Blacks/African Americans, 0.4% Asian Americans, and 1.4% Hispanics/Latinos (U.S. Bureau of Labor Statistics, 2019), which presents an urgent need for organizations to develop and implement effective diversity and inclusion initiatives. The skewed gender and racial representation in the industry also contributes to the existence of a pay gap between men and women (Chitkara, 2018). Such pay gap becomes even greater when comparing white PR professionals to non-whites when all other variables are held constant such as tenure, education, location, job type, gender, etc. (Shah, 2017).

When reviewing communication leadership research done in the most recent years, results from the past three Leadership Report Card studies released by The Plank Center for Leadership in Public Relations found that men and women in PR actually value the dimensions of public relations leadership similarly (Meng, Berger, Heyman & Reber, 2019). Nearly three thousand of surveyed public relations and communication executives in the U.S. in the past five years (i.e. 2015 to 2019) agreed that an effective leader in public relations should demonstrate a strong and consistent performance in:

1. Developing and sharing a compelling vision in communication,
2. Demonstrating a strong ethical orientation to guide communication actions,
3. Leading work teams to successfully resolve issues,
4. Developing productive relationships and coalitions,
5. Participating in organization's strategic decision-making processes, and
6. Developing effective communication strategies, plans and measurements to make valuable contributions (Meng, et al., 2019).

Comparable to what has found in business and corporate leadership research, men and women working in the public relations profession also share similar perceptions of leadership value (e.g. Meng & Berger, 2013a). However, when it is time to evaluate the performance of their top communication leader in the leadership dimensions mentioned earlier, sharp gender gaps arise between men and women in public relations. In general, men ranked their top communication leader's performance significantly higher than women did on all six leadership dimensions (Meng et al., 2019).

The more discouraging truth is this significant evaluation gap based on gender perceptions has not changed nor improved much in the public relations profession in the past five years, based on results from three Leadership Report Card studies. More sharp gender gaps are also found in job engagement, trust in the workplace, job satisfaction, organizational culture in supporting two-way communication, and stress factors in their jobs (Meng, Reber, Berger, Gower & Zerfass, 2019). In general, women in public relations feel less engaged, less satisfied with their current job status, and less optimistic about their future career development. They also feel less confident in their work cultures in sharing decision making and less trusting of their organizations in taking their opinions into account when making decisions.

Not surprisingly, the unbalanced gender scene has existed in the public relations industry for a few decades as witnessed by several benchmark studies done by pioneering feminist scholars in public relations research (e.g. Aldoory & Toth, 2002; Cline et al., 1986; Grunig, 2006; Hon, 1995; Toth & Cline, 1989, 1991; Toth & Grunig, 1993; Wrigley, 2002). The stream of feminist scholarship in public relations research has significantly contributed to our understanding of women's experience and perspectives in the public relations profession and the challenges faced by women working in the profession. Several recurring themes are confirmed by these early studies on gender issues in public relations. Some major ones include: 1) The noticeable salary disparity between men and women is prevalent (e.g. Toth & Cline, 1991); 2) The socialization problems of women who want careers steer women to self-select technical roles, as opposed to managerial roles (e.g. Cline et al., 1986; Toth & Cline, 1989); 3) The existence of institutional factors and barriers (or the glass ceiling) prevents women from being promoted or limits their advancement opportunities (e.g. Wright et al., 1991); and 4) The double standards women are facing between work and family force unfair choices and result in unfair treatment (e.g. Hon, 1995; Wrigley, 2002).

In their pioneering research examining the influence of gender on public relations practice, Grunig, Toth and Hon (2001) addressed the fact that with an influx of women into the practice of public relations in the past 20 years, the scene of a "new female majority" has created many professional opportunities and offered great potential for women in a profession "once considered a male bastion" (p. 6). However, over the years, women in public relations as competent individuals are still blocked from senior executive positions by invisible artificial barriers, or what we often refer to as a "glass ceiling" to describe the persistent barriers caused by attitudinal, structural and societal prejudices deeply rooted in the unconscious gender bias that women do not belong in senior leadership positions. The disturbing fact that the percentage of women in senior leadership roles in the public relations industry remains unchanged or without significant growth over the years makes it a compelling story to tell as well as an insurmountable obstacle to overcome.

In later studies of feminist scholarship in public relations research, the notion of promoting an integrative approach to help communication professionals, both men and women, balance work-life issues has become a new focus (e.g. Aldoory, Jiang, Toth & Sha, 2008; Grunig, 2006). Scholars have recommended a more contextual approach to consider the lives of men and women in public relations not only as practitioners but also as individuals. Scholars propose it is critical to have a work-personal balance continuum so communication professionals can measure their place on the continuum in various contexts to maintain health (Aldoory et al., 2008).

Recent scholarship in public relations research has widened the lens to explore more identity-related challenges for both men and women, including but not limited to race, class, sexuality, sexual orientation, country of origin, age, etc. (e.g. Daymon & Demetrious, 2013; Pompper, 2013; Vardeman-Winter & Tindall, 2010; Waymer, 2010; Waymer & Dyson, 2011). Scholars propose the intersectionality theory of public relations to present cases of how identities at various levels shall be understood in public relations practice (e.g. Vardeman-Winter & Tindall, 2010; Vardeman-Winter, Tindall & Jiang, 2013). Intersectionality theory focuses on how we have multiple "social identities," or categories to which we are socially recognized as belonging (Owens, 2003), so neither gender nor race alone would explain the entire story of an individual's lived experiences and access to opportunities (Collins, 1990; 2000; Mattis et al., 2008; Weber, 2001).

Research using this lens calls for efforts at multiple levels within the profession of public relations in order to create equal opportunities for all public relations professionals who operate diverse functions in public relations practice (e.g. Vardeman-Winter & Tindall, 2010). Scholars in this stream of research emphasize the ethical advocacy function in public relations practice (e.g. Fitzpatrick & Bronstein, 2006). They argue that public relations practitioners serve the publics' interests; they shall act as one of the responsible advocates for clients.

More recently, Golombisky's (2015) research updates feminist theory in public relations by defining gender with regard to performativity, accommodating "intersectionality as theory and method of accounting for positionality" (p. 390), and expanding the boundaries of public relations to embrace social justice to facilitate change and influence social transformation. These different streams of scholarship in public relations do not only enrich our knowledge in understanding the complexity of public relations as an evolving profession, but more importantly, they help the profession strengthen its identification in a meaningful, integral, and diverse approach.

Unfortunately, many of the challenges and issues identified and highlighted in feminist and extended scholarship in public relations continue to be present in today's profession. FitzPatrick (2013) calls for attention and actions to include more female professionals at the top level. Although women hold roughly 75% of the PR jobs in the industry, men still occupy approximately 80% of the senior leadership roles in various types of organizations. With the achievement of educational equality and changes in social attitudes towards men's and women's roles, one would assume that women in PR (or the "new female majority" as named by Grunig, Toth and Hon, 2001) would quickly move up the career ladder and create an inclusive scene at top leadership. However, we still face the reality that women in public relations have not achieved equality in communication leadership. So what's holding women in public relations back from top leadership positions?

Many of the challenges are well recognized as we addressed in the impressive literature of feminist scholarship and extended research in the past decades. But for women in public relations who have demanding careers, their work and personal lives are deeply intertwined while insufficient solutions are available. Such challenging reality inspires our thinking path and stimulates this research. By turning our focus on women in public relations and examining the ethical and leadership challenges they are facing, our original research has one primary purpose—to stimulate serious scholarly research from the perspective of leadership development and advancement that supports teaching, stimulates change, informs practice, and transforms the profession to be more diverse, equal and inclusive.

In short, our research is significant as it is grounded in relevant social scientific literature relating to women in public relations and leadership. We aim at expanding the exploration of leadership development by adding the perspective of ethical advocacy because we believe ethical leadership and effective leadership are interrelated. If women's capacity for leadership does not simply depend on their individual initiatives of goals and identities, how can they address other contextual factors within which opportunities for leadership rise? We use this fundamental question to consider both individual and contextual influences on leadership development and its outcomes. More specifically, we raise five important research questions to guide this research:

1. What do female professionals believe are the most critical attitudinal, structural, and social barriers affecting their leadership advancement in the profession?
2. What do female professionals believe are the top issues contributing to the underrepresentation of women in leadership in the profession?
3. How do female professionals define influence in their leadership path and develop strategies to build and enact their influence when providing leadership and ethics counseling?
4. What do female professionals believe can be done to help them balance the identity transitions between professional and family responsibilities?
5. How do female professionals perceive the role of mentoring as a key career-building strategy in leadership advancement?

As scholars and educators, we are obligated to be at the forefront of teaching and research on diversity, inclusion, talent management, and leadership in public relations education. The profession has an enormous need in ensuring equal access to leadership opportunities at both the developmental and participative levels. To make that possible, we need more knowledge about women's capacity and desire for leadership and how we can help improve the representation and advance the opportunities. Drawing on recent theory about leadership excellence in public relations and developing leadership expertise, our goal is to offer formal propositions in order to advance future research. We hope to build upon and extend previous work that has been conducted in this area as well as stimulate interest in scholarship in women and leadership in public relations.

The State of Leadership Research in Public Relations: Perspectives and Trends

Leadership is a "complex multifaceted phenomenon" (Yukl, 1989, p. 253). As communication is growing in strategic importance for organizations due to the rapid diffusion of new information, communication technologies, global competition, ethical dilemmas, employee trust and engagement challenges, and the growing demands from stakeholders for greater transparency and information sharing, the public relations industry is crying out for better leadership (Meng et al., 2019). Leaders in public relations are vital to the profession's and their organization's success, image, and future. Recent research on public relations leadership has confirmed that excellent leaders in public relations are crucial to leverage the strategic influence and value of public relations within and beyond the organization (e.g. Aldoory & Toth, 2004; Meng & Berger, 2013a; Werder & Holtzhausen, 2009).

Given the vast volume of the corresponding leadership literature from different perspectives and across multiple disciplines, including organization behavior, psychology, sociology, history, education, and political science, it is impossible for us to present all of them here. Our goal in this chapter is to provide a variety of perspectives on different streams of leadership research in public relations. We consider research that resides at the intersection of public relations and leadership. Within this broad category, we review recent research that conceptualizes, develops and investigates a "leadership" construct in public relations. Following this direction, we have adopted the definition of public relations leadership developed by Meng and Berger (2013a). According to their research, public relations leadership is "a dynamic process that encompasses a complex mix of individual skills and personal attributes, values and behaviors that consistently produce ethical and effective communication practice" (Meng & Berger, 2013a, p. 143). Consequently, excellent public relations leadership "fuels and guides successful communication teams, helps organizations achieve their goals, and legitimizes organizations in society" (p. 143).

In recent years, the topic of public relations leadership has received significant attention from scholars in public relations and communication management. Such research interest is evidenced by a plethora of research in public relations (e.g. Aldoory & Toth, 2004; Berger & Meng, 2014; Berger, Reber & Heyman, 2007; Gregory & Willis, 2013; Grunig, Grunig & Dozier, 2002; Meng, 2014; Meng et al., 2012; Meng & Berger, 2013a, 2013b; Werder & Holtzhausen, 2009; Zerfass & Huck, 2007). Previous research has focused on various aspects of leadership and its role in supporting public relations professionals as they apply different sets of leadership skills and knowledge (i.e. strategic decision making, ethical leadership, role and identity development, and transformational leadership) to enhance practice, participate in strategic decision making, and develop future leaders.

With its roots in the Excellence research in public relations, managerial leadership research, and organizational communication studies, the concept of public relations leadership is implicit in several theoretical perspectives in the field as investigated by different groups of scholars. In our review, we attempt to cover briefly those major perspectives to clarify the state of leadership research in public relations. We particularly extend our literature review to analyze the scope of research on women and leadership in public relations, and thereby to convey its complexity and challenges.

We hope to build upon and extend previous work that has been conducted in this area but with a strong focus on the developmental efforts in women's leadership advancement at both the individual and organizational levels. By placing gender-related issues and barriers in a leadership developmental context, we hope our research will address some of the profession's most pressing concerns, inform effective leadership practice, and stimulate changes that demonstrate some authentic progress on achieving diversity, equity, and inclusion (DE&I), not only among top leadership positions but also in the public relations profession.

Excellence and Role Theories

As one of the most comprehensive research projects in the field, the IABC Excellence Study identified key characteristics of excellence in public relations and provided a conceptual framework of public relations principles (Grunig, 1992; Grunig, Grunig & Dozier, 2002; Lee & Evatt, 2005). The well-known principles reflect characteristics and values that a public relations unit could (and should) have at the program, departmental, organizational, and economic levels. We also can view the principles as a conceptual framework for leadership as it implicitly recognizes the importance of leadership and its application in communication practice. Applying some of the generic principles to leadership, for example, we might conclude that: 1) public relations leaders should be involved in strategic management of the organization, 2) senior public relations executives should be empowered as members of the dominant coalition, 3) public relations leaders should possess a managerial worldview and professional knowledge and experience, and 4) public relations leaders should use and model two-way communication (Broom & Dozier, 1986; Dozier & Broom, 1995; Grunig, 1992).

This theoretical perspective suggests that, to achieve excellence in public relations and communication management, public relations leaders have a responsibility to explain "*why* public relations contributes to organizational effectiveness and *to what extent* by asserting that public relations has monetary value to the organization" (Grunig, Grunig & Dozier, 2002, p. 10). Specifically, researchers suggest that organizations must empower public relations as a critical management function, and relevant managerial role activities should be carried out (e.g. Broom, 1982; Dozier, 1984, 1992).

Dozier (1992) advocated that the leadership role must become a central part of a public relations manager's identity that facilitates communication between management and publics and is accountable for supporting a "rational problem-solving process" for the organization (p. 333). These identified managerial role activities reflect characteristics and values that a public relations unit should present as a managerial function to contribute to organizational effectiveness. Excellence theorists also concluded that an organization's structure and culture influence the role and effectiveness of public relations. They advocated for a "culture for communication," which is characterized by a participative work environment, a symmetrical system of internal communication, and equal opportunities (Grunig, Grunig & Dozier, 2002).

In addition, role theory in public relations research also explores gender issues as part of the early feminist scholarship. Roles research found that women were outnumbered by men in managerial roles as women were more often residing as technician roles (e.g. Broom, 1982). This widely accepted phenomenon also resulted in salary disparity between men and women as reviewed earlier and significantly increased women's frustrations (Broom & Dozier, 1986). Such gender role differences arise from the mismatch between the qualities traditionally associated with male leaders and those traditionally associated with women (e.g. Catalyst, 2007). Roles research in public relations makes clears that women's underrepresentation in leadership positions can be partly attributed to traditional gender expectations and roles (Broom, 1982).

The Contingency Approaches in Public Relations Leadership

Cameron and colleagues (e.g. Cameron, Cropp & Reber, 2001; Reber & Cameron, 2003; Shin, Cameron & Cropp, 2006) developed and tested contingency theory, which focuses on strategic and conflicted relationships between an organization and its publics. Extended from the contingency theory of strategic conflict management, the contingent perspective of public relations leadership emphasizes the uniqueness of each leadership situation by recognizing there is no universal model or a single best way to lead.

Contingency theorists propose that communication could be examined through a continuum "whereby organizations practice a variety of stances at a given time for a given public depending on the circumstance" to reflect the reality (Pang, Jin & Cameron, 2010, p. 18). Therefore, leadership effectiveness and the application of leadership skills must be contingent on the specifics of any given situation. Public relations leaders help strategically manage their organizations by making choices based on issues and actors in the external environment. These choices fall within an organization-public relationship continuum that ranges from pure advocacy to pure accommodation. Public relations may be accommodative in one situation but adversarial in another.

The contingent view of leadership suggests that public relations leaders must be able to assess external threats and opportunities, choose the right position on the continuum, and advocate effectively for their choices with organizational leaders. These contingency approaches highlight how leadership might vary across different types of situational variables. Presumably, such approaches reflect a situational theory of leadership (Waller, Smith & Warnock, 1989), where leaders also change and adapt their style, depending on the environment and circumstances. The contingent perspective is also reflected on individual traits and characteristics of the leader, ranging from gender, race and other background variables.

Power and Leadership in PR

Leadership involves influence. Therefore, the relationship between power and leadership is "inextricably intertwined" (Nye, 2010, p. 305). An effective leader combines the right amounts of hard and soft power skills in a social relationship to create and achieve shared goals. This perspective of leadership research in public relations explores how power can make public relations units more active, effective, and ethical in organization's decision making (Berger & Reber, 2006). Power relations scholars claimed that public relations is inherently political, and argued that "individual professionals can increase their influence if they become more politically astute, employ more diverse influence resources and tactics, and exert greater political will in organizational arenas where decisions are shaped through power relations" (Berger & Reber, 2006, p. 2).

Berger, Reber, and Heyman (2007) further explored factors which help public relations leaders achieve professional success and maintain their leadership positions. They found a complex set of factors and patterns linked to success, including communication and rhetorical skills; diverse experiences and assignments; a proactive nature; and strong relationship building, networking, and interpersonal skills. This perspective of leadership research emphasizes the importance of understanding how to combine power resources and leadership styles in different contexts in order to achieve the shared goals. Just as Nye (2010) addressed in power and leadership, "One cannot lead without power" (p. 306).

PR Leadership as an Integrated Process and Its Global Implication

Scholars in this perspective of leadership research adopted an integrated approach to develop and define the construct of leadership in public relations (e.g. Meng, 2014; Meng & Berger, 2013a; Meng & Berger, 2019), which is also the basis of the definition of public relations leadership we adopted as the foundation for this research project. Comprehensive research done by Meng and colleagues suggests that excellent leadership in public relations is a complex mix of six interrelated dimensions: self-dynamics, team collaboration, ethical orientation, relationship-building skills, strategic decision-making capability, and communication knowledge management and expertise (Meng & Berger, 2013a).

By taking a theory construction approach, Meng and colleagues proposed and tested the integrated leadership model in public relations and confirmed that all six dimensions of the leadership construct are largely complementary and related in a meaningful way (Meng, 2014; Meng & Berger, 2013a). Public relations leadership will not be effective in any isolated perspective, but rather, it should be seen and developed in a comprehensive and balanced manner. Through the integration of the leadership dimensions, public relations leaders will effectively embed organizational knowledge through the development of specific and strategic routines designed to manage communication practice and leverage the value of public relations practice to advance an organization's effective performance (Meng & Berger, 2019).

Testing and validating the six dimensions provides a foundation to develop a theoretical framework for excellent leadership in public relations. Drawing from existing public relations leadership research, Berger and Meng extended the integrated leadership perspective in a global context (Berger & Meng, 2014). As an extensive global research project, Berger and colleagues investigated the appropriate and effective leadership strategies and skills public relations leaders working in 23 countries in Europe, Asia, and North and South America could apply to manage key issues and challenges the profession faces.

Ethical Leadership in PR

Both industry leaders and scholars have advocated for public relations professionals to provide ethical leadership in their organizations, a role sometimes referred to as an "ethical conscience" (e.g. Bivins, 1992; Bowen, 2008, 2009; Fitzpatrick, 1996; Fitzpatrick & Gauthier, 2001; Ryan & Martinson, 1983). This perspective of leadership research develops the foundation that in the workplace, public relations leaders should be a central source of ethical conduct and guidance. This ethical leadership role is described as encompassing both ethics counsel regarding the concerns of various stakeholders and communication about values (Bowen, 2004; 2008; Neill, 2016; Neill & Drumwright, 2012).

The role of acting as an ethical conscience or counselor in public relations is consistent with the responsibility of issues management in public relations. With the purpose of preventing crises and protecting organizational reputation

(Wartick & Rude, 1986), public relations professionals serve in a leadership role by providing ethics counseling. The second responsibility associated with ethical leadership in public relations is values communication. Research in this area suggests it is important to develop communication strategies and programs to promote an organization's core values. It is even more critical to actually routinely disseminate those messages through various internal communication channels to promote the values of the organization (Neill, 2016; Sison, 2010).

Ethical leadership scholars emphasize that leaders must communicate their values and ethics because "if people do not hear about ethics and values from the top, it is not clear to employees that ethics and values are important" (Trevino, Hartman & Brown, 2000, p. 135). Consistent with this perspective, ethical leadership involves "the demonstration of normatively appropriate conduct through personal actions and interpersonal relations, and the promotion of such conduct to followers through two-way communication, reinforcement and decision-making" (Brown, Trevino & Harrison, 2005, p. 120). Based on these normative roles embedded in public relations leaders, it is appropriate and necessary to study exemplars from the perspective of ethical leadership in public relations.

Leadership Styles and Gender

In our review presented at the beginning of this chapter, we have summarized the stream of feminist scholarship in public relations that investigates the impact of gender on the profession. Taking a closer look, we were able to identify feminist scholarship that has specifically examined similarities and differences between men and women when applying leadership styles in public relations practice. For example, Aldoory (1998) interviewed female leaders in public relations to examine their language and leadership style. Aldoory found that women exhibited transformational and interactive styles of leadership, grounded in a situational context. Aldoory and Toth (2004) conducted one of the few studies that focused directly on gender and leadership in the field. They examined which leadership styles are the most effective for public relations and how leadership perceptions vary by gender. They found that practitioners strongly favored transformational leadership style over transactional style.

Overall, research done by Aldoory and Toth (2014) revealed few differences between female and male participants and their preference for leadership style. Public relations professionals have a strong preference of the transformational leadership style, but they also agree that the situational leadership style works well in various situations. Public relations professionals also mentioned the fact that women have fewer opportunities for leadership positions in the industry, though they believed that women make better leaders due to their perceived empathy, collaborative efforts and relationship-building skills.

Another pioneering study done by earlier feminist scholars (L. Grunig, Toth & Hon, 2001) documents the evolution of gender research in public relations. Although women today represent about 70% of the professional workforce, the pay gap is still a prominent issue. Scholars argued that issues of gender bias are the essential key drivers contributing to the skewed gender representation at top leadership level. Their research also documented the journey to top leadership is more difficult for women due to a number of historical and societal factors rooted in gendered stereotypes.

More recent research on women and leadership in public relations explores the dynamics of leadership and gender in the public relations industry by asking why women occupy fewer leadership and senior management roles in public relations (e.g. Place & Vardeman-Winter, 2018; Vardeman-Winter et al., 2014; Vardeman-Winter & Place, 2017). By analyzing existing literature, Place and Vardeman-Winter (2018) found several key themes in gender-related research in public relations leadership, which include: 1) lack of presence of women in senior leadership roles, 2) social constructions of gendered assumptions in assigning leadership roles, 3) gendered leadership styles associated with female leaders (i.e. the application of a transformational leadership style over other leadership styles), and 4) organization's reporting structure and its limitation in enabling women's leadership roles. Based on the review, they make a strong argument that "increasing women's presence in leadership roles in public relations is crucial to the overall success and progression of the industry" (Place & Vardeman-Winter, 2018, p. 168).

In short, previous research in public relations leadership suggests that leaders are crucial to: 1) increasing the value of public relations, 2) achieving effectiveness in and for organizations, and 3) helping organizations make good strategic choices and do the right thing. However, such conclusions do not reflect the imbalance between men and women in senior leadership positions in the profession. We do have some benchmark research addressing the marginalization of public relations women in senior leadership, but we need to reinvigorate serious research that undertakes the organizational, professional and social issues of women's under-representation in leadership positions in our profession.

Being successful in the field is still a challenge for women as reflected in the actual pay gap, the limited leadership advancement opportunities, as well as the ongoing battle to be involved, heard and respected in the organizational decision-making process. Therefore, our research is significant because it provides a unique and timely contribution on this topic by providing the rigorous theory-based social scientific study. Public relations women in leadership is a topic that has great potential for academic researchers and professionals. More pragmatically, by understanding the attitudinal, structural and social barriers women in public relations are facing, we hope our research could contribute to effective leadership development for women in PR who aspire to build their leadership capacity along their career path.

This book is thoroughly grounded in rich empirical evidence gained through two phases of original research conducted in the field. In the first phase, we designed and conducted a series of 51 in-depth interviews with current women leaders in public relations. The interviews provide compelling individual stories on (1) their own experiences in leadership advancement, (2) their challenges in navigating through organizational structure in building influence and achieving leadership roles, (3) their strategies to provide ethics counseling to senior leadership, and (4) the role of mentoring in supporting their leadership advancement.

The second phase of our research involves the design and recruitment of a national panel via an online survey. A total of more than 500 female public relations and communication professionals at different levels and with different years of professional experience were recruited. Through this online survey, multiple topics as related to women and leadership are investigated, including barriers to women's leadership roles in the profession, factors causing the underrepresentation, the meaning of having influence for female professionals, ethical leadership and consideration, female professionals' perceptions on organizations' efforts in making change, and their perceptions on work-family conflict and coping strategies. We understand that such challenges might be more intense for women of color in public relations. Therefore, that factor is carefully weighed into our sampling strategy and design by deliberately specifying the quotas on ethnicity and a few other demographic control variables. More detailed explanation on research design and demographic profiles is presented in Chapter Two.

Overall, we are confident that results from the two research phases will provide a current and compelling picture of women and leadership in public relations. By presenting insights based on current female executive's leadership developmental paths and leadership achievement experience, we want to highlight the role of mentoring in supporting female professionals' leadership development efforts and provide recommendations to younger generations and women of color in terms of leadership advancement and achievement. Joint efforts are needed to push for change and create opportunities. The profession is facing the trends that Baby Boomers are retiring at high levels while Millennials are moving into advanced levels of responsibility and leadership and Gen Z are beginning to enter the workforce. Therefore, advice and recommendations from current senior women executives will benefit those who aspire to reach senior levels. In short, by understanding the landscape of leadership challenges female professionals in the public relations industry are facing, we call for real actions to build a constructive ecosystem within the organization and the profession to embrace leadership for women in public relations.

Outline of the Book

The book presents and discusses current issues and knowledge around the subject of women and leadership in public relations. It is organized into four sections. Although each chapter focuses on a well-defined aspect of public relations leadership, many of these topics are interconnected at both the individual and organizational levels. As we suggest solutions and approaches to help guide future research and practice, we rely on a key underlying theme of the book—that women's leadership advancement in public relations shall be put into a developmental context and participative phase to drive change and track progress.

Our discussion of women and leadership in public relations begins in Chapter One with an overview of the book. By reviewing the current state of women in leadership in the public relations industry, we introduce five research questions on which this book is based. The review of different perspectives of leadership research in public relations provides a useful lens on organizing this vast field by emphasizing the need for more rigorous scholarship focusing on women and leadership in public relations. We present the case that the gender inequality in senior leadership in our profession is prevalent and deserves serious attention. Such underrepresentation in senior leadership positions for female PR professionals raises a fundamental challenge for current and future generations to overcome the leadership barriers along their career paths. Chapter Two outlines our two-phase research design, research methods and participants' demographic profiles.

Chapter Three addresses the longtime issues blocking women in achieving senior leadership positions. In the reality, some women achieve leadership positions in spite of attitudinal, structural and social barriers. Nonetheless, those barriers play a significant role in shaping their leadership development and coping experiences. Data from our research presents current situational issues and barriers as addressed by female professionals. Their perceptions on potential improvements of such issues and barriers within the next three years are also presented, leading to a discussion of what we can do to stimulate change and influence practice.

Chapter Four argues that the role of effective leaders is best understood not only in terms of their direct impact on decision making and organizational outcomes but more through their indirect influence to shape and achieve shared goals. In this chapter, we focus specifically on defining the meaning of having influence as female leaders in public relations. We investigate women's adoption of strategies in building and enacting influence when providing leadership and ethics counseling to senior leadership within the organization.

Chapter Five details leadership development efforts as perceived and expected by female professionals in public relations. We agree that the ultimate goal of studying leadership is to enable the development of leaders and contribute to effective leadership practice. Research on organization's leadership development is abundant, and this chapter tries to make sense of what has been done and what is more needed from the perspective of women in PR. To address the underlying theme of the book, which is to place leadership achievement into a developmental context, we particularly emphasize our analysis and discussion on leadership participation. We argue that leadership development is a prerequisite in leadership achievement. Conceptually and structurally, organizations are willing to allocate resources to build leadership training and advancement programs. However, perhaps most important, leadership participation is the real force that makes it happen.

In Chapter Six, we broaden our view of women and leadership by exploring how to balance professional and family responsibilities and how to build instrumental support at the organizational level. We also investigate coping strategies as the set of cognitive and behavioral processes initiated by female professionals in response to stress caused by work-life conflict. We argue that it is important to explore solution-based strategies as related to the coping situation in work-life conflict in order to maintain job engagement and inspire proactive strategy-seeking behaviors. Women in public relations specifically address the critical supporting role of mentorship in various coping situations, as well as along their overall career development.

Chapters Seven, Eight and Nine each focus on specific areas of women's leadership challenges: the deep meaning of leadership and influence as interpreted by current female leaders in public relations, examples of influence in actual practice, the obstacles women in general face in achieving influence, the unique challenges faced by women of color, the strategies they use to define and enact their leadership role as ethics counselors, and the roles of mentors in supporting their leadership development and achievement. By presenting our deep conversations with current female leaders in the industry, these three chapters provide more vivid examples and stories to further illustrate our findings outlined in Section III.

As a concluding chapter, Chapter Ten builds on all the earlier ones and summarizes our research findings and provides advice for young professionals. Key themes are presented by making an argument regarding how individuals, organizations, the profession, and the society can use some joint collaboration and persistent efforts in removing gender inequalities in leadership practice in the public relations profession.

In sum, the book is optimistic, portraying women and leadership as a stream of research within public relations. Such research efforts will not only address one of the profession's pressing concerns (i.e. the skewed gender representation in top leadership), but also help provide a deep understanding of how and why we study women in leadership. Despite the scale and the scope of the topic, we do not pretend for a moment that this book is comprehensive or covers all aspects of the topic. However, by providing empirically research-based insights, we believe our book offers a practical perspective for scholars, practitioners and educators seeking to integrate the subject of women and leadership development into their own research, practice, and teaching. It is clear that there still is much more we need to know and do to change this unbalanced leadership scene in public relations. This challenge poses a great opportunity not only for women but also for men. We hope that our research helps create a new future for women in public relations who aspire to reach the top and be a great leader. We hope that our efforts delivered in this book inspire more research, practice and teaching of gender-related leadership knowledge to develop better leaders for a better, diverse, equal, and inclusive profession.

References

Aldoory, L. (1998). The language of leadership for female public relations professionals. *Journal of Public Relations Research*, *10*(2), 73–101.

Aldoory, L., & Toth, E. (2002). Gender discrepancies in a gendered profession: A developing theory for public relations. *Journal of Public Relations Research*, *14*(2), 103–126.

Aldoory, L., & Toth, E. (2004). Leadership and gender in public relations: Perceived effectiveness of transformational and transactional leadership styles. *Journal of Public Relations Research*, *16*, 157–183.

Aldoory, L., Jiang, H., Toth, E. L., & Sha, B. L. (2008). Is it still just a women's issue? A study of work-life balance among men and women in public relations. *Public Relations Journal*, *2*(4), 1–20.

Berger, B. K., & Meng, J. (2014). *Public relations leaders as sensemakers: A global study of leadership in public relations and communication management*. New York: Routledge.

Berger, B. K., & Reber, B. H. (2006). *Gaining influence in public relations: The role of resistance in practice*. Mahwah, NJ: LEA Publishers.

Berger, B. K., Reber, B. H., & Heyman, W. C. (2007). You can't homogenize success in communication management: PR leaders take diverse paths to top. *International Journal of Strategic Communication*, *1*(1), 53–71.

Bivins, T. H. (1992). A systems model for ethical decision making in public relations. *Public Relations Review*, *18*, 365–383.

Bowen, S. A. (2004). Organizational factors encouraging ethical decision making: An exploration into the case of an exemplar, *Journal of Business Ethics*, *52*(4), 311–324.

Bowen, S. A. (2008). A state of neglect: Public relations as 'corporate conscience' or ethics counsel. *Journal of Public Relations Research*, *20*, 271–296.

Bowen, S. A. (2009). What communication professionals tell us regarding dominant coalition access and gaining membership. *Journal of Applied Communication Research*, *37*(4), 418–443.

Broom, G. M. (1982). A comparison of sex roles in public relations. *Public Relations Review*, *8*(3), 17–22.

Broom, G. M., & Dozier, D. M. (1986). Advancement for public relations role models. *Public Relations Review*, *12*(1), 37–56.

Brown, M. E., Trevino, L. K., & Harrison, D. A. (2005). Ethical leadership: A social learning perspective for construct development and testing. *Organizational Behavior and Human Decision Processes*, *97*(2), 117–134.

Cameron, G. T., Cropp, F., & Reber, B. H. (2001). Getting past platitudes: Factors limiting accommodation in public relations. *Journal of Communication Management*, *5*(3), 242–261.

Catalyst. (2007). *The double blind dilemma for women in leadership: Damned if you do; doomed if you don't*. New York: Catalyst.

Chitkara, A. (April 12, 2018). PR agencies need to be more diverse and inclusive: Here's how to start. Blog post. *Harvard Business Review*, available at https://hbr.org/2018/04/pr-agencies-need-to-be-more-diverse-and-inclusive-heres-how-to-start. Access date: October 15, 2019.

Cline, C. G., Toth, E. L., Turk, J. V., Walters, L. M., Johnson, N., & Smith, H. (1986). *The velvet ghetto: The impact of the increasing percentage of women in public relations and business communication*. San Francisco: IABC Foundation.

Collins, P. H. (1990). *Black feminist thought: Knowledge, consciousness and the politics of empowerment*. London: Harper Collins.

Collins, P. H. (2000). Gender, black feminism, and black political economy. *The Annals of the American Academy of Political and Social Science*, *568*(1), 41–53.

Daymon, C., & Demetrious, K. (2013). Introduction: Gender and public relations: Making meaning, challenging assumptions. In C. Daymon & K. Demetrious (Eds.), *Gender and public relations: Critical perspectives on voice, image and identity* (pp. 83–102). London: Routledge.

Dozier, D. M. (1984). Program evaluation and roles of practitioners. *Public Relations Review*, *10*(2), 13–21.

Dozier, D. M. (1992). The organizational roles of communications and public relations practitioners. In J. E. Grunig (Ed.), *Excellence in public relations and communication management* (pp. 327–355). Hillsdale, NJ: Lawrence Erlbaum Associates.

Dozier, D. M., & Broom, G. M. (1995). Evolution of the manager role in public relations practice. *Journal of Public Relations Research, 7*(1), 3–26.

Fitzpatrick, K. (1996). The role of public relations in the institutionalization of ethics. *Public Relations Review, 22*(3), 249–258.

Fitzpatrick, K., & Bronstein, C. (Eds.). (2006). *Ethics in public relations: Responsible advocacy.* Thousand Oaks, CA: Sage Publications.

Fitzpatrick, K., & Gauthier, C. (2001). Toward a professional responsibility theory of public relations ethics. *Journal of Mass Media Ethics, 16,* 193–212.

FitzPatrick, M. (2013, February 01). A strong case for female inclusion at the top level. *PRWeek,* retrieved from https://www.prweek.com/article/1276818/strong-case-female-inclusion-top-level. Access date: October 15, 2019.

Golombisky, K. (2015). Renewing the commitments of feminist public relations theory from velvet ghetto to social justice. *Journal of Public Relations Research, 27*(5), 389–415.

Gregory, A., & Willis, P. (2013). *Strategic public relations leadership.* New York: Routledge.

Grunig, J. E. (Ed.). (1992). *Excellence in public relations and communication management: Contributions to effective organizations.* Hillsdale, NJ: Lawrence Erlbaum Associates.

Grunig, L. A. (2006). Feminist phase analysis in public relations: Where have we been? Where do we need to be? *Journal of Public Relations Research, 18*(2), 115–140.

Grunig, L. A., Grunig, J. E., & Dozier, D. M. (2002). *Excellent public relations and effective organizations: A study of communication management in three countries.* Mahwah, NJ: Lawrence Erlbaum Associates.

Grunig, L. A., Toth, E. L., & Hon, L. C. (2001). *Women in public relations: How gender influences practice.* New York: The Guilford Press.

Hon, L. C. (1995). Toward a feminist theory of public relations. *Journal of public relations research, 7*(1), 27–88.

Lee, S., & Evatt, D. S. (2005). An empirical comparison of the predictors of excellence in public relations. *Corporate Reputation Review, 8*(1), 31–43.

Mattis, J. S., Grayman, N. A., Cowie, S. A., Winston, C., Watson, C., & Jackson, D. (2008). Intersectional identities and the politics of altruistic care in a low-income, urban community. *Sex Roles, 59*(5/6), 418–428.

Meng, J. (2014). Unpacking the relationship between organizational culture and excellent leadership in public relations: An empirical investigation. *Journal of Communication Management, 18*(4), 363–385.

Meng, J., & Berger, B. K. (2013a). An integrated model of excellent leadership in public relations: Dimensions, measurement, and validation. *Journal of Public Relations Research, 25*(2), 141–167.

Meng, J., & Berger, B. K. (2013b). What they say and what they do: Executives affect organizational reputation through effective communication. In Craig E. Carroll (Ed.), *The handbook of communication and corporate reputation* (pp. 306–317). Malden, MA: John Wiley & Sons, Inc.

Meng, J., & Berger, B. K. (2019). The impact of organizational culture and leadership performance on PR professionals' job satisfaction: Testing the joint mediating effects of engagement and trust. *Public Relations Review, 45*, 64–75.

Meng, J., Berger, B. K., Gower, K. K., & Heyman, W. C. (2012). A test of excellent leadership in public relations: Key qualities, valuable sources, and distinctive leadership perceptions. *Journal of Public Relations Research, 24*(1), 18–36.

Meng, J., Berger, B. K., Heyman, W. C., & Reber, B. H. (2019). *Public relations leaders earn a "C+" in The Plank Center's Report Card 2019: Is improving leadership even on the radar screen in the profession?* Tuscaloosa, AL: The Plank Center for Leadership in Public Relations.

Meng, J., Reber, B. H., Berger, B. K., Gower, K. K., & Zerfass, A. (2019). *North American Communication Monitor 2018–2019. Tracking trends in fake news, issues management, leadership performance, work stress, social media skills, job satisfaction and work environment.* Tuscaloosa, AL: The Plank Center for Leadership in Public Relations.

Neill, M. S. (2016). The influence of employer branding in internal communication. *Research Journal of the Institute for Public Relations, 3*(1). Available online: http://www.institute-forpr.org/influence-employer-branding-internal-communication. Access date: October 21, 2019.

Neill, M. S., & Drumwright, M. E. (2012). PR professionals as organizational conscience. *Journal of Mass Media Ethics, 27*(4), 220–234.

Nye, J. S. (2010). Power and leadership. In Nitin Nohria & Rakesh Khurana (Eds.), *Handbook of leadership theory and practice* (pp. 305–332). Boston, MA: Harvard Business Press.

Owens, T. J. (2003). Self and identity. In DeLamater, J. D. (Ed.) *Handbook of social psychology* (pp. 205–232). New York: Kluwer/Plenum.

Pang, A., Jin, Y., & Cameron, G. T. (2010). Strategic management of communication: Insights from the contingency theory of strategic conflict management. In R. L. Heath (Ed.), *Handbook of public relations* (2nd ed., pp. 17–34). Thousand Oaks, CA: Sage.

Place, K. R., & Vardeman-Winter, J. (2018). Where are the women? An examination of research on women and leadership in public relations. *Public Relations Review, 44*(1), 165–173.

Pompper, D. (2013). Interrogating inequalities perpetuated in a feminized field: Using Critical Race Theory and the intersectionality lens to render visible that which should not be disaggregated. In C. Daymon & K. Demetrious (Eds.), *Gender and public relations: Critical perspectives on voice, image and identity* (pp. 83–102). London: Routledge.

Reber, B. H., & Cameron, G. T. (2003). Measuring contingencies: Using scales to measure public relations practitioner limits to accommodation. *Journalism & Mass Communication Quarterly, 80*(2), 431–446.

Ryan, M., & Martinson, D. L. (1983). The PR officer as corporate conscience. *Public Relations Quarterly, 28*(2), 20–23.

Shah, A. (April 16, 2015). *Why aren't there more female CEOs in PR?* PRovoke Media, premium content retrieved from https://www.provokemedia.com/long-reads/article/why-aren't-there-more-female-ceos-in-pr. Access date: October 15, 2019.

Shah, A. (September 12, 2017). *Why do PR firms pay women, people of color less?* PRovoke Media, retrieved from https://www.provokemedia.com/long-reads/article/why-do-pr-firms-pay-women-people-of-color-less. Access date: October 15, 2019.

Shin, J., Cameron, G. T., & Cropp, F. (2006). Occam's Razor in the contingency theory: A national survey of 86 contingent variables. *Public Relations Review, 32*, 282–286.

Sison, M. D. (2010). Recasting public relations roles: Agents of compliance, control or conscience. *Journal of Communication Management, 14*(4), 319–336.

Toth, E. L., & Cline, C. G. (Eds.). (1989). *Beyond the velvet ghetto.* San Francisco, CA: IABC Research Foundation.

Toth, E. L., & Cline, C. G. (1991). Public relations practitioner attitudes toward gender issues: A benchmark study. *Public Relations Review, 17*(2), 161–174.

Toth, E. L., & Grunig, L. A. (1993). The missing story of women in public relations. *Journal of Public Relations Research, 5*(3), 153–175.

Trevino, L. K., Hartman, L., & Brown, M. (2000). Moral person and moral manager: How executives develop a reputation for ethical leadership. *California Management Review, 42*(4), 128–142.

U.S. Bureau of Labor Statistics (2019). Available at https://www.bls.gov/cps/cpsaat11.htm. Access date: October 1, 2019.

Vardeman-Winter, J., & Place, K. (2017). Still a lily-white field of women: The state of workforce diversity in public relations practice and research. *Public Relations Review, 43*, 326–336.

Vardeman-Winter, J., & Tindall, N. (2010). Toward an intersectional theory of public relations. In R. L. Heath (Ed.), *Handbook of public relations* (2nd ed., pp. 223–235). Thousand Oaks, CA: Sage.

Vardeman-Winter, J., Jiang, H., & Tindall, N. (2014). "Mammography at age 40 to 49 saves lives; just not enough of them": Gendered political intersections in communicating breast cancer screening policy to publics. In D. Daymon & K. Demetrious (Eds.), *Gender and public relations: Critical perspectives on voice, image, and identity* (pp. 221–246). London, England: Routledge.

Vardeman-Winter, J., Tindall, N., & Jiang, H. (2013). Intersectionality and publics: How exploring publics' multiple identities questions basic public relations concepts. *Public Relations Inquiry, 2*(3), 279–304.

Waller, D. J., Smith, S. R., & Warnock, J. T. (1989). Situational theory of leadership. *American Journal of Hospital Pharmacology, 46*, 2335–2341.

Wartick, S. L., & Rude, R. E. (1986). Issues management: Corporate fad or corporate function? *California Management Review, 29*(1), 124–140.

Waymer, D. (2010). Does public relations scholarship have a place in race? In R. L. Heath (Ed.), *Handbook of public relations* (2nd ed., pp. 237–246). Thousand Oaks, CA: Sage.

Waymer, D., & Dyson, O. (2011). The journey into an unfamiliar and uncomfortable territory: Exploring the role and approaches of race in PR education. *Journal of Public Relations Research, 23*(4), 458–477.

Weber, L. (2001) *Understanding race, class, gender, and sexuality: A conceptual framework.* Boston: McGraw-Hill.

Werder, K. P., & Holtzhausen, D. (2009). An analysis of the influence of public relations department leadership style on public relations strategy use and effectiveness. *Journal of Public Relations Research, 21*(4), 404–427.

Women and leadership: Public says women are equally qualified, but barriers persist. (2015, January 14). *Pew Research Center.* Retrieved from www.pewreearch.org. Access date: September 21, 2019.

Wright, D. K., Grunig, L. A., Springston, J. K., & Toth, E. L. (1991). *Under the glass ceiling* (monograph). New York: Public Relations Society of America (PRSA) Foundation.

Wrigley, B. J. (2002). Glass ceiling? What glass ceiling? A qualitative study of how women view the glass ceiling in public relations and communications management. *Journal of Public Relations Research, 14*(1), 27–55.

Yukl, G. A. (1989). Managerial leadership: A review of theory and research. *Journal of Management, 15*, 251–289.

Zenger, J., & Folkman, J. (2012, Mar. 15). Are women better leaders than men? Blog post. *Harvard Business Review.* Available at: https://hbr.org/2012/03/a-study-in-leadership-women-do. Access date: October 15, 2019.

Zenger, J., & Folkman, J. (2019, June 25). Research: Women score higher than men in most leadership skills. Blog post. *Harvard Business Review,* retrieved from https://hbr.org/2019/06/research-women-score-higher-than-men-in-most-leadership-skills. Access date: October 15, 2019.

Zerfass, A., & Huck, S. (2007). Innovation, communication, and leadership: New developments in strategic communication. *International Journal of Strategic Communication, 1*(2), 107–122.

CHAPTER TWO

Research Design and Methods

How We Approach This Subject

This chapter explains the research design and methods used in this project. In order to obtain a deep understanding of the subject, we used both qualitative (i.e. in-depth interviews) and quantitative (i.e. cross-sectional online survey) research methods to collect responses from targeted populations nationwide. This chapter is organized by two large sections. Section 1 provides a detailed description of the qualitative phase of our research design and the profiles of the interviewees. Section 2 explains the quantitative phase of the research. Detailed demographic profiles of our survey participants are documented in this section as well.

Research Design and Methods

A mixed research design and combined methodology is used in this project in order to obtain comprehensive knowledge. The two-phase study, jointly funded by The Plank Center for Leadership in Public Relations and The Arthur W. Page Center for Integrity in Communication, included in-depth interviews of top female executives in public relations and communication management and a national online survey of female professionals in public relations and communication management at various stages of their professional career across different types of organizations.

Phase 1: In-Depth Interviews of Top Female Executives in Communication Profession

To gain a deep understanding of how women in public relations define influence, the challenges they face in achieving positions in leadership and how they have overcome those challenges, we conducted 51 in-depth interviews with women working in mid-management and senior executive level positions. Interviews are an appropriate research method when the subject matter is confidential, when group pressure could discourage honest responses, and when there is a desire to understand attitudes, behaviors and motivations (Davis, 2012).

The participants were recruited using both purposive and snowball sampling strategies. To be eligible for the study, potential participants were expected to be working in either mid-management or senior leadership roles in public relations and communication management. We began our study by reaching out to female executives we personally knew who currently hold leadership positions in public relations and/or communication in their organization and are members of prominent professional organizations such as the Public Relations Society of America (PRSA) and the Arthur W. Page Society. Upon completion of the interviews, we asked these senior female executives for referrals to continue recruiting qualified participants for the interviews. We used the same interview guide for all participants. Given the geographic diversity, the majority of the interviews were conducted by telephone, although a few were conducted in person when possible, between October 2018 and April 2019.

The interview guide was reviewed by two industry professionals prior to the beginning of the study and revised based on their feedback. The interview topics included influence and leadership, professional and personal challenges, influence in actual practice, ethical leadership, mentoring, and practical advice. The study followed IRB guidelines and was IRB approved. All participants were provided consent forms detailing actions to preserve confidentiality. The interviews were audio-recorded and transcribed for analysis producing 592 pages of typed, singled-spaced text, representing almost 46 hours of interviews or an average of 54 minutes per interview.

Data Analysis

The data were analyzed by using standard approaches for qualitative data analysis (Miles & Huberman, 1994), which involves three steps: data reduction, data display, conclusions and verification. The qualitative researcher coded each interview individually under broad categories based on the conceptual framework and key variables under study. Composite code sheets were then created electronically by using a qualitative research software reflecting all respondents' comments related to each category. To confirm reliability of the categories, a random sample of 20% of the transcripts was independently coded by the qualitative research investigator and a research assistant using a code book and QDA Miner software, which calculated inter-rater reliability as 93.8% agreement. After data reduction, each category was then qualitatively analyzed by the qualitative researcher who wrote memos and analyzed the data further to identify additional insights, which were discussed and agreed upon by both authors. The data analysis also included negative or discrepant case analysis to identify any examples that disconfirmed or challenged emerging findings (Merriam, 2002), which supported triangulation.

Phase 2: A National Online Survey of Female Professionals in PR/ Communication

The second phase of the project involved designing and conducting a national online survey of female professionals working in public relations, communication management and other related areas in the communication profession. In order to obtain a representative national sample of the targeted population, we used the audience database of Qualtrics and its online survey platform. A few key demographic parameters were pre-specified as sampling criteria for our audience panel recruitment. Qualified respondents must satisfy all of the following demographic parameters:

1. Be equal or older than 21;
2. Be a woman;
3. Be a full-time employee in current employment status.
4. Identify herself as a communication professional and perform a major communication role in her current job, including but not limited to public relations, communications, public affairs, digital and social media, marketing communication, fundraising, etc.

In addition, we pre-specified three important demographic quotas (i.e. leadership position, years of professional experience, and ethnicity) as part of our sampling strategies to obtain a more balanced national sample of female professionals in the public relations industry as suggested by social science researchers when designing cross-sectional survey research (Singleton & Straits, 2005). Specifically, the leadership position quota requires the final usable sample must have at least 100 respondents (20.0%) to self-identify themselves as having a defined leadership role. For years of professional experience, we specified three categories: about 40% of respondents having up to five years of experience in communication, 30% having 6–10 years of professional experience, and 30% having more than ten years of professional experience in communication. One last quota we used is ethnicity in order to recruit more qualified minority groups in the sample that will help understand the perceptions and challenges of women of color in the profession. Specifically, about 70% of respondents in the sample shall be whites as pre-specified, followed by 20% of Blacks/African Americans and 10% of other minority groups including Asian Americans, Hispanics/Latinos, Native Americans, Multiracial and other.

The survey questionnaire was designed in April and pretested in May, 2019 by using a group of graduate students majoring in public relations (n =12) to ensure the face validity of investigated constructs and topics in the survey. Revisions and updates were applied to questions and statements in the survey questionnaire based on collected feedback. We also modified the structure of the questionnaire based on collected feedback to improve the survey flow and enhance users' survey experience.

A pilot test was carried out by using a small group of qualified respondents from Qualtrics (n = 20). Pre-specified demographic parameters (i.e. age, gender, employment status, and communication function in the job) were also applied to the pilot testing group to ensure the quality of the results. The goal of the pilot test was to evaluate respondents' overall impression of survey language, their understanding of our questions and topics, the skipping functions we built in to screen out unqualified respondents, the validation we set up for certain questions, as well as the survey flow. Results from the pilot test further confirmed the face validity of our questionnaire design and programming. After inspecting the results of the pilot test, we made minor revisions to certain questions and added a few more validation options to ensure the final sample quality. All 20 responses were discarded after the pilot test and those 20 respondents were excluded from final recruitment.

The final survey was launched in July and remained active from July 19 to August 19, 2019. Qualtrics managed the online survey access and sent the invitation to potential participants in their audience panel database. The data collection was finished in four weeks. Over the four-week period of data collection, we had a total of 10,099 valid clicks from Qualtrics' database that opened the survey link after reading the introduction and consent form page. Unqualified respondents were screened out after finishing the first part of screening section. Qualified respondents were directed to the main questionnaire once they passed all screening questions and met our sampling criteria. After we met the pre-specified demographic quotas and the targeted sample size, the survey link was deactivated. All responses were anonymous.

The exported raw data file included 515 complete cases. After data clean and re-coding, three cases were excluded from the analysis due to conflicting answers and failure to pass validations. Therefore, the final sample for our Phase II study consists of 512 complete responses. The average duration for qualified respondents to complete the questionnaire was 1,260 seconds (about 21 minutes). The average age of respondents was 36.2 (*S.D.* = 10.67) ranging from 22 to 66 in the sample. Detailed sample profiles will be described later in the chapter.

Profiles of Interview and Survey Participants

Sample Profiles of Interviewed Female Professionals

Overall, a total of 51 in-depth interviews were completed for the project. The average years of experience for the sample was 24 years, and 17 (33.3%) of the participants were classified as mid-career (10–19 years of experience), and the remaining 34 (66.6%) participants had 20 or more years of professional experience in public relations. Because one of our study goals was to understand the additional challenges that women of color may face in advancing into leadership positions, we made a strategic effort to recruit an ethnically diverse sample. A total of 15 (29.0%) participants identified themselves as African American, seven (13.7%) as Hispanic/Latina, and five (9.8%) as Asian, with women of color representing 53% of the total sample. The women interviewed represented 15 different states and the District of Columbia including Alaska, California, Connecticut, Florida, Hawaii, Illinois, Maryland, Minnesota, New Jersey, New York, North Carolina, Tennessee, Texas, Virginia, and Washington. They also worked in a variety of sectors including public relations firms, education, corporate, government/military, and independent consultants. A summary of interviewees' demographic profiles is listed in Table 2.1. More details about the qualitative findings are included in Section III of this book.

Sample Profiles of Surveyed Female Professionals

The final survey sample consists of 512 female public relations and communication professionals in the United States. The final sample met pre-specified demographic parameters. All 512 valid respondents are women and full-time employees in their current employment status. They self-identified as communication professionals performing a major communication role in their current position. Specifically, the sample has 24.2% (n = 124) of respondents indicating performing a major role in public relations, 21.1% (n = 108) in communications,

Table 2.1. Demographic profiles of interviewed female executives (N = 51)

Job Title	Years of Experience	Geographic Location
CCO	29	Alaska
Sr. Manager, Corporate Communications	15	Alaska
Vice President, Integrated Marketing Communications	28	Alaska
Senior VP, Global Corporate Communications	26	California
Founder	34	California
CEO/GM	30	California
VP, Global Diversity, Inclusion & Engagement	35	Connecticut
Director, Advancement Communications	23	Connecticut
Assistant Vice President, Internal Communications	24	Connecticut
Executive Director of Marketing & Communication	26	Connecticut
VP Corporate Communication	34	Florida
Strategic Communications Officer	16	Florida
Co-Founder	18	Florida
Program Director	26	Georgia
Operations Chief Planner	20	Hawaii
Sr. Consultant	38	Illinois
President	28	Illinois
President/Managing Director	20	Illinois
CCO	30	Illinois
Executive Director of Growth	25	Illinois
Vice President, Global Communications	34	Illinois
Director	42	Maryland
VP	30	Minnesota
CCO	30	Minnesota
Consultant	15	New Jersey
Head of Digital & Social Analytics Practice	15	New York
Senior Vice President, Media Relations	15	New York
VP Global Communication	17	New York
Director, External Comm. and Community Relations	30	North Carolina
Vice President	25	Tennessee
SVP	18	Texas
Director of External Communications	18	Texas
Founder	15	Texas
SVP/CCO	26	Texas
Associate Vice Chancellor	17	Texas

Table 2.1. *Continued*

Job Title	Years of Experience	Geographic Location
Partner	20	Texas
Director, Media and Public Relations	12	Texas
Vice President, Communications	31	Texas
Executive Director	34	Texas
Chief Experience Officer	18	Texas
President & CEO	45	Texas
VP of Marketing & Communications	12	Texas
Strategic Communication Manager	16	Texas
Public Affairs Officer	10	Texas
Associate VP for Development	30	Virginia
President & CEO	15	Washington
Communications Director	23	Washington
Regional Director, Advocacy and Public Affairs	20	Washington, D.C.
Executive Vice President	23	Washington, D.C.
President	40	Washington, D.C.
Deputy Chief of Information	20	Washington, D.C.

20.9% (n = 107) in marketing communication, 10.5% (n = 54) in public affairs, 6.4% (n = 33) in corporate communication, 6.4% (n = 33) in digital and social media, 6.1% (n = 31) in media, and 4.3% (n = 22) in advertising in current organization. To further validate their communication role in current job, we asked respondents to select up to three primary areas of job responsibilities and/or functions in communication. The top three areas of their job functions in communication are: 1) marketing, brand and consumer communication (n = 118; 23.0%), 2) overall communication (generalist) (n = 103; 20.1%), and 3) community relations (n = 100; 19.5%). Across the entire sample, respondents presented a wide range of job responsibilities and functions in communication. See Table 2.2 for a detailed display.

Some other basic demographic information we collected include age, ethnicity, years of experience, reporting level in their current job, types of organization, years of tenure in their current organization, level of education, and ranges of basic annual salary.

- *Age.* Four age categories are identified based on respondents' answers: 38.1% (n = 195) of respondents are in the range of 21 to 30, followed by 30.9% (n = 158) in the age range of 31–40, 19.5% (n = 100) in the range of 41–50, and 11.5% (n = 59) being older than 50.

Table 2.2. Primary areas of job responsibilities in communication

Primary areas of responsibilities in communication	Frequencies	Percentages
Marketing, brand & consumer communication	118	23.0%
Overall communication (generalist)	103	20.1%
Community relations	100	19.5%
Event planning	77	15.0%
Online communication, social media	68	13.3%
Internal communication/employee relations	63	12.3%
Government relations, public affairs & lobbying	56	10.9%
Monitoring, measurement & evaluation	51	10.0%
Corporate communication, media & publications	50	9.8%
Strategy and coordination of the communication function	45	8.8%
Crisis communication	41	8.0%
Consultancy, advising, coaching & key account	36	7.0%
Corporate media design, graphics & photography	36	7.0%
Financial communication/investor relations	27	5.3%
Media relations and/or press spokesperson	20	3.9%
International communication	20	3.9%
Corporate social responsibility/sustainability	20	3.9%
Sponsor relations	14	2.7%

- *Ethnicity.* The sample included a reasonably balanced mix of ethnic groups as pre-specified in our demographic quotas. We were able to recruit 360 white female professionals (70.3%), 100 African Americans (19.5%) and 52 other minority groups (10.2%). A detailed ethnicity breakdown is listed in Table 2.3.
- *Years of Professional Experience.* Overall, the sample showed a normal span in terms of years of professional experience. We had 41.0% of respondents having up to 5 years of experience in communication (n = 210), 29.9% (n = 153) having 6–10 years of experience, and 29.1% (n = 149) having more than 10 years of experience in the field. In addition, we asked respondents to share their years of tenure (see Table 2.4) in currently employed organization, nearly 50% of those surveyed (n = 250) have worked in current organization for more than 5 years.
- *Reporting Level.* We asked respondents to share the reporting levels between herself and the highest ranked PR/communication leader in current organization. Results indicated 8.2% of respondents (n = 42) served as the top leader in public relations and communication in their current

Table 2.3. Respondents' ethnicity (N = 512)

Ethnicity	Frequencies	Percentages
Caucasian or White	360	70.3%
African American, African descent, Black	100	19.5%
Other minority groups	52	10.2%
Hispanic, Latino, Spanish descent	*23*	*4.5%*
Asian, Asian American, Pacific Islander	*14*	*2.7%*
Multiracial	*11*	*2.1%*
Native American, American Indian	*4*	*0.8%*
Total	512	100.0%

Table 2.4. Respondents' tenure in current organization

Years of tenure in current organization	Frequencies	Percentages
Less than one year	52	10.2%
More than one year but less than 5 years	210	41.0%
More than 5 years but less than 10 years	143	27.9%
More than 10 years	107	20.9%
Total	512	100.0%

organization. We had 39.1% of them (n = 200) who reported directly to the top communication leader, which is one reporting level. The rest of the sample (n = 270 or 52.7%) reported staying at the lower level of the reporting hierarchy, meaning two and plus reporting levels. Since our project is interested in exploring women in different ethnic groups and their leadership status, we also looked at the distribution of these two demographic variables (see Table 2.5 for details).

• *Type of Organization.* Respondents in our survey reported working in various types of organizations. The largest category is working in private or state-owned companies (194 or 37.9%), followed by the category of non-profit, governmental, educational or political organizations (155 or 30.3%), the publicly held corporation (stock ownership) type (106 or 20.7%), and the category of communication or public relations agencies (56 or 10.9%). We only had one respondent selected the option of "other." However, no further information was specified by the respondent. Therefore, we cannot recode the one case into any of the above-mentioned categories.

Table 2.5. Reporting level and ethnicity

Reporting level/Ethnicity	White or Caucasian	African American	Other minority groups
Zero (I am the top leader) (n=42; 8.2%)	26 (7.2%)	13 (13.0%)	3 (5.8%)
One reporting level (n=200; 39.1%))	137 (38.1%)	36 (36.0%)	27 (51.9%)
Two and plus reporting levels (n=197; 52.7%)	197 (54.7%)	51 (51.0%)	22 (42.3%)
Total (n=512; 100.0%)	360 (70.3%)	100 (19.5%)	52 (10.2%)

Note: percentage listed in each cell indicates the percentage within the specific ethnicity category.

Table 2.6. Respondents' education levels

Education	Frequencies	Percentages
Senior High Diploma or below	77	15.0%
Associate Degree	96	18.8%
Bachelor Degree (e.g. formal education in a 4-year college)	219	42.8%
Master Degree (e.g. M.A., M.S., MBA)	106	20.7%
Doctoral Degree (e.g. Ph.D., DBA, JD)	13	2.5%
Other	1	0.2%
Total	512	100.0%

- *Level of Education.* In general, as shown in Table 2.6, surveyed professionals in our sample are well educated with 42.8% of them possessing a Bachelor's degree and 20.7% having a Master's degree.
- *Ranges of Basic Annual Salary.* We collected data on salaries of surveyed female communication professionals in order to see the ranges and variations across different types of organizations and leadership reporting levels. Overall, every fifth respondent (108 or 21.2%) earns over $90,000 annually. Within this top group, 6.3% (n = 32) make over $120,000 and 4.9% (n = 25) over $150,000 per year. On the other hand, more than half (276 or 53.9%) of surveyed female professionals earn no more than $60,000, and 12.7% (n = 65) of them earn only up to $30,000. The sample showed there is 22.9% of respondents (n = 117) reporting their basic annual salary staying in the category of $60,001 to $90,000. We had 2.1% (n = 11) that chose not to share such information.

Table 2.7. Salary range by organizational type (N=501)

Type of organization	Under $30,000	$30,001-$60,000	$60,001-$90,000	$90,001-$120,000	$120,001-$150,000	$150,000 & plus
Publicly held organization (n=103)	10 (9.7%)	46 (44.7%)	23 (22.3%)	16 (15.5%)	2 (1.9%)	6 (5.8%)
Private or state-owned company (n=189)	26 (13.8%)	78 (41.3%)	38 (20.1%)	21 (11.1%)	14 (7.4%)	12 (6.3%)
Communication or PR agency (n=55)	7 (12.7%)	13 (23.6%)	16 (29.1%)	7 (12.7%)	9 (16.4%)	3 (5.5%)
Nonprofit, governmental, educational or political organization (n=153)	22 (14.4%)	73 (47.7%)	40 (26.1%)	7 (4.6%)	7 (4.6%)	4 (2.6%)

A close analysis by looking at the organization type and the distribution of salary range found that communication or PR agencies pay better, with 34.6% in this category reporting earning over $90,000 annually. Joint stock and private companies also pay well with a similar percentage reporting their earnings above $90,000 annually (23.2% for joint stock companies and 24.8% for private companies), while nonprofit, governmental, educational or political organizations are lagging behind. See Table 2.7 for details.

Our analysis on annual salary information also revealed a similar pattern that top line managers and/or communication leaders reported a much higher percentage in the higher end of the salary range, for example, with an annual salary of $90,000 and more (Zerfass, Vercic, Verhoeven, Moreno & Tench, 2019), as shown in Table 2.8. Although our sample was limited to female communication professionals and the gender pay differences were not reflected in the results, we have linked our surveyed salary results to other recently published work related to gender discussions and the debate on gender pay gaps (e.g. Place & Vardeman-Winter, 2018; Toth & Aldoory, 2017).

- *Defined Leadership Role.* As reviewed in Chapter One, this research project was designed to explore in depth the topic of women's leadership challenges in public relations and communication management, and especially how

Table 2.8. Salary range by hierarchical reporting level (N=501)

Hierarchical reporting level	Under $30,000	$30,001-$60,000	$60,001-$90,000	$90,001-$120,000	$120,001-$150,000	$150,000 & plus
Zero (top leader) (n=41)	3 (7.3%)	7 (17.1%)	8 (19.5%)	11 (26.8%)	8 (19.5%)	4 (9.8%)
One reporting level (n=197)	21 (10.7%)	81 (41.1%)	44 (22.3%)	24 (12.2%)	15 (7.6%)	12 (6.1%)
Two and plus reporting levels (n=263)	65 (13.0%)	211 (42.1%)	13.0% (23.4%)	51 (10.2%)	32 (6.4%)	25 (5.0%)

female communication professionals navigate through barriers in advancing their leadership roles within the organization and building influence both within and beyond the organization. Therefore, we designed a few demographic questions to capture the leadership landscape among surveyed professionals. Particularly, we asked qualified respondents to share whether they have an official *and* a well-defined leadership role in their current job with current organization. More than half of surveyed respondents (291 or 56.8%) indicated they have an official and defined leadership role in current job. The rest (221 or 43.2%) selected "not having an official and defined leadership role."

To validate such self-reported information, as well as to obtain a more accurate picture of leadership roles and functions, we further asked respondents to select the level that best matches the scope of their current leadership role. The results show that nearly one in four respondents (25.5%) is having a defined leadership role at the senior manager level or above: 5.3% hold their leadership role and function at the C-Suite level or equivalent; 6.1% are at the top executive level or equivalent; and 14.1% are at the senior manager level or equivalent. This does not only reveal the high quality of the sample but also presents a balanced sample with mixed leadership roles and functions as shown in Table 2.9.

Some recent literature discusses the importance of pursuing diversity in executive development and building effective interventions to remove barriers to enable the success of women and people of color in corporate environments (e.g. Chitkara, 2018; McCarty Kilian, Hukai & Elizabeth McCarty, 2005). We also looked into the percentage of women of color in public relations and communication management who are in a defined leadership role in their current job. The demographics showed similar patterns across the three ethnic groups we

Table 2.9. Scope of leadership roles and functions

	Having a defined leadership role & function	Not having a defined leadership role & function
At the C-Suite level	27 (5.3%)	–
At top executive level	31 (6.1%)	–
At senior manager level	72 (14.1%)	–
At unit/departmental level	85 (16.6%)	41 (8.0%)
At team/project level	45 (8.8%)	73 (14.3%)
At general employee level	31 (6.1%)	106 (20.7%)
Other	–	1 (0.2%)
Total	291 (56.8%)	221 (43.2%)

recoded: 56.1% of White/Caucasian respondents reported having a defined leadership role, followed by a slight increase for African American women (58.0%) and respondents in other minority groups (59.6%).

We used the Statistical Package for the Social Sciences (SPSS) for data analysis. More details about the analysis and results as related to our survey are presented and documented in Section II of this book.

References

Chitkara, A. (April 12, 2018). PR agencies need to be more diverse and inclusive: Here's how to start. Blog post. *Harvard Business Review*, available at https://hbr.org/2018/04/pr-agencies-need-to-be-more-diverse-and-inclusive-heres-how-to-start. Access date: October 20, 2019.

Davis, J. (2012). *Advertising research theory and practice*. Upper Saddle River, NJ: Prentice Hall.

McCarty Kilian, C., Hukai, D., & Elizabeth McCarty, C. (2005). Building diversity in the pipeline to corporate leadership. *Journal of Management Development, 24*(2), 155–168.

Merriam, S. B. (2002). Introduction to qualitative research. *Qualitative Research in Practice: Examples for Discussion and Analysis, 1*(1), 1–17.

Miles, M. B., & Huberman, A. M. (1994). *Qualitative data analysis*. Thousand Oaks, CA: Sage.

Place, K. R., & Vardeman-Winter, J. (2018). Where are the women? An examination of research on women and leadership in public relations. *Public Relations Review, 44*(1), 165–173.

Singleton, R. A., & Straits, B. C. (2005). *Approaches to social research* (4th Ed.). New York: Oxford University Press.

Toth, E. L., & Aldoory, L. (2017). Looking back, looking forward: 20 years and more of gender theory of public relations practice. In B. R. Yook, Y. G. Ji, & Z. F. Chen (Eds.),

Looking back, looking forward: 20 years of developing theory & practice. Proceedings of the 20th International Public Relations Research Conference (pp. 353–364). Orlando, FL: IPRRC.

Zerfass, A., Vercic, D., Verhoeven, P., Moreno, A., & Tench, R. (2019). *European Communication Monitor 2019. Exploring trust in the profession, transparency, artificial intelligence and new content strategies. Results of a survey in 46 countries.* Brussels: EACD/EUPRERA, Quadriga Media Berlin.

A Grand Landscaping

National Survey Results on PR Women's Leadership and Ethical Challenges

This section provides detailed information and results from our national survey of female professionals working in the public relations and communication profession.

Chapter Three explores current situational issues and barriers to women's leadership advancement in public relations. It also presents female professionals' perceptions on potential improvements of such issues and barriers in the next three years. Chapter Four defines the meaning of leadership influence from the perspective of our surveyed female professionals and presents their strategies to build and enact influence in the workplace. In Chapter Four, we also discuss how female professionals perceive their personal readiness to provide ethics counseling to senior leadership and their evaluation of principled behaviors in ethical leadership. Chapter Five discusses organizations' efforts in leadership development and participation. Top leaders' performance is evaluated with a focus on improvements in the near future. Challenges in balancing work-family conflict, female communication professionals' coping strategies, as well as the role of mentorship in leadership advancement are profiled in Chapter Six.

CHAPTER THREE

Situational Barriers to PR Women's Leadership Advancement

Women in public relations leadership are historically underreported, underrepresented and unrecognized (Cline et al., 1986). Although historically women comprise nearly 70–75% of the jobs in the public relations profession, only a small percentage (approximately 20–30%) have made gains in achieving senior leadership positions in the last several years (Place & Vardeman-Winter, 2018; Shah, 2015). Not surprisingly, women have not been historically identified as pioneers or figures in the history of public relations in the United States. According to a recent webinar published by The Plank Center for Leadership in Public Relations, among the 17 pioneers identified in the history of public relations in the United States, there are only two women, and those two women are presented in relation to the men with whom they worked (as cited in *Hidden figures in public relations*, May 4, 2017). There are no minorities nor female public relations professionals that were considered pioneers when reviewing the history of public relations in the United States (Brunner, 2006; also as cited in *Hidden figures in public relations*, May 4, 2017).

As reviewed in Chapter One, now many organizations have recognized the need to diversify their employee base and leadership team. Therefore, organizations have started making efforts in developing deliberate diversity and inclusion strategies. However, a most recent industry report states women still make up less than half of the executive leadership positions in large public relations firms and only four women lead public relations agencies with more than $100 million in global revenue (Lee, 2011). Such reality makes us to wonder what the experience of being in senior leadership in the public relations profession looks like for women. Why does the gender representation for senior leadership still lag far behind in corporate and elite professional settings? What are the critical situational issues and barriers to women's leadership advancement in the public relations profession?

In this chapter, we focus on exploring the critical situational issues and barriers that are likely to influence female public relations professionals' leadership advancement along their career paths. In the reality and various business settings, we do see some female leaders who achieve leadership positions in spite of societal, structural and attitudinal barriers. Nonetheless, situational issues and barriers at multiple levels still play a significant role in forming and shaping female professionals' developmental and leadership experiences. We would like to report those critical situational issues and barriers reflected by our surveyed female professionals via their own practice and experiences in today's communication profession. More importantly, we would like to gain their perspectives on the anticipated improvements as related to those situational issues and barriers in the next three years. We hope such findings could help the industry to make real progress in advancing women to leadership and board positions and minimize the leadership gaps between men and women in the communication profession in the near future.

The Skewed Gender Representation in Top Leadership

In our survey, we asked a few leadership pipeline questions in order to obtain a bigger picture of gender representation in the public relations profession. We asked our female public relations professionals to report the gender of their direct supervisor or manager in their current position in the organization. Six out of ten female professionals report that their direct supervisor is a woman (n = 317; 61.9%). The rest report their direct supervisor is a man (n=195; 38.1%). When breaking down by types of organizations, a similar pattern emerged: more women serve as *direct* supervisors than men. Many parallels were found across the four major types of organizations we investigated (i.e. publicly held corporations, private companies, communication agencies, and the group of nonprofit, governmental, educational or political organizations). They were similar in terms of the percentage differences (approximately 5%) between women and men direct supervisors except for the group of nonprofit, governmental, educational or political organizations. Women significantly outnumbered men as direct supervisors by almost 10% in this category. Table 3.1 displays the details.

A similar pattern emerged when breaking down the gender representation by ethnicity. As explained in the research design in Chapter Two, we deliberately designed a few demographic quotas in our sample to ensure women of color in the profession are represented. According to Catalyst's most recent report (2018), women of color remain underrepresented in business leadership positions in the United States and in 2015, women of color made up 5.0% of executive/senior-level officials and managers in the *S&P 500* (as cited in *Catalyst: Women of color in the United States*, 2018). Therefore, we perceive the urgent need to examine the proportion of gender and leadership among women of color in the public relations profession. Not surprisingly, data reported by our national panel reflect similar trends: We found that more women (42.2%) than men (28.1%) serve as direct supervisors as reported by white women. For Black women, the percentage dropped to 13.3% (as women direct supervisors) versus 6.3% (as men direct supervisors). The difference reported by other minority women further reduced to 6.4% (as women direct supervisors) versus 3.7% (as men direct supervisors).

Another similar pattern was found along the age line. However, it is interesting to observe that as the age of surveyed female public relations professionals goes up, the percentage gap between female direct supervisors and male ones decreases. For example, professionals in the youngest group in our sample (i.e. those younger than 30) reported approximately a 10% difference between having a female direct supervisor (24.0%) vs. a male one (14.1%). While the gap almost disappeared among the professionals in the group of "older than 50" (6.1% vs. 5.5%).

Table 3.1. Organizational type vs. gender of direct supervisor/manager

Organizational type	Gender of *direct* supervisor/manager		*Percentage diff.*
	A woman	A man	
Publicly held corporation	65 (12.7%)	41 (8.0%)	4.7%
Private or state-owned company	110 (21.5%)	84 (16.4%)	5.1%
Communication or PR agency	40 (7.8%)	16 (3.1%)	4.7%
Nonprofit, governmental, educational or political organization	101 (19.8%)	54 (10.6%)	9.2%

Note: the categories of "self-employed" and "other" were excluded in this cross-tabulation analysis.

We analyzed the gender representation at the level of senior leadership as well. We asked a similar leadership pipeline question but shifted the focus to *the highest ranked communication leader* in their current organization. The big picture of gender-representation flipped at the level of senior communication leadership. Overall, surveyed public relations professionals reported a much higher percentage of men serving in top leadership roles in communication (n = 288; 56.3%) than women (n = 224; 43.8%). When breaking down by organizational type, communication or public relations agencies are in a relatively better position in achieving the gender balance at the top leadership level. This finding echoes the results that have been shared by Shah (2018) in her article, which addressed that most leading PR firms have been looking for approaches to achieve diversity via employee resource groups. According to our data analysis, the widest gap exists in the category of private or state-owned companies with a much higher percentage of men residing as the highest ranked communication leader in the organization. Similar patterns exist for publicly held corporations and for the category of non-profits. Table 3.2 displays the detailed results on our percentage analysis.

The pattern of men outnumbering women in senior communication leadership is also identified among different ethnic groups and age groups. More men lead as the top communication leaders as reported by white women (40.8% vs. 29.5%) and other minority groups (6.3% vs. 3.9%) in their current organization. Female African American professionals reported to have slightly more women (10.4%) than men (9.2%) as the top communication leaders in their current organization. Similar gaps in gender representation remain stable among the four age groups we investigated except for professionals in the age bracket 41–50. Professionals in this group reported having equal numbers of women and men leading as the top communication leader in their current organization.

Table 3.2. Organizational type vs. gender of the highest ranked communication leader

Organizational type	Gender of the highest ranked communication leader		
	A woman	A man	*Percentage diff.*
Publicly held corporation	45 (8.8%)	61 (11.9%)	-3.1%
Private or state-owned company	80 (15.7%)	114 (22.3%)	-6.6%
Communication or PR agency	28 (5.5%)	28 (5.5%)	--
Nonprofit, governmental, educational or political organization	70 (13.7%)	85 (16.6%)	-2.9%

Note: the categories of "self-employed" and "other" were excluded in this cross-tabulation analysis.

Despite some statistical limitations of our data addressed earlier in Chapter Two, the results clearly show a pattern of women holding a smaller portion of senior leadership positions compared with their male counterparts. Such figures do not match women's overall share of the labor force in the public relations and communication profession as women make up more than 70% of the labor force in the public relations industry (Becker, 2014; U.S. Bureau of Labor Statistics, 2019).

Our results also provide a baseline picture of the gender representation at the lower level of leadership in various organizations. We do see a substantial percentage of women serving as direct supervisors at junior and middle management levels to fill in the pipeline. However, these statistics also point out the fact that women in that pipeline are not moving quickly enough nor in sufficient numbers into the senior leadership level of line or executive positions to balance the gender representation and foster an environment of inclusiveness. Women still lag behind in gaining senior leadership roles and reaching the top, even though they often have greater opportunities at junior or middle management levels. Men still constitute a much higher percentage of top leadership positions in communication and public relations in various organizations in the United States.

Identifiable Barriers to Leadership Advancement

As considerable data and reports exist to address the firewalls and barriers that block women's leadership advancement in various business and professional settings (Kottke & Pelletier, 2013), we focus on current critical issues and barriers as identified by female public relations professionals as related to the public relations profession in this research project. In order to lay the foundation to investigate this tough subject of gender inequality, which seems to be a general issue across all elite and professional settings, we reviewed the series of research on women's advancement in U.S. corporate leadership designed and conducted by Catalyst in the past decade. We rely on Catalyst's series of research to obtain a list of potential barriers and issues for women in business and professional settings in leadership advancement (Catalyst, 1996, 2003, 2004, 2005, 2007). Substantial research does not only identify various structural and attitudinal barriers to women's leadership advancement, but more importantly, it also speculates about their long-term effects on women's leadership career patterns (e.g. Eagly, 2005, 2007; Ely & Rhode, 2010; Rudman & Kilianski, 2000; Schein, 2001). Results from previous research help us build the list of ten potential critical situational barriers that may influence women's leadership advancement opportunities along their career paths, especially for minority women in the public relations profession. The list of ten potential critical barriers we investigated is displayed in Table 3.3.

In this section of survey, we asked respondents to rate the list of barriers (all appeared in random order) regarding their potential influence on women's advancement to senior leadership positions in the public relations and communication profession. As displayed in Table 3.3, based on female professionals' overall assessment, the top three situational barriers influencing women's leadership advancement are:

1. Workplace structures (4.78/7.0),
2. Double standards in domestic roles and professional demands (4.66/7.0), and
3. Social attitudes towards female professionals (4.62/7.0).

When comparing female professionals' perceptions on situational barriers by different types of organizations, we found that professionals in publicly held corporations rated several situational barriers higher if compared to those working in other types of organizations. The one item receiving the highest rating is the situational barrier of "workplace structures (4.91/7.0)." Such rating echoes the reality that fewer women than men are in the boardroom of *Fortune 500* companies (Catalyst, 2007).

Table 3.3. Assessment of situational barriers and their influence on women's advancement

Potential critical situational barriers	*Mean*	*S.D.*
Workplace structures	4.78	1.67
Double standards in domestic roles and professional demands	4.66	1.90
Social attitudes towards female professionals	4.62	1.82
Occupational stereotypes in clustering more women in staff functions than line functions	4.50	1.79
Conventional assumptions of gender identity at work	4.45	1.88
Disadvantaged by gender-based stereotypes	4.45	1.88
Male stereotyping and preconceptions	4.39	1.91
Occupational segregation in limiting women to advance careers in professional services	4.32	1.87
An inhospitable corporate culture of male dominance	4.30	1.91
Disadvantaged by race-based stereotypes	4.18	1.97

Note: all items were measured by using a seven-point Likert-type scale with "1 = no influence at all" and "7 = influence a great deal." The items in the table were sorted by mean score, from high to low.

Female professionals in publicly held corporations also rated the situational barriers of "double standards in domestic roles and professional demands" high (4.78/7.0), making it the second highest one for this group of respondents. Such a result is especially relevant to the role congruity theory when evaluating female leaders (Eagly & Karau, 2002). The propositions of role congruity theory address less desirable evaluations of women's potential for taking leadership roles because leadership ability is perceived as prototypical of men but not of women. Such prejudices toward women in leadership roles expose the inherent incongruity between the expected gender roles of women (e.g. family roles and responsibilities) and the role of leaders (e.g. increasing working pace, competitiveness and line responsibilities). Such incongruity perpetuates unequal leadership opportunities, particularly experienced by female professionals working in large corporations with complicated organizational structures.

Professionals in communication and public relations agencies rated almost all situational barriers the lowest, except for the one addressing "an inhospitable organizational culture of male dominance" (4.41/7.0), if compared to professionals in other types of organizations.

Professionals in the group of nonprofit, governmental, educational and political organizations gave four situational factors the highest scores among others. They are: 1) occupational stereotypes in clustering more women in staff functions than line functions (4.65/7.0), 2) conventional assumptions of gender identity at work (4.61/7.0), 3) male stereotyping and preconceptions (4.52/7.0), and 4) disadvantaged by race-based stereotypes (4.30/7.0). Meanwhile, professionals in private or state-owned companies rated the situational barrier of "occupational segregation in limiting women to advance careers in professional services" the highest (4.40/7.0) but gave the item of "disadvantaged by race-based stereotypes" the lowest score (4.03/7.0).

Situational Barriers and Women of Color

When evaluating the potential influence of the listed situational barriers, women of color rated all items consistently high but significantly higher on the following five situational barriers, including:

1. Workplace structures (5.33/7.0),
2. Social attitudes towards female professionals (5.29/7.0),
3. Disadvantaged by race-based stereotypes (5.13/7.0),
4. Occupational stereotypes in clustering more women in staff functions than line functions (5.08/7.0), and
5. An inhospitable organizational culture of male dominance (4.92/7.0).

Since few women gain access to the highest positions as executive head of organizations' strategic communication, many would assume their perceptions of situational barriers will be different from those at junior levels and/or those in the pipeline to reach the top executive level. Our results confirmed such perceptions. It is important to find that current top female leaders in communication actually rated almost all situational barriers the highest except for three items (i.e. disadvantaged by gender-based stereotypes, workplace structures, and occupational stereotypes in clustering more women in staff functions than line functions). Professionals holding a one-reporting-level status rated gender-based stereotypes and workplace structures the highest, while those at lower reporting level (i.e. in the group of "two and more reporting levels") rated occupational stereotypes the highest.

Even though the proportion of top female leaders in communication is small (8.2% in our sample), that is, those in the category of "zero reporting level (I am the top leader)," their ratings on the list of situational barriers are actually much higher. Such results may be a reflection of their professional development path. The existence of those situational barriers may have significantly shaped their leadership advancement experiences.

Independent sample *t*-tests were run between *leaders* and *non-leaders* to test the different perceptions. Similar to the patterns reflected in our mean comparisons across three groups by reporting levels, we found that professionals who reported they have an official and defined leadership role and functions in their current job actually reported much higher scores on all situational barriers than those who identified themselves as non-leaders. Particularly, professionals in the leader group rated the situational barrier of having an inhospitable organizational culture of male dominance significantly higher than the non-leader group (4.48 vs. 4.08). Figure 3.1 displays the specific ratings of situational barriers as perceived by *leaders* and *non-leaders*. Again, this brought up the similar reflecting question: Are the perceptual differences the reflections of the true leadership advancement journey as reported by our respondents?

Based on the ratings on leadership advancement barriers from leaders and non-leaders as we presented above, we further looked into respondents' ratings by the scope of their leadership and managerial roles or functions to further validate the results. As explained in our research design (Chapter Two), we asked respondents to report the scope of their current leadership and managerial roles/ functions in their organization and the answers indicated different levels, ranging from "at the C-Suite level or equivalent" to "at general employee level or equivalent" (see Table 2.8 in Chapter Two for details).

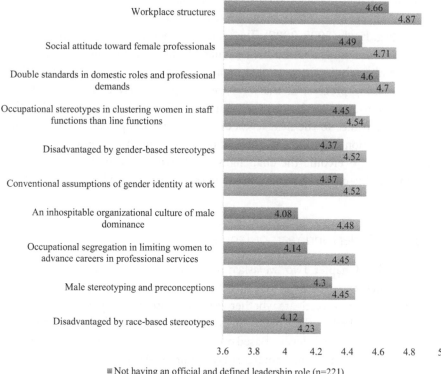

Figure 3.1. Leaders' vs. non-leaders' perceptions on situational barriers

Consistent high ratings were found in two senior leadership groups: 1) those who identified themselves holding leadership roles/functions at *the C-Suite level or equivalent*, and 2) those who identified themselves holding leadership roles/functions at *top executive level or equivalent*. Professionals in these two groups rated all situational and structural barriers the highest. As the scope of leadership roles and functions declines, for example, at senior management level, at unit/departmental level, at team/project level, etc., the scores on barriers also decreased. For example, respondents at the C-Suite level or equivalent rated double standards in domestic roles and professional demands the highest (5.26/7.0), followed by a 4.81-rating by professionals at top executive level or equivalent. Such perception started decreasing as the scope of leadership declines. Professionals identified themselves at general employee level or equivalent rated this situational barrier the lowest (4.43/7.0).

Such a pattern helps validate the speculation about situational barriers' long-term effects on women's leadership career patterns as addressed in previous research (e.g. Eagly, 2005, 2007). The societal, structural and attitudinal barriers identified in our study showed their influence and impact on female professionals at several levels: in the ways that organizations structured leadership and the decision-making process, in the ways that people perceived women leaders in public relations, and in the ways women in public relations perceive what they must do to advance to the next levels of leadership roles/positions either within their organization or in the communication profession. It is even more true that only when you overcome the challenges and barriers, you will have a stronger sense and feeling of the existence of such barriers, as reflected by our respondents' ratings.

Situational Barriers and Years of Tenure

As reported in Chapter Two, we asked respondents to share their overall length of professional experience (in years) in the communication profession. In addition, we wanted to investigate whether years of tenure in one position within the organization will affect their perceptions and experiences on leadership advancement barriers at multiple levels. Based on the results of the mean comparisons, we found two interesting trends among surveyed professionals as indicated by years of tenure in their current organization.

Two groups (i.e. the group with less than one year and the group with more than 5 years but less than 10 years in their tenure in current organization) rated all situational barriers much higher. They take turns in getting top rating scores on surveyed items. For example, the group with the minimal tenure experience (i.e. less than one year) rated five situational barriers the highest among all four groups. Such barriers include:

1. Double standards in domestic roles and professional demands (5.04/7.0)
2. Social attitudes towards female professionals (5.00/7.0)
3. Women in communication being disadvantaged by gender-based stereotypes (4.71/7.0)
4. Perceived occupational segregation in limiting women to advance careers in professional services (4.65/7.0)
5. Women in communication being disadvantaged by race-based stereotypes (4.58/7.0)

The group within the mid-range of tenure (i.e. more than 5 but less than 10 years) gave the other half of measured items the highest ratings, including:

1. Workplace structures (4.99/7.0)
2. Perceived occupational stereotypes in clustering women in staff functions than line functions (4.75/7.0)
3. Conventional assumptions of gender identity at work (4.68/7.0)
4. Existing male stereotyping and preconceptions (4.68/7.0)
5. An inhospitable organizational culture of male dominance (4.63/7.0)

It is also interesting to find that the group with the longest years of tenure (i.e. more than 10 years) in their current organization rated all items the lowest. We wondered why years of tenure presented such interesting patterns toward female professionals' interpretation of various barriers in leadership advancement. With the relatively smaller cell size of the group with less than one-year tenure experience, we need to carefully interpret their rating scores and perceptions. The high scores on certain items may be influenced and explained by the critique of gender inequality existing in the public relations industry, both online and offline, as part of pre-existing information, impressions and assumptions. The group within the mid-range of tenure rated five different items the highest as listed above, besides their high ratings on other items as well. Such results further reinforced the reality of existing barriers as mid-career professionals reflect on their challenges along their career path.

Impact of Situational Barriers

In order to get a bigger picture to reflect the general perceptions of female professionals on investigated situational barriers, we also did percentage analysis to gauge the trends. The scale for all ten items were re-coded and re-grouped into categorical variables with *disagreement* representing scale points 1–3, *neutral* representing scale point of 4, and *agreement* representing scale points 5–7. Based on our percentage analysis of frequency, surveyed professionals agreed that listed situational barriers present a serious impact on women's leadership advancement journey in the communication profession. In Figure 3.2, we list the situational barriers by the perceived impact level as rated by our surveyed female professionals. Here, we highlight three of the most noteworthy barriers as rated by surveyed professionals.

Consistently, female professionals state that double standards in domestic roles and professional demands is the top barrier which has a direct impact on their leadership advancement (58.6% in agreement), followed by social attitudes toward female professionals (57.4%), and workplace structures (57.2%). Six out of ten female professionals acknowledged the above-mentioned three situational

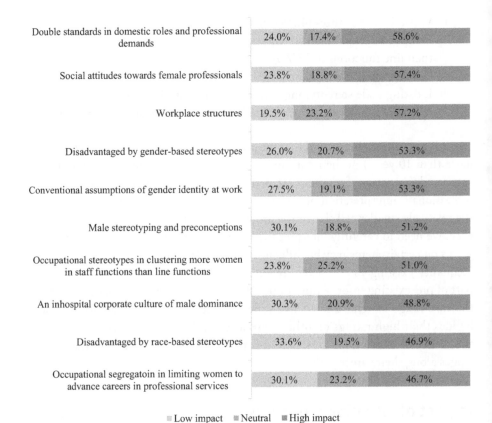

	Low impact	Neutral	High impact
Double standards in domestic roles and professional demands	24.0%	17.4%	58.6%
Social attitudes towards female professionals	23.8%	18.8%	57.4%
Workplace structures	19.5%	23.2%	57.2%
Disadvantaged by gender-based stereotypes	26.0%	20.7%	53.3%
Conventional assumptions of gender identity at work	27.5%	19.1%	53.3%
Male stereotyping and preconceptions	30.1%	18.8%	51.2%
Occupational stereotypes in clustering more women in staff functions than line functions	23.8%	25.2%	51.0%
An inhospital corporate culture of male dominance	30.3%	20.9%	48.8%
Disadvantaged by race-based stereotypes	33.6%	19.5%	46.9%
Occupational segregatoin in limiting women to advance careers in professional services	30.1%	23.2%	46.7%

■ Low impact ■ Neutral ■ High impact

Figure 3.2. The impact of situational barriers on women's leadership advancement in public relations

barriers have the highest impact on their leadership advancement along their career path. Probably it is more concerning that our results showed almost five out of ten female professionals (50.0%) believe the listed situational barriers would hurdle their leadership advancement at certain levels.

Issues Causing the Underrepresentation of Women in Top Leadership

Knowing the professionals' perceptions on some societal, structural and attitudinal barriers that influence women's advancement to leadership positions is important. However, we would argue that knowing the existence of such perceptions is not sufficient. One of the key questions we asked in this section of the questionnaire is what the most important issues causing the underrepresentation of women in leadership positions in the public relations industry are. Summarized from some of the most recent trade publications and research in the field focusing on women and leadership (e.g. Catalyst, 2005, 2007), we generated a list of ten potential current issues that may cause or explain why such underrepresentation exists in our profession.

We asked surveyed professionals to select the top-3 issues that are currently the most important reasons causing or contributing to the reality that women are underrepresented in various leadership positions in the communication profession. Our survey results show that the top-3 issues as rated by female professionals are:

1. Lack of sufficient numbers of women as role models in high-level decision-making positions (n = 222; 43.4%),
2. Lack of work-family balance (n = 189; 36.9%), and
3. Lack of position power of authority or control over important resources such as staffing and budgets (n = 180; 35.2%).

Apparently, lack of sufficient female role models in top leadership positions in the field is now considered more problematic than ever, which may further link back to those situational barriers we have examined earlier in this chapter. This was mentioned by Chitkara in her interviews of 18 CEOs who lead firms in the top 100 Global PR Agencies. According to Chitkara's research (2018), the interviewed CEOs acknowledged that the retention of diverse talent is particularly challenging and some of them believed that the lack of diverse mentors and role models in senior leader positions contributes to the problem.

It is worth mentioning that professionals also rated two other issues quite high: lack of support in childcare and other domestic tasks (n = 175; 34.2%) and lack of opportunities in getting desirable work assignments (n = 173; 33.8%). These two issues are closely lined up with the second (i.e. lack of work-family balance) and the third (i.e. lack of position power of authority or control over important resources) issues. The rating results further showed that today's female communication professionals have their working and family lives deeply intertwined. Such a reality causes female professionals not only being stressed but facing unique challenges as they scramble to build careers while carrying out traditional domestic responsibilities. We highlight the causing factors in Figure 3.3 based on the ratings from our surveyed professionals.

Besides the three top issues and the other two extended top issues, a second group of issues can be identified based on our frequency report. Those issues are mentioned in the 20–32% range by our surveyed professionals. This group includes three issues:

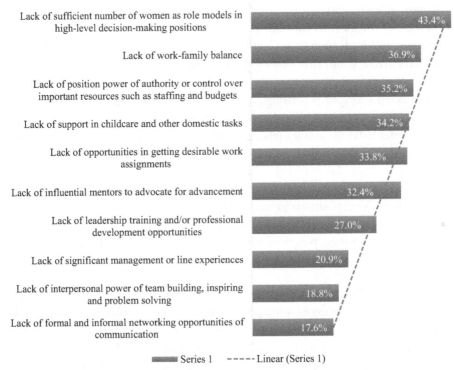

Figure 3.3. Top issues causing the underrepresentation of PR women in leadership

1. Lack of influential mentors to advocate for advancement (n = 166; 32.4%),
2. Lack of leadership training and/or professional development opportunities (n = 138; 27.0%), and
3. Lack of significant management or line experience (n = 107; 20.9%).

Among the ten current issues we ask our respondents to evaluate, two issues (i.e. interpersonal power of team building, inspiring and problem solving, and networking opportunities in communication) seem to be less concerning for female professionals in the field. Such results reflect the traditional gender ideology, expectations and practices associated with women in the field: women as a group are generally positive, competent in relationship building with external stakeholders, and possess desirable social skills (e.g. Eagly, et al., 2007; Grunig, Toth & Hon, 2001).

A close look at the top five most ranked issues by different types of organization revealed the following trends. Professionals working in publicly held corporations and private companies focus more on the fact of lacking sufficient number of women as role models in high-level decision-making positions. Meanwhile, female professionals working in nonprofit, governmental, educational and political organizations are more concerned about balancing work and family demands. In addition, professionals in this category mention that the issue of lacking opportunities in getting desirable work assignments also presents challenges in leadership advancement. At the same time, female professionals in private companies have to deal with the reality of lacking position power of authority or control over important resources such as staffing and budgets.

Similar trends were revealed along the hierarchy line of reporting levels. Lack of sufficient number of female role models is an issue for all professionals regardless of their reporting levels. Lack of support in childcare and domestic tasks is more of an issue for professionals who identified themselves as top communication leaders. Professionals staying at the one reporting level are more concerned about lacking position power of authority, while professionals at other lower reporting levels are facing the issue of lacking work-family balance.

For African American professionals, the top issues are:

1. Lack of sufficient number of women as role models (46.0%),
2. Lack of opportunities in getting desirable work assignments (41.0%),
3. Lack of position power of authority (35.0%), and
4. Lack of leadership training and/or professional development opportunities (35.0%).

Comparative analysis across three ethnic groups (i.e. whites, Blacks/African Americans, and other minorities) we coded in this study finds African American women rated two issues particularly high: 1) lack of female role models (46.0%), and 2) lack of opportunities in getting desirable work assignments (41.0%), if compared to the other two ethnic groups. Similar challenges are also presented to professionals in the group of "other minorities," but the results show lack of work-family balance and lack of childcare support and other domestic tasks have become the next big concern for white women.

One most noteworthy issue as highlighted by respondents in all three ethnic groups is they all feel lack of position power of authority over important resources or line responsibilities. The percentages on this item are consistently high (35.3% for white women, 35.0% for Black women, and 34.6% for other women of color). Such frustration expressed by female professionals, in turn, reflects the reality that women receive fewer line responsibilities and get fewer assignments that would demonstrate their leadership abilities, which are critical and expected to lead them to top executive positions (Wellington, Kropf & Gerkovich, 2003).

When gender-based stereotypes are combined with race-based stereotypes, it presents even greater challenges for women of color in business settings than those faced by white women.

Overall, our surveyed female professionals are less concerned with the interpersonal power of team building and problem solving. Instead, they don't see themselves getting sufficient opportunities in having authority or position power to control important resources. Such perceptions reflect the gender-based stereotypical traits for men being task-oriented while women being people-oriented (e.g. Eagly & Johannesen-Schmidt, 2001). The "taking-care" perspective of leadership assumption (e.g. team building, inspiring, and networking) and the "taking-charge" perspective of leadership behavior (e.g. delegating, staffing, budgeting, and problem solving) have formed the rationale to withhold leadership positions and opportunities from women.

Projection of Improvements in Next Three Years

To fully understand the current issues causing or explaining the underrepresentation of women in leadership positions in communication, we also asked female professionals to project issues that will get improved within *the next three years* based on their expectations. The results show female professionals believe the improvement of the following three issues is expected to take place in the next three years:

1. Having improved work-life balance (n=199; 38.9%)
2. Having more women as role models in high-level decision-making positions (n=192; 37.5%)
3. Having more influential mentors to advocate for advancement (n=179; 35.0%)

It is critical to note the top-3 issues to be improved are *different* from female professionals' ratings of the top-3 issues causing the leadership underrepresentation, if we compare Figure 3.4 to Figure 3.3. Professionals rated lack of sufficient female role models in top leadership positions in the field as the number one issue. However, they don't anticipate this issue to be the number one being solved or improved in the next three years. Based on the results, respondents seem to set a more reasonable goal to achieve in the next three years, which is to have improved work-life balance (38.9%). At the same time, surveyed women still have their faith that the profession will make progress to have more women taking on senior leadership roles in the near future (37.5%).

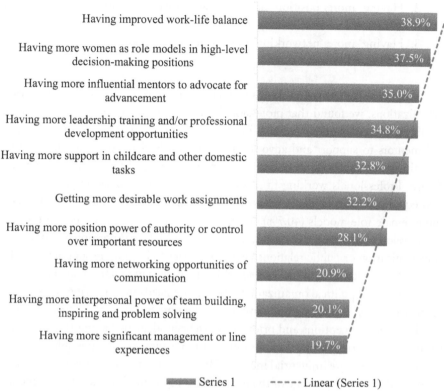

Figure 3.4. Professionals' projection of issues to be improved in next three years

Lack of position power of authority was widely rated among the top-3 issues causing leadership underrepresentation by surveyed professionals. However, the issue itself did not make the list of top-3 improvements. Only about three out of ten professionals think it will be improved (28.1%) in the near future. The third potential improvement is linked to mentors and mentorship. Female professionals believe it is important to have influential mentors to help women advocate for leadership advancement (35.0%). See Figure 3.4 for a bar chart showing female professionals' projection of issues to be improved in next three years.

Female professionals also believe they will have more leadership training and professional development opportunities (34.8%), as well as receive growing support in childcare and domestic tasks (32.8%). Similarly, a second group of issues to be improved is identified based on our frequency report. Those issues are mentioned in the 20–32% range by our surveyed professionals, including:

1. Having more opportunities in getting desirable work assignment (n = 165; 32.2%),

2. Having more position power of authority or control over important resources (n = 144; 28.1%), and

3. Having more networking opportunities of communication (n = 107; 20.9%).

When looking at the rankings of issues to be improved by different types of organizations, we found that professionals have their own priorities. For example, 43.4% of professionals in publicly held corporations hope to have more influential mentors to support and advocate for them for leadership advancement. They also think the challenge in balancing work and life will be improved in the near future. Professionals working in private companies hope to see improvements in two equally important issues: improved work-family balance (40.7%) and having more female role models (40.7%). They also hope to get more leadership training and development opportunities in the near future (40.2%). Professionals working in communication or public relations agencies project to have more support in childcare and other domestic tasks (39.3%), while their peers in nonprofit, governmental, educational and political organizations show more needs in improving work-family balance (38.7%) and having more influential mentors to advocate for them (36.1%).

Different perceptions and priorities have been identified along the hierarchical line of reporting levels. Top communication leaders see the possible improvement in having more influential mentors (38.1%) in next three years. Professionals in the middle to upper range of the hierarchical reporting line (i.e. the one reporting level) show their need in getting more leadership training and development opportunities (43.5%). Professionals at the lower level along the reporting line (i.e. two and more reporting levels) call for improvement in having more female role models in high-level decision-making positions (40.4%).

Ratings from different ethnic groups also reflect their priorities. White women need to have an improved work-family balance (41.7%), followed by having more female role models (36.7%). Black women set the priority to increase the number of women as role models in top leadership (43.0%). They also expect to have more influential mentors (37.0%) and leadership training opportunities (37.0%) to reflect the profession's improvement. Other women of color believe that the work-family balance will be improved in next three years (40.4%) while more leadership training will be provided (34.6%).

Conclusion

In this chapter, we have identified and discussed the common situational barriers women in public relations face when building up their own career path and seeking to advance into top leadership positions. We presented a grand picture depicting the gender representation at both the lower and higher level of leadership among the national sample we recruited. We examined these barriers horizontally and vertically by looking into a few key situational variables such as the type of organizations and the hierarchical line of reporting levels. We also compared the perceptions of professionals who have a defined and official leadership role and functions to those who don't in order to test how situational barriers may have shaped their leadership development experiences. Women who have overcome the situational barriers to reach the top leadership positions reported a much stronger impression and opinion when evaluating the potential impact of such barriers. Similar patterns also are identified among women of color.

Further, we looked into the potential causing factors that may explain the underrepresentation of women in top leadership positions in public relations. Similarly, the horizontal and vertical comparisons allow us to identify issues in hindering upward progress of women in public relations. The bright side of the story is we do have a substantial percentage of women who are currently taking on junior or middle management roles along the leadership pipeline. At the same time, we also need to admit that the profession itself does not have a sufficient number of women as role models in top leadership positions. Such a fact does not only discourage aspired junior female professionals. More critically, it may also slow down the progress of qualified women advancing into senior leadership in organizations because there are not enough role models and/or influential mentors to advocate for them.

Despite the persistent challenges in overcoming situational barriers, women in public relations have projected areas that may make potential progress in the near future. As noted in this chapter, it is our hope that the projected improvements will push for more changing scenes that will restructure the composition of top leadership tiers in the public relations profession. There is much more for us to do to recognize and advance more female leaders and showcase their talents.

References

Becker, G. (2014, Aug. 11). *Now the Atlantic should ask: Where are the women leaders in PR?* https://www.huffpost.com/entry/now-the-atlantic-should-a_b_5668635, retrieved on September 9, 2019.

Brunner, B. (2006). Where are the women? A content analysis of introductory public relations textbooks. *Public Relations Quarterly, 51*(3), 43–47.

Catalyst. (1996). *Women in corporate leadership: Progress and prospects.* New York: Catalyst.

Catalyst. (2003). *Women in U.S. corporate leadership.* New York: Catalyst.

Catalyst. (2004). *Women and men in the U.S. corporate leadership: Same workplace, different realities?* New York: Catalyst.

Catalyst. (2005). *Women take care, men take charge: Stereotyping of business leaders exposed.* New York: Catalyst.

Catalyst. (2007). *The double blind dilemma for women in leadership: Damned if you do; doomed if you don't.* New York: Catalyst.

Catalyst. (2018, Nov. 07). *Women of color in the United States: Quick take.* New York: Catalyst.

Chitkara, A. (April 12, 2018). PR agencies need to be more diverse and inclusive: Here's how to start. Blog post. *Harvard Business Review*, available at https://hbr.org/2018/04/pr-agencies-need-to-be-more-diverse-and-inclusive-heres-how-to-start. Access date: October 20, 2019.

Cline, C. G., Toth, E. L., Turk, J. V., Walters, L. M., Johnson, N., & Smith, H. (1986). *The velvet ghetto: The impact of the increasing percentage of women in public relations and business communication.* San Francisco: IABC Foundation.

Eagly, A. H. (2005). Achieving relational authenticity in leadership: Does gender matter? *The Leadership Quarterly, 16*(3), 459–474.

Eagly, A. H. (2007). *Through the labyrinth: The truth about how women become leaders.* Boston: Harvard Business School Press.

Eagly, A. H., & Johannesen-Schmidt, M. C. (2001). The leadership styles of women and men. *Journal of Social Issues, 57*(4), 781–797.

Eagly, A. H., & Karau, S. J. (2002). Role congruity theory of prejudice toward female leaders. *Psychological Review, 109*, 573–598.

Eagly, A. H., Eagly, L. L. C. A. H., & Carli, L. L. (2007). *Through the labyrinth: The truth about how women become leaders.* Boston, MA: Harvard Business School Press.

Ely, R. J., & Rhode, D. L. (2010). Women and leadership. In Nitin Nohria & Rakesh Khurana (Eds.), *Handbook of leadership theory and practice* (pp. 377–410). Boston, MA: Harvard Business Press.

Grunig, L. A., Toth, E. L., & Hon, L. C. (2001). *Women in public relations: How gender influences practice.* New York: The Guilford Press.

Hidden figures in public relations: Putting a long-overdue spotlight on African-American PR pioneers (2017, May 4). *Plank Center Webinar*, published by The Plank Center for Leadership in Public Relations online via SlideShare: https://www.slideshare.net/plankcenter/hidden-figures-of-pr-putting-a-longoverdue-spotlight-on-african-american-pr-practitioners. Access date: September 21, 2019.

Kottke, J. L., & Pelletier, K. L. (2013). Advancing women into leadership: A global perspective on overcoming barriers. In M. A., Paludi (Ed.), *Women and Management Worldwide: Global Issues and Promising Solutions* (pp. 55–85). Santa Barbara, CA: Praeger.

Lee, J. (2011, Mar. 4). Diversity of agency leadership remains up for debate. *PRWeek*. Retrieved from https://www.prweek.com/article/1264912/diversity-agency-leadership-remains-debate on September 15 2019.

Place, K. R., & Vardeman-Winter, J. (2018). Where are the women? An examination of research on women and leadership in public relations. *Public Relations Review, 44*(1), 165–173.

Rudman, L. A., & Kilianski, S. E. (2000). Implicit and explicit attitudes toward female authority. *Personality and Social Psychology Bulletin, 26*(11), 1315–1328.

Schein, V. E. (2001). A global look at psychological barriers to women's progress in management. *Journal of Social Issues, 57*(4), 675–688.

Shah, A. (April 16, 2015). *Why aren't there more female CEOs in PR?* PRovoke Media, retrieved from https://www.provokemedia.com/long-reads/article/why-aren't-there-more-female-ceos-in-pr on September 20, 2019

Shah, A. (Jan. 18, 2018). *Why the PR industry's diversity initiatives fail?* PRovoke Media, retrieved from https://www.provokemedia.com/long-reads/article/why-the-pr-industry's-diversity-initiatives-fail on September 20, 2019.

U.S. Bureau of Labor Statistics (2019). Available at https://www.bls.gov/cps/cpsaat11.htm. Access date: October 5, 2019.

Wellington, S., Kropf, S. B., & Gerkovich, P. (2003, June). What's holding women back? *Harvard Business Review, 81*(6), 18–19.

CHAPTER FOUR

Ethical Leadership and the Meaning of Building Influence to Women in PR

If leadership is "a process whereby an individual influences a group of individuals to achieve a common goal" (Northouse, 2018, p. 7), it is hard to argue against the propositions that leadership involves influence (Yukl, 2002), creates meaning for the members (Selznick, 1984), performs specific social functions (Guillén, 2010), and seeks constructive change (Northouse, 2018). In this chapter, we focus on defining the meaning of building influence to women in public relations. We aim at defining influence from a more descriptive perspective so that we can better understand what characterizes influence for women in public relations. By positioning the role of public relations professionals with particular emphasis on ethical advocacy, we assess how building influence relates to female professionals' adoption of strategies when providing leadership and ethics counseling to the senior leadership team within the organization. We hope to uncover the role of ethical leadership in supporting female professionals to overcome situational hurdles when building and enacting influence, with an ultimate goal of achieving leadership success and effectiveness.

According to Bandura's (1977, 1986) social learning theory, for leaders to be seen as ethical leaders by their subordinates, they must be attractive and credible role models. Similarly, Moberg (2000) listed ideal characteristics of an ethical role model as demographic similarity, relevancy, and attainability. Leaders influence the ethical conduct of followers or subordinates via modeling as most individuals look outside themselves to other individuals for ethical guidance (Brown, Trevino & Harrison, 2005). By taking a more descriptive approach to define influence, ethics and leadership, we are adopting Brown et al.'s (2005) definition of ethical leadership in this research project. According to their systematical conceptualization, ethical leadership is defined as "the demonstration of normatively appropriate conduct through personal actions and interpersonal relationships, and the promotion of such conduct to followers through two-way communication, reinforcement, and decision-making" (Brown et al., 2005, p. 120).

At a more descriptive level, ethical leaders are thought to be honest and trustworthy. They make fair and principled decisions that bring constructive changes to people and the broader society. Ethical leaders also behave ethically in their personal lives and maintain that consistency in their professional lives. Brown and associates (2005, 2006) characterize these personal traits as the *moral person* aspect of ethical leadership.

At the same time, since both leaders and managers are engaged in influencing people toward goal accomplishment (Northouse, 2018), there is also the *moral manager* aspect of ethical leadership (Brown et al., 2005). The *moral manager* aspect depicts ethical leaders' proactive efforts to communicate ethics and values messages, intentionally demonstrate role modeling ethical behavior, and use appropriate rewards and punishments to hold followers accountable for ethical conduct (Brown et al., 2005; Trevino et al., 2003).

To characterize influence, we adopt the definition developed by Berger and Reber (2006) and focus on exploring how female professionals in public relations use their power to become more active and effective leaders who are ready to provide leadership and ethics counseling to guide organizational decision making. In their research, the terms of power and influence are interchangeable and influence is defined as "the ability to get things done by affecting the perceptions, attitudes, beliefs, opinions, decisions, statements, and behaviors of others" (Berger & Reber, 2006, p. 5). According to Berger and Reber's research, influence in public relations is characterized most often as *holding a seat at the decision-making table* (p. 17), followed by *delivering tangible results to support the organization* (p. 19) and *managing the communication production process* (p. 19). The researchers also emphasize that public relations professionals define influence in diverse ways and should have access to "an equally diverse set of influence resources" (p. 21). However, it seems professionals rely on relatively few resources to build their influence or gain their power in reality.

Therefore, the fundamental questions guiding and relating to this chapter become: How do women in public relations define influence? What strategies do women in public relations use to build and enact their influence? How can such established influence help women in public relations become active agents in promoting ethical leadership behaviors and providing leadership and ethics counseling?

Defining the Meaning of Having Influence as a Female PR Leader

As revealed in Chapter Three, women in public relations feel they lack position power of authority in making important decisions such as staffing and budgeting. This naturally links to our questions related to how to define and build up influence to reach the top. In our survey, we designed and built in a section that asks female professionals at all levels of institutional leadership to define the meaning of having influence as a female leader in public relations or communication. We developed and built the list of empowerment and influence items based on a series of industry research on gender representation (e.g. Catalyst, 2003, 2004, 2005, 2007), professional publications (e.g. Zenger & Folkman, 2012), and scholarly research which has particularly focused on the topic of empowerment and influence building (e.g. Berger & Reber, 2006; Eagly, 2005; Ely, 1995; O'Neil, 2003, 2004).

The first key question we asked in this section of the survey is how female professionals define the meaning of having influence as a leader in public relations and communication. Across the entire sample, the top-3 characteristics describing the nature of having influence as a public relations leader include:

1. Being seen as a trusted advisor (5.92/7.0),
2. Having career advancement opportunities (5.87/7.0), and
3. Having a voice that colleagues and co-workers listen to (5.81/7.0).

Besides the top-3 characteristics, a second group of features also frame female professionals' interpretation of empowerment and influence building. Surveyed professionals rate those characteristics in the 5.50–5.80 range, on a seven-point Likert-type scale. This group includes seven critical capabilities:

1. Demonstrating expertise (5.79/7.0),
2. Cultivating a reputation for effectiveness that exceeds expectations (5.77/7.0),
3. Advocating for other women's opportunities (5.77/7.0),
4. Having competitive financial compensation (5.76/7.0),

5. Gaining visibility through senior leadership positions (5.70/7.0),
6. Performing more take-charge actions of delegating, problem solving and influencing upward (5.62/7.0), and
7. Performing in high-visibility assignments (5.60/7.0).

There are two items that received relatively lower ratings from our surveyed professionals, if compared with other influencing characteristics being defined. These two items include: 1) developing informal relationships with influential colleagues and clients (5.45/7.0) and 2) performing more take-care actions of supporting, consulting and rewarding (5.44/7.0).

Our frequency analysis showed similar patterns. The top-4 characteristics of having influence as a female leader in public relations deal with being a trusted advisor (85.7%), having career advancement opportunities (84.0%), demonstrating expertise (83.0%), and having a voice being heard (82.8%) as displayed in Table 4.1.

Table 4.1. Defining the meaning of having influence: Perspectives from women in PR

Having influence means …	Disagreement	Neutral	Agreement
Being seen as a trusted advisor	6.4%	7.8%	85.7%
Having career advancement opportunities	6.1%	10.0%	84.0%
Demonstrating expertise	5.5%	11.5%	83.0%
Having a voice that colleagues and co-workers listen to	6.4%	10.7%	82.8%
Cultivating a reputation for effectiveness that exceeds expectations	5.5%	12.9%	81.6%
Gaining visibility through senior leadership positions	7.00%	11.9%	81.1%
Having competitive financial compensation	8.6%	10.7%	80.7%
Advocating for other women's opportunities	9.0%	10.5%	80.5%
Performing in high-visibility assignments	7.00%	13.3%	79.7%
Performing more take-charge actions of delegating, problem solving and influencing upward	7.8%	13.3%	78.9%
Developing informal relationships with influential colleagues and clients	9.0%	13.5%	77.5%
Performing more take-care actions of supporting, consulting and rewarding	9.2%	16.6%	74.2%

Note: all items were evaluated based on a seven-point Likert-type scale with "1 = not important at all" and "7 = extremely important." The scale for all items was recoded and re-grouped into categorical variables with disagreement representing scale points of 1–3, neutral representing scale point of 4, and agreement representing scale points of 5–7.

PR Women in Different Types of Organizations Define Influence Differently

Our mean comparisons indicated that female professionals working in different types of organizations define influence in different ways. A consistent pattern shows that female professionals working in the category of nonprofit, governmental, educational and political organizations rated almost all characteristics describing influence the highest, if compared with professionals working in other types of organizations. Particularly, they rated the following five items significantly higher:

1. Having competitive financial compensation (6.10/7.0),
2. Having a voice that colleagues and co-workers listen to (6.06/7.0),
3. Having career advancement opportunities (6.03/7.0),
4. Demonstrating expertise (6.00/7.0), and
5. Cultivating a reputation for effectiveness that exceeds expectations (5.90/7.0).

Professionals working in publicly held corporations rated one item, performing in high-visibility assignments, particularly higher than peers in other types of organizations did. Overall, professionals working in public relations and communication agencies showed relatively the lowest scores on items interpreting the meaning of having influence.

Women of Color Define Influence with Strong Opinions

Results of mean comparisons showed that women of color in general expressed a strong opinion when defining influence and framing important capabilities for being a female leader in public relations. They rated all items describing having influence higher than white women did. Eight items out of 12 received significantly higher scores as displayed in Table 4.2. Women of color particularly valued three characteristics when defining influence, including:

1. Demonstrating expertise (6.10/7.0),
2. Being seen as a trusted advisor (6.10/7.0), and
3. Gaining visibility through senior leadership positions (6.02/7.0).

In addition, women of color defined influence from a different perspective. They believe that having influence will bring better career advancement opportunities to them (5.98/7.0). They can cultivate a reputation for effectiveness that

Table 4.2. Women of color define the meaning of having influence with strong opinions

	White women (n=360)	Black women (n=100)	Other women (n=52)	F-value
Having career advancement opportunities	5.93	5.50	5.98	4.27**
Having competitive financial compensation	5.80	5.61	5.81	.68
Gaining visibility through senior leadership positions	5.77	5.30	6.02	6.28**
Demonstrating expertise	5.84	5.46	6.10	4.64**
Performing in high-visibility assignments	5.64	5.42	5.75	1.24
Performing more take-charge actions of delegating, problem solving and influencing upward	5.69	5.29	5.77	3.51*
Performing more take-care actions of supporting, consulting and rewarding	5.52	4.96	5.90	8.85**
Developing informal relationships with influential colleagues and clients	5.53	5.05	5.69	5.44**
Cultivating a reputation for effectiveness that exceeds expectations	5.85	5.42	5.90	4.06*
Having a voice that colleagues and co-workers listen to	5.87	5.53	5.98	2.63
Being seen as a trusted advisor	5.98	5.62	6.10	3.36*
Advocating for other women's opportunities	5.82	5.52	5.98	2.20

Note: $* p < .05$; $** p < .01$.

exceeds expectations (5.90/7.0) and perform more take-care actions of supporting, consulting and rewarding (5.90/7.0).

PR Women at Lower Level of Leadership Define Influence with Different Emphasis

Not surprisingly, when we look at definitions of influence by different levels of hierarchical reporting relationships, female professionals at the lower reporting levels rated all influence characteristics higher than those who have made it to the top. Professionals at the lower level of leadership perceive getting more career advancement opportunities and being seen as a trusted advisor as their immediate needs to build influence and establish reputation. However, independent sample t-tests did not show significant differences between the group of professionals who have an official and defined leadership title and functions and the group who does not, when rating the meaning of having influence as a female leader in public relations.

Years of Experience Impact the Interpretation of Influence

Professionals' years of experience revealed different perceptions when defining influence. The group with the longest professional experience (i.e. having more than 10 years of experience in communication) defines having influence as a major drive to have better career advancement opportunities (5.99/7.0, F-value = 3.92, $p < .05$). This group also defines influence as having their voice being heard by their colleagues and co-workers (5.92/7.0, F-value = 3.53, $p < .05$). This evaluation is consistent with the perception of being a trusted advisor. With more than ten years of professional experience, they define having influence as being trusted by colleagues and co-workers as a reliable advisor (6.03/7.0, F-value = 4.50, $p < .01$). They also believe having influence is an indicator that one could establish a solid reputation of being effective as a female leader in public relations. Such evaluations can be a reflection of the positive outcomes resulted from established influence from the most experienced group of female professionals.

On the other hand, professionals with less than 5 years of professional experience define influence from the unconscious dynamics that underlie their career path and expectations on leadership advancement. For example, they define having influence as an indicator to gain visibility through senior leadership positions and perform in high-visibility assignments. This group of professionals also indicates having influence means; as female communication professionals, you will perform more take-care actions such as supporting, consulting and rewarding. As the least-experienced group, they also believe that advocating for other women to gain opportunities shall be part of the leadership efforts in empowering women. You establish your influence as a leader by coaching and advocating for other group members. This finding highlights the importance of having mentors and sponsors in early stages of leadership development. Such essential elements of building influence contribute to a deeper understanding of the proposition that leadership involves influence.

Using Strategies to Build and Enact Influence

We asked surveyed professionals to evaluate how likely they are to use certain strategies to provide leadership and ethics counseling to senior leadership team within the organization, if this is part of their strategic efforts in establishing and enacting their influence. Based on the ratings of potential strategies we adapted from some recent industry reports (e.g. Catalyst, 2005, 2007), the most used and valued strategy is to invite questions and build up a dialogue (5.45/7.0), with the goal that the issue can be discussed and resolved. Surveyed female professionals think the building-a-dialogue strategy is a positive approach to establish influence and obtain desired outcomes. The strategy that receives the second highest rating score is referring to the core values of the organization and addressing what is right or lawful (5.23/7.0) when providing ethics and leadership counseling. Another common strategy rated by surveyed professionals is to provide scenarios, discuss potential consequences, and provide alternative solutions (5.19/7.0). Professionals also prefer to use research results such as case studies, benchmark reports, and surveys (5.15/7.0) to provide persuasive and scientific evidence.

Surveyed professionals' ratings also reflect some less-used strategies when providing leadership and ethics counseling, including raising concerns of stakeholders (4.70/7.0), recruiting allies or forming coalitions (4.74/7.0), and getting buy-in from team members (4.83/7.0). Professionals indicated they do use personal experience with a combined strategy of emotional appeals (5.07/7.0). They also feel using a direct approach to apply pressure or show persistence may help them build and enact their influence (4.88/7.0).

The percentage analysis shows that female professionals do use various strategies when providing leadership and ethics counseling to the senior leadership team in the organization. The strategy of inviting questions and having a dialogue is rated as the top strategy, agreed by 74.0% of the respondents. The strategy of making legitimacy appeals by referring to core values of organizations or addressing what is right or lawful is the second most valued strategy as mentioned by 70.1% of respondents. The third strategy that has been used widely is to provide scenarios, present potential consequences, or suggest alternatives as mentioned by 69.5% of respondents. Figure 4.1 shows the percentage changes that are based on our survey respondents' evaluations over a range of strategies they would use when providing leadership and ethics counseling to the senior leadership team. Overall, our results have confirmed a preferred trend in using discussion- and research-dominated proactive strategies has gone hand-in-hand with a less-preferred and relational approach in recruiting allies or raising concerns.

When comparing how female professionals working in different types of organizations use strategies to build influence, different preferences appeared. Female professionals in different types of organizations are in favor of different strategies to build and enact influence. Professionals in private or state-owned

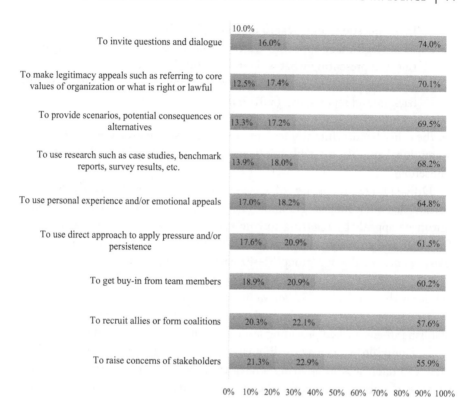

Figure 4.1. Using strategies to build and expand influence when providing leadership and ethics counseling

companies are in favor of using research results and making legitimacy appeals to provide leadership and ethics counseling. Professionals in the group of non-profits, governmental, educational and political organizations focus on building a dialogue to invite questions and have a discussion. Agency-based professionals lead on using a combination of various strategies in making their cases, including providing scenarios, using a direct approach of being persistent, sharing personal experiences, recruiting allies, and getting buy-in from team members.

Minority women use a wide variety of strategies when providing leadership and ethical counseling. When comparing the likelihood of using influence-building strategies by looking at different ethnic groups, minority women do not only lead on the overall ratings of most strategies but also show differences in the extent to which the strategies are preferred. For example, women of color are in favor of three strategies particularly:

1. Invite questions and create a dialogue (5.75/7.0),
2. Make legitimacy appeals by referring to the core values of the organization and presenting what is right or lawful (5.35/7.0), and
3. Use research such as case studies, benchmark reports, survey results, background reports, etc. (5.31/7.0).

On the other hand, white women are in favor of using personal experience and/or emotional appeals to establish influence when providing leadership and ethics counseling.

Different age groups use influence-building strategies differently. Statistics indicate that the youngest group of female professionals are in favor of making legitimacy appeals by referring to core values (5.33/7.0), using research results (5.27/7.0), and providing scenarios (5.26/7.0). Besides the three most valued strategies, women in the age group 31–40 particularly prefer using the strategy of inviting questions and creating a dialogue for discussion (5.54/7.0) to establish and enact their influence. Senior women (e.g. those in the group of more than 50 years) prefer to use personal experiences and/or emotional appeals (5.12/7.0) to establish influence when providing leadership and ethics counseling.

Not only do women with different years of professional experiences have different preferences in applying strategies in building and exerting influence, but there are also differences in the extent to which they are represented along the hierarchical reporting line. We found that the hierarchical reporting level influences female professionals' selection and application of influence-building strategies. Professionals at the lower levels rated all influence-building strategies higher than those at higher levels but particularly higher on two strategies, which are creating a dialogue for discussion (5.63/7.0) and using personal experience and/or emotional appeals (5.23/7.0). On the other hand, professionals at the top level (e.g. top leaders in communication) have given all strategies consistent and average ratings without showing any strong preferences.

Readiness to Provide Leadership and Ethics Counseling

As part of the research design, we asked female professionals whether they feel prepared to provide leadership and ethics counseling on issues related to public relations and communication to the senior leadership team in their organization. As a related topic, we also asked female professionals to evaluate their top communication leaders' principled behaviors as addressed in ethical leadership.

Descriptive results showed that overall female professionals feel they are ready to provide leadership and ethics counseling when needed, with a mean score of 5.01 ($S.D.$ = 1.48) on a seven-point Likert-type scale. When we analyzed the results by percentage, we found that almost three out of four female professionals (72.5%) indicated that she feels prepared to provide leadership and ethics counseling on issues related to public relations and/or communication to the senior leadership team if needed.

The nature of women's positions along the hierarchical line is a major factor prohibiting women from providing leadership and ethics counseling. Female respondents who identify themselves as top communication leaders in our sample are most confident with their preparedness to provide leadership and ethics counseling (M = 5.60, $S.D.$ = 1.17). Respondents with two or more reporting levels feel less prepared to do so (M = 4.80, $S.D.$ = 1.50). When female professionals face more reporting levels in their current position, they feel less confident in demonstrating leadership and ethics counseling functions (F-value = 7.21, $d.f.$ =2, $p < .01$).

Such confidence gap is also found between white women and women of color, but reversely. White women are less confident or feel less prepared (4.90/7.0) to provide leadership and ethics counseling to the senior leadership team, if compared with women of color (5.20/7.0) (F-value = 3.25, $d.f.$ =2, $p < .05$). Female African American professionals in our sample are the most prepared and confident group who are ready to provide leadership and ethics counseling based on their own evaluation (5.33/7.0) while women in other minority groups lag behind slightly (5.06/7.0). The percentage analysis (see Figure 4.2) also shows that Black women feel more ready and prepared to act as leadership and ethics counselors when issues are related to public relations and communication.

Principled Behaviors of Ethical Leadership

Given the fact that many prominent ethical scandals happened in virtually all types of organizations, it is obvious that emphasizing the ethical dimension of leadership in public relations practice is not only necessary but also urgent. Some recent research in public relations leadership has confirmed the growing demands from stakeholders for transparency in communication (e.g. Berger & Meng, 2014). When stakeholders expect organizations to communicate directly with external groups to address transparency, organizations should prioritize ethical leadership and consideration to implement strategies and actions to increase transparency, both within and beyond the organization (Reber, 2014). Research

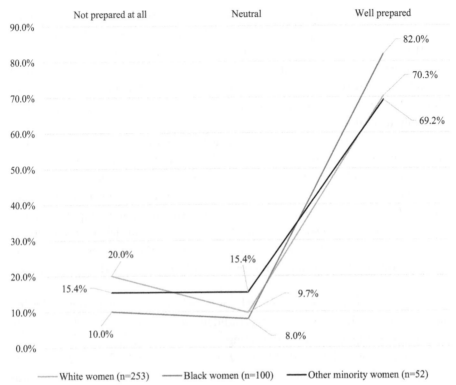

Figure 4.2. Readiness for providing leadership and ethics counseling by race (in percentages)

also suggests organizations shall constantly monitor stakeholder communications to identify transparency concerns (Berger & Meng, 2014; Reber, 2014). When leaders are one of the key sources of ethical guidance for employees, the demonstration of principled ethical behaviors through personal actions, communication, and interpersonal relationships will reinforce the importance of ethical conduct to followers (Brown & Trevino, 2006).

Building on this work, as well as the collective responses from our surveyed professionals in the current study, we further investigate what the term ethical leadership means to female professionals at different phases of their professional career. Through their evaluations of seven principled behaviors which reflect the domain of ethical leadership (Brown et al., 2005), we obtain their reflective perspective of ethical leadership by examining their perceptions of the ethical conduct of the highest ranked public relations or communication leader in their organization. In this way, we can better understand what characterizes ethical leadership from the perspective of public relations practice, and how it relates to female professionals' strategies and efforts in establishing and enacting influence.

Brown and associates' (2005) systematically conceptualize and develop an ethical leadership construct by using social learning theory as the theoretical basis to explain why and how ethical leaders influence their followers. Based on their research, ethical leaders are seen as honest and trustworthy advisors. They are fair and principled decision-makers. They also behave ethically in their personal and professional lives. As briefly reviewed earlier, Brown et al. (2005, 2006) characterized this as the *moral person aspect* of ethical leadership. Systematically, they also define the *moral manager aspect* of ethical leadership, which describes the leader's proactive efforts to influence followers through ethical conduct and consideration. The *moral manager* aspect emphasizes the leader's actions of communicating an ethics and values message, demonstrating visibly and intentionally role modeling ethical behavior, and using the reward system to hold followers accountable for ethical conduct. According Brown et al. (2006), ethical leaders always walk the talk as "they practice what they preach and are proactive role models for ethical conduct" (p. 597).

By using the Ethical Leadership Scale (ELS) developed by Brown et al. (2005), we asked female professionals to evaluate the ethical conduct of their highest ranked public relations or communication leader based on their observation and the working relationship with the leader in the workplace. We selected seven items out of the ten-item instrument of ELS as these seven items "were rated significantly more likely to reflect the domain of ethical leadership than consideration" (p. 125). The content of the seven items represent principled behaviors in ethical leadership. Table 4.3 illustrates female professionals' evaluations on their top public relations or communication leaders' ethical leadership. Top leaders received a relatively high score on two principled behaviors, which are:

1. Conduct his/her personal life in an ethical manner (5.22/7.0), and
2. Sets an example of how to do things the right way in terms of ethics (5.16/7.0).

Besides these top two exemplars, a second group of ethical behaviors with mediocre performance can be identified. Those are rated just above 5.0, based on a seven-point Likert-type scale. They include behaviors like making fair and balanced decisions (5.07/7.0), defining success not just by results but also the way that they are obtained (5.07/7.0), and discussing business ethics or values with employees (5.01/7.0). Both the top group and second group of principled ethical behaviors are assessed differently by types of organization, by professionals' leadership level, and by professionals' ethnic background, which will be reported later in this chapter.

Table 4.3. Assessment of principled behaviors of ethical leadership as demonstrated by the highest ranked communication leader

The highest ranked communication leader in my organization ...	Mean	S.D.
Conducts his/her personal life in an ethical manner	5.22	1.60
Sets an example of how to do things the right way in terms of ethics	5.16	1.71
Makes fair and balanced decisions	5.07	1.67
Defines success not just by results but also the way that they are obtained	5.07	1.64
Discusses business ethics or values with employees	5.01	1.76
Asks "what is the right thing to do?" when making decisions	4.98	1.75
Disciplines employees who violate ethical standards	4.81	1.72

Note: items are evaluated based on a seven-point Likert-type scale with "1 = never" and "7 = always."

Two principled behaviors that receive passing scores may raise some concerns, which include asking "what is the right thing to do" when making decisions (4.98/7.0) and disciplining employees who violate ethical standards (4.81/7.0). Figure 4.3 illustrates female professionals' evaluations of top communication leaders' ethical leadership. The decrease in percentage is similar to their overall ratings on leaders' principled ethical behaviors as displayed in Table 4.3. The figure also reveals the behaviors that have been less endorsed (showing as "disagreement" in percentage) by top leaders. For example, our respondents don't think their top leaders have put sufficient efforts in discussing business ethics or values with group members nor coming up right solutions when there are employees who violate ethical standards.

Demographics and the Underlying Influence on Ethical Leadership

In order to test whether female professionals' demographics are associated their perceptions and evaluations of leaders' ethical behaviors, we conducted several tests to look for evidence. We looked at a few demographics such as age, race, organizational type, hierarchical reporting levels and leadership role in order to find out how they relate to respondents' perceptions of ethical leadership.

Leadership Role and Ethical Conduct

When looking at respondents' evaluation of top communication leaders' principled ethical behaviors, it is interesting to find that professionals who currently

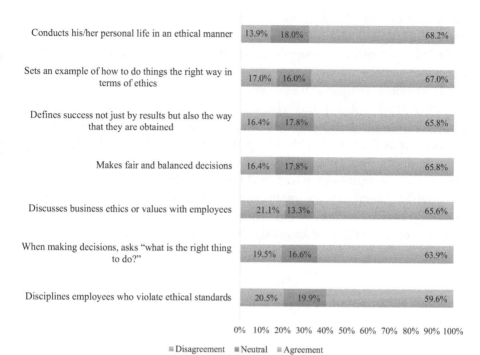

Figure 4.3. Do top communication leaders demonstrate ethical behaviors? Opinions of surveyed female professionals (in percentages)

have an official and defined leadership position rated their top leaders' ethical conduct much higher than those who don't. There are two principled behaviors that received significantly higher scores from professionals having an official and defined leadership position. They agree that their top leaders define success not only by results but also by looking at the process to obtain such success (5.20 vs. 4.89, F-value = 4.58, $p < .05$). They also agree that their top leaders would ask "what is the right thing to do" when making decisions (5.20 vs. 4.89, F-value = 4.89, $p < .05$). Overall, the results indicate respondents who are already in a leadership position, regardless of the scope and the level of that leadership role (ranging from the C-Suite level to the team/project level), would give their top leader higher scores on ethical conduct than those who are not in a defined leadership position.

Reporting Level and Ethical Leadership

By comparing the ratings from respondents at different levels along the hierarchical reporting line, we found perceptual gaps when evaluating top leaders' principled ethical behaviors. Self-identified top leaders think they make fair and balanced decisions (5.57/7.0), ask "what is the right thing to do" when making decisions (5.31/7.0), and define success not only by results but also by process (5.29/7.0). The top-leader group also agrees that ethical leadership would involves disciplining employees who violate ethical standards (5.05/7.0).

Respondents residing at the one-reporting level gave their top leaders mediocre scores on principled ethical behaviors, while respondents having two or more reporting levels rated more harshly when evaluating leaders' performance on ethical conduct as illustrated by the line pattern in Figure 4.4. Given the existing research on employee cynicism, the prevalence of employee cynicism does affect the perceived integrity of top leaders (Dean et al., 1998). It is not surprising to see lower-level employees (i.e. professionals with two or more reporting levels in this study) may be inclined to rate senior executives or leaders with whom they have little contact or limited knowledge (i.e. the top communication leader in the

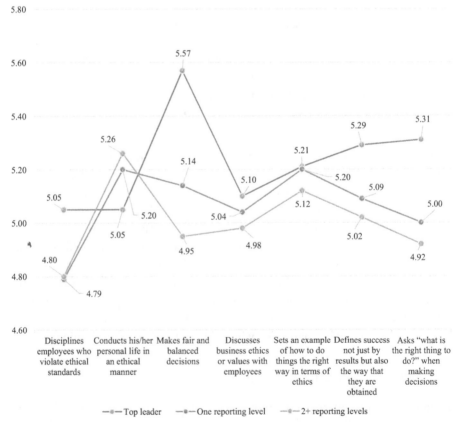

Figure 4.4. Perceptual gaps on ethical leadership along the hierarchy reporting line

organization) harshly in terms of ethical leadership performance since no direction interaction nor collaboration is involved.

However, there is one item rated much higher by junior professionals. They do agree their top communication leader conducts his/her personal life in an ethical manner (5.26/7.0). Such finding shows promising outcomes that when general employees or junior professionals are looking outside themselves to senior leaders for ethical guidance, the ethical dimension of leadership as demonstrated by top communication leaders at an individual level is accountable.

At the same time, we also raise the question regarding what top leaders can do to decrease the perceptual gaps that may have been caused by employee cynicism on their ethical leadership performance? If ethical leaders exert a great influence on employees such as their pro-social behavior, job satisfaction and performance (Brown & Trevino, 2006), it is critical to create and establish the visibility of executive ethical leadership and make sure such behavioral influence is well received at both group and individual levels. Such efforts may neutralize lower-level employees' cynical attitudes with the ultimate goal of creating favorable reputations for ethical leadership.

Organizational Types and Ethical Leadership

Certain aspects of ethical leadership are likely to vary depending on the type of organization and its affiliated industry. Although we didn't further differentiate respondents' organizations by industry in this project, we did find professionals working in different types of organizations rated their top communication leaders' principled behaviors differently. Results from our mean comparisons show that top communication leaders in publicly held corporations demonstrate ethical leadership better as they received relatively higher scores on all seven principled behaviors. On the other hand, top communication leaders in the category of nonprofit, governmental, educational and political organizations received the lowest ratings on ethical leadership from their fellow employees. More work and research will be required to find out why and how ethical leadership differs depending upon the types of organizations.

Race and Ethical Leadership

The perceptual gaps on ethical leadership are also reflected on different ethnic groups' ratings on their top communication leaders. White women (70.3% in our sample) gave their top leaders mediocre ratings on principled behaviors, ranging from 4.80 to 5.26 over the seven items. There is a significantly divided viewpoint between black women and other minority women. Black women gave the lowest ratings on ethical leadership while other minority women rated top leaders the highest on five out of seven items. The content of the two items that received relatively low scores from other minority women represents the actions of setting ethical examples as role models and asking "what is the right thing to do" when making decisions. Figure 4.5 depicts the trend lines of the ratings, as well as shows the different perceptions from three ethnic groups we defined in this study.

In recent years, diversity, equity, and inclusion (DE&I) management are important in terms of its effectiveness in promoting equality and fostering an inclusive corporate environment. It responds to different needs, career aspirations, contributions and lifestyles of employees by recognizing employees' differences and potential (Wirth, 2001). Literature on DE&I management suggests that to practice diversity, equity, and inclusion more effectively, leaders shall be responsible for continually developing themselves and their employees. It is important for leaders to use an upward-appraisal approach to receive feedback on their performance from their subordinates and peers (Kandola & Fullerton, 1994). This approach has implications in improving the mutual understanding of ethical leadership as well. Due to the distance (e.g. physical distance, social distance, or frequency of task interaction) between leaders and subordinates, it is critical for leaders to improve their communication with employees about ethical leadership.

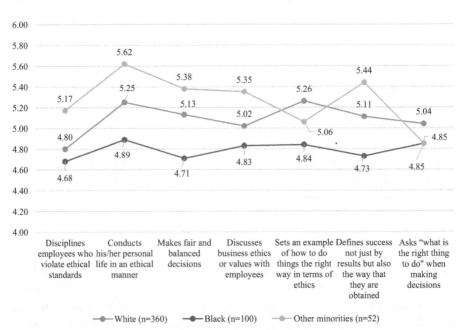

Figure 4.5. Assessment of principled behaviors of ethical leadership by race

Leaders need to make sure their demonstration of principled ethical behaviors is consistent and perceived well if no or limited direct observation or interaction with subordinates is offered (Antonakis & Atwater, 2002).

Conclusion

As mentioned at the beginning of this chapter, leadership involves influence (Yukl, 2002). We began this chapter by reviewing relevant literature on influence, empowerment, ethics and leadership. We identified the meaning of having influence as a female leader in public relations and communication. Our surveyed female professionals shared their interpretation of influencing characteristics based on their demographic backgrounds (e.g. age, reporting level, organizational type). Defining influence shall be an initial step for female professionals to be empowered and to rise above the leadership hurdle along their career paths.

We further explored the strategies female professionals used (or could use) to establish and exert their influence. Results indicated inviting questions and creating a dialogue for discussion is the most used and valued strategy in building influence. Using research results and making legitimacy appeals also help female professionals make their case when providing leadership and ethics counseling to the senior leadership team when the issues are related to public relations and communication.

Ethical practice has always been one of the core values for the public relations profession. For public relations professionals, the PRSA Code of Ethics is central to the ethical practice of public relations. While ethical concerns and scandals occur daily, they also raise important questions about the role of leadership in cultivating ethical conduct. Despite its normative perspective embedded in transformational and charismatic leadership domains, ethical leadership is a topic that has great potential for academic research and practice in public relations.

In this chapter, we did not only explore female professionals' readiness in providing leadership and ethics counseling. We also asked female professionals to evaluate their top communication leaders' performance on ethical leadership based on their personal observations and task interaction. We found that professionals' demographics (such as race, leadership status, reporting levels, etc.) presented some underlying influence on their perceptions of top leaders' ethical leadership. More research is needed to explore top leaders' demographic profiles and how these would be associated with ethical leadership. The public relations profession and organizations are striving to select, develop and retain ethical leaders. Knowing the perceptual gaps in ethical leadership could be a beginning step to make ethical leadership a part of research and training agendas.

References

Antonakis, J., & Atwater, L. (2002). Leader distance: A review and proposed theory. *The Leadership Quarterly, 13*, 673–704.

Bandura, A. (1977). *Social learning theory.* Englewood Cliffs, NJ: Prentice Hall.

Bandura, A. (1986). *Social foundations of thought and action.* Englewood Cliffs, NJ: Prentice Hall.

Berger, B. K., & Meng, J. (2014). *Public relations leaders as sensemakers: A global study of leadership in public relations and communication management.* New York: Routledge.

Berger, B. K., & Reber, B. H. (2006). *Gaining influence in public relations: The role of resistance in practice.* Mahwah, NJ: LEA Publishers.

Brown, M. E., & Trevino, L. K. (2006). Ethical leadership: A review and future directions. *The Leadership Quarterly, 17*(6), 595–616.

Brown, M. E., Trevino, L. K., & Harrison, D. A. (2005). Ethical leadership: A social learning perspective for construct development and testing. *Organizational behavior and human decision processes, 97*(2), 117–134.

Catalyst. (2003). *Women in U.S. corporate leadership.* New York: Catalyst.

Catalyst. (2004). *Women and men in the U.S. corporate leadership: Same workplace, different realities?* New York: Catalyst.

Catalyst. (2005). *Women take care, men take charge: Stereotyping of business leaders exposed.* New York: Catalyst.

Catalyst. (2007). *The double blind dilemma for women in leadership: Damned if you do; doomed if you don't.* New York: Catalyst.

Dean, J. W., Brandes, P., & Dharwadkar, R. (1998). Organizational cynicism. *Academy of Management Review, 23*, 341–352.

Eagly, A. H. (2005). Achieving relational authenticity in leadership: Does gender matter? *The Leadership Quarterly, 16*(3), 459–474.

Ely, R. J. (1995). The power in demography: Women's social constructions of gender identity at work. *Academy of Management Journal, 38*(3), 589–634.

Guillén, M. F. (2010). Classical sociological approaches to the study of leadership. In N. Nohria & R. Khurana (Eds.), *Handbook of leadership theory and practice* (pp. 223–238). Boston, MA: Harvard Business Press.

Kandola, R., & Fullerton, J. (1994). Diversity: More than just an empty slogan. *Personnel Management, 26*(4), 46.

Moberg, D. J. (2000). Role models and moral exemplars: How do employees acquire virtues by observing others? *Business Ethics Quarterly, 10*(3), 675–696.

Northouse, P. G. (2018). *Introduction to leadership: Concepts and practice* (4th Ed.). Thousand Oaks, CA: SAGE publications.

O'Neil, J. (2003). An investigation of the sources of influence of corporate public relations practitioners. *Public Relations Review, 29*(2), 159–169.

O'Neil, J. (2004). Effects of gender and power on PR managers' upward influence. *Journal of Managerial Issues, 16*(1), 127–144.

Reber, B. H. (2014). Strategies and tactics leaders use to manage issues. In Berger, B. K., & Meng, J. (Eds.). *Public relations leaders as sensemakers: A global study of leadership in public relations and communication management* (pp. 80–94). New York: Routledge.

Selznick, P. (1984). *Leadership in administration: A sociological interpretation.* Berkeley, CA: University of California Press.

Trevino, L. K., Brown, M., & Hartman, L. P. (2003). A quantitative investigation of perceived executive ethical leadership: Perceptions from inside and outside the executive suite. *Human Relations, 55,* 5–37.

Wirth, L. (2001). *Breaking through the glass ceiling: Women in management.* Geneva: International Labour Organization.

Yukl, G. A. (2002). *Leadership in organizations* (5th Ed.). Englewood Cliffs, NJ: Prentice Hall.

Zenger, J., & Folkman, J. (2012, Mar. 15). Are women better leaders than men? Blog post. *Harvard Business Review.* Retrieved from https://hbr.org/2012/03/a-study-in-leadership-women-do on September 20, 2019.

CHAPTER FIVE

PR Women's Leadership Development and Participation Opportunities

We agree that the purpose of studying leadership is to enable the development of leaders to enhance effective leadership practice. Previous research on leadership development suggests that some best-practice organizations (e.g. Johnson & Johnson, GE) view leadership development as a critical way to increase competitive advantage and support organizational strategies (Fulmer & Glodsmith, 2001). Similarly, one of the most important factors to facilitate the advancement of the public relations profession is to enable the development of highly qualified professionals who will become future leaders not only in the organization but also for the profession.

Are women capable to lead? This is an age-old question deeply rooted in gender-based stereotypes when discussing the development of leaders (e.g. Catalyst, 2003; Ely & Rhode, 2010; Mumford, Zaccaro, Connelly & Marks, 2000). We fully acknowledge that women (and men) may start with different levels of inherited leadership capabilities, especially at the individual level of personal attributes or psychological perspectives (e.g. Chatman & Kennedy, 2010). At the same time, we also strongly believe that leadership skills can be learned and leadership competency can be improved especially in the public relations profession, as it is such a dynamic profession experiencing rapid development at an ever-fast changing pace and under the influence of media, cultural, and social changes (Servaes, 2012).

Therefore, this chapter focuses on investigating female professionals' perceptions on leadership development and leadership participation opportunities based on their observations and experience in the workplace. We ask questions to gain their perspectives on their organization's efforts in supporting women's leadership advancement in the past three years. Knowing their experiences and opportunities helps gauge whether progress has made. We are also interested in their projection of future improvement, if there's any, in women's leadership development and participation. We hope to connect the *knowing*, *doing*, and *being* dimensions in leadership development based on the perceptions and expectations of female professionals in the field. By doing so, we hope to help organizations create sustainable development-and-participation leadership initiatives, interventions, and programs as part of their strategic planning to drive operations and change.

Leadership Development: From Knowing to Being

Leadership development can be defined as "the expansion of the organization's capacity to enact the basic leadership tasks needed for collective work: setting direction, creating alignment, and maintaining commitment" (Van Velsor & McCauley, 2004, p. 18). Thus, leadership development should be seen as a continuous journey or process that can improve a person's leadership capacity and competency. This is a contrasting view to *management* development, which aims at helping managers to acquire the specific knowledge and skills needed to enhance task performance in the management role (Day, 2000). Van Velsor and McCauley (2004) also distinguished between *leader* development and *leadership* development. Leader development refers to individual growth and skill advancement that expand one's leadership capacity and improve performance, while leadership development focuses more on an organization's attempt to enhance its team of leaders to strengthen their overall organizational performance.

Rather than focusing on technical job skills, leadership development initiatives usually pay more attention to broader capabilities and competencies in an interpersonal context, such as flexibility, conflict management, team building, change management, self-awareness, and/or interpersonal skills (e.g. Day & Harrison, 2007). Such initiatives see leadership development as a process involving cultivating and leveraging strengths while understanding and minimizing weaknesses (Hernez-Broome & Hughes, 2004).

Previous research on leadership development has focused on three major categories: the "knowing," the "doing," and the "being" dimensions of becoming a leader. The "knowing" dimension highlights the cognitive capabilities and multiple intelligences such as analytical intelligence, social intelligence, emotional intelligence, and contextual intelligence a leader is required to possess (e.g. Riggio, Murphy & Pirozzolo, 2001). The "doing" dimension highlights the behavioral components or skills such as problem-solving skills, conflict management, or adaptive skills a leader could demonstrate to group members in varied institutional contexts (e.g. Mumford et al., 2000). The "being" dimension addresses a unique perspective of looking into leadership development from the concept of self-identity, which enables someone to think of him- or herself as a leader and to interact with the team from that identity (e.g. Ibarra, Snook, & Guillén Ramo, 2010). Such self-perception will generate an identity-based model of leader development to enlist the followers.

Leadership development literature also suggests that experience plays a critical role in developing leadership talent. Research confirms that an individual's naturally occurring life experiences and what he or she learns from those experiences can generate a significant impact on the development of leaders (Bennis, 2009). Scholars who study leadership development also found that organizations are critical in helping talented employees get the right experiences at the right time to accelerate their development as leaders (e.g. McCall, 2010; McCauley et al., 1994). For example, McCall (2010) identified five leveraging points organizations can use to create a supportive institutional context for leadership learning and development: (1) identifying developmental experiences; (2) identifying people with potential to be leaders; (3) developing processes for getting the right learning experience; (4) increasing the odds that learning will occur; and (5) taking a career-long perspective with a focus on critical career transitions.

Research on formal leadership development initiatives generated similar results with a heavy focus on the role of organizations in such efforts. For example, Conger (2010) suggested that it is important for organizations to create formal leadership development initiatives and interventions. These leadership development initiatives shall not only focus on individual skill development. But more importantly, such initiatives shall emphasize integrating the corporate vision and values, adding strategic interventions to promote major changes, and designing active learning approaches to address organizational challenges and opportunities with the ultimate goal of enhancing the overall quality of leadership in an organization (Conger, 2010).

Avolio (2010) also argues that, in order to develop authentic leadership, it is important for organizations to accelerate the development of positive leadership for sustainable impact not only focused on individuals, but also groups, communities, and societies. In addition, Kegan and Lahey (2010) argued that past research has over-emphasized leadership while underemphasized development.

They suggested that the emphasis of leadership development should be on the process of *development* in order to build up an ecosystem motivation rather than an ego-system of self-worth validation.

Overall, the broad literature in the field has suggested best-practice organizations view leadership development programs as a way to increase competitive advantage and support corporate strategy (e.g. Fulmer & Goldsmith, 2001). The literature on leadership development also confirms that leaders develop in multiple approaches: an individual's experiences, formal or structured leadership development programs, educational programs or other types of interventions, formal training developed by organizations, and the influence of role models, mentors and coaches (e.g. Conger & Fulmer, 2003). The possibility of various formats of leadership development initiatives echoes the complicated nature of leadership itself.

As mentioned earlier, the focus of this chapter is to explore the challenges and barriers female public relations professionals face as they seek leadership development and participation opportunities. Particularly, we are interested in organizations' support and efforts in such leadership programs and initiatives to advance female communication professionals who are aspired to take on leadership roles. Thus, the central questions for us to address in this chapter include: How can organizations support female professionals who have *the desire* and *the ability* to develop leadership competency? Can organizations design and launch leadership development initiatives and interventions to help women reach the top by increasing their leadership participation?

Resources for Leadership Development

Leadership development is an essential prerequisite and a continued effort in leadership progression as it allows organizations to maximize members' contribution at various stages of their professional career (Conger, 2010). On-the-job training offers immediate learning opportunities at the individual level for individual skill and leadership development. From the perspective of sustainable development, it is equally critical to enable female communication professionals' access to formal and informal leadership development programs and resources for leadership advancement. Some action learning approaches also suggest to have individuals take ownership for leading change initiatives at their level of the organization in order to facilitate a major change, namely learning by doing (e.g. Conger, 1992; Dotlich & Noel, 1998).

For women who have the desire and the ability to achieve leadership positions and move up the ladder in managerial jobs at senior levels, access to formal leadership training and development programs both internally and externally is critical. Some informal processes such as mentoring and networking, both within and beyond the organization, are also crucial. Therefore, in order to obtain a picture of leadership development approaches, we asked our respondents to share their experience and observations in terms of what leadership development resources are available via their organization.

Results indicate the majority of female professionals (63.9%) agreed that their organization has built in some on-the-job training programs to improve qualifications and skills required for higher-level jobs or a wide range of tasks. A similar portion of female professionals—six out of ten—reported that their organization provides access to both internal and external leadership training and development programs (62.7% and 60.5%, respectively). More than half of surveyed professionals (55.7%) indicated their organization allows them to work with a mentor for leadership development. The only approach that received the divided answer is engaging female professionals in continued and/or formal leadership education at a college or university (28.5% in disagreement and 54.5% in agreement). Figure 5.1 displays survey results on how organizations help "women like me" develop leadership competencies.

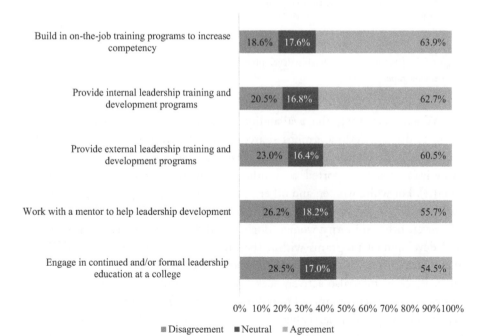

Figure 5.1. Resources for leadership development supported by organization as observed by female professionals (in percentages)

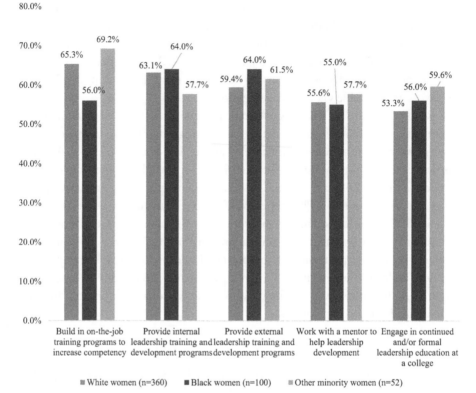

Figure 5.2. Resources for leadership development as perceived by different ethnic groups (agreement in percentages)

When examining the availability of leadership development approaches by race, different ethnic groups shared different perceptions. As illustrated in Figure 5.2, the biggest gap exists in *the on-the-job training programs* as African American women reported a significantly smaller percentage of agreement (56.0%). For white women and other minority women, the percentages of agreement on *on-the-job training programs* jumped to 65.3% and 69.2%, respectively. However, other minority women don't feel there are many leadership training and development programs within the organization suitable for them (57.7%), if compared with white women (63.1%) and Black women (64.0%). At the same time, Black women also actively seek leadership training and development programs outside their organization (64.0%). Women from all three ethnic groups report relatively lower percentages of agreement on two things: working with a mentor to help leadership development and engaging in continued and/or formal leadership education.

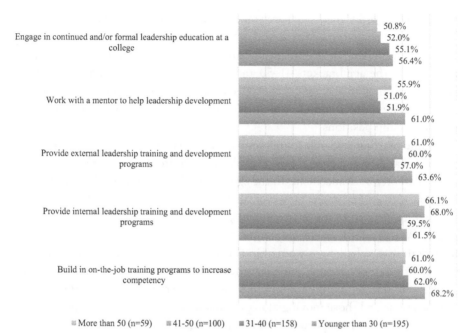

Engage in continued and/or formal leadership education at a college
- 50.8%
- 52.0%
- 55.1%
- 56.4%

Work with a mentor to help leadership development
- 55.9%
- 51.0%
- 51.9%
- 61.0%

Provide external leadership training and development programs
- 61.0%
- 60.0%
- 57.0%
- 63.6%

Provide internal leadership training and development programs
- 66.1%
- 68.0%
- 59.5%
- 61.5%

Build in on-the-job training programs to increase competency
- 61.0%
- 60.0%
- 62.0%
- 68.2%

■ More than 50 (n=59)   ■ 41-50 (n=100)   ■ 31-40 (n=158)   ■ Younger than 30 (n=195)

Figure 5.3. Resources for leadership development as perceived by age (in percentages)

When breaking down the resources for leadership development by types of organizations, different gaps also emerged. Female professionals working in public relations or communication agencies seem to be short of internal development resources in several ways, including internal leadership training and development programs, mentorship opportunities, and on-the-job training programs to increase competency, if compared to their colleagues working in other types of organizations. At the same time, agency-based professionals report to have more resources externally for leadership development such as external training programs and continued/formal leadership education. Female professionals working in corporations report to have more internal leadership training and development programs but they also indicate a relative shortage in mentoring programs for leadership development. Half of professionals working in private companies report having no access to continued and/or formal leadership education resources at a college.

The fact of insufficient leadership development resources is particularly noticeable for women in the 31–40 age bracket as illustrated in Figure 5.3. Female professionals in the age group 31–40 report to have less access or opportunities for mentorship support, continued leadership education, as well as leadership training and development programs, both internally and externally. On the other hand, female professionals who are younger than 30 years report the highest percentage of agreement in all listed leadership development resources. The situation of lacking leadership development resources is improved slightly for female professionals in the age brackets 41–50 and more than 50. The constraints that are placed on women in the age bracket 31–40 can seriously hamper their efforts to establish their careers and can be particularly discouraging for them aspiring to hold leadership positions.

Some existing research found similar facts that women's advancement into leadership and/or managerial positions slows down from age 35 onward, if compared with men's advancement. In the age group 25–34, there was little difference between women and men. However, in the age bracket 35–44, the percentage for men moving up to top management positions nearly doubled (e.g. 45.4% vs. 27.1%) (Wirth, 2001). One may argue that such career interruption may be a reflection of the challenges women in this age group are generally facing: planning the timing of training, job assignments and promotion while taking on the traditional allocated family responsibility and gendered roles. Women in leadership positions and those moving along the managerial ladder may be particularly affected by this. It is important that organizations ensure the resources for leadership development are allocated appropriately across different age groups and develop initiatives to help professionals balance work and family. We hope that those different perceptions on leadership development resources can be treated as areas for improvement so organizations can intentionally develop initiatives to minimize the gaps and offer equal opportunities.

The Intertwined Relationship between Leadership Development and Participation

If leadership development is a prerequisite to women's leadership advancement, then there is a need for benchmarking in actual leadership participation. The purpose of being involved in various leadership training and development initiatives is to help female professionals overcome skill- or competency-based obstacles in leadership advancement. Consequently, leadership participation is the action learning intervention which exposes future leaders to emerging issues and challenges facing the organization (Conger, 2010).

Leadership participation is part of the perceived leadership construct conceptualized in the path-goal theory of leadership (House, 1971, 1996). This perspective of leadership research suggests leaders focus on subordinates' involvement and participation in sharing decision making. A participative leadership addresses the issue of low involvement and improve the level of employee engagement. Leaders invite subordinates to share decision making (e.g. in the ways and means of getting things done). They work to establish a climate or culture that is open to new and diverse opinions and perspectives. By creating that diverse climate, leaders obtain subordinates' ideas and opinions and allow them to influence decisions. In this way, subordinates have various levels of participation into the decision-making process regarding how the team and organization shall proceed.

Female professionals' capacity for leadership does not only depend on their individual leadership development efforts as discussed earlier when reviewing leadership development approaches, but more importantly on the organizational contexts within which the opportunities for leadership participation arise. Leadership development and participation ideally shall go hand-in-hand to ensure the balance of diversity, development, and participation. As illustrated in Figure 5.4, the majority of our surveyed respondents agree that their organization helps "women like me" bring different experiences and perspectives to the workplace (63.9%) and take on leadership roles on various committee service (63.7%). These opportunities may open the door for leadership participation and advancement.

However, as the line responsibility and the decision-making power increase, the opportunities to participate in leadership initiatives decrease. Four out of ten female professionals don't think (or take a neutral stand on) they've been given

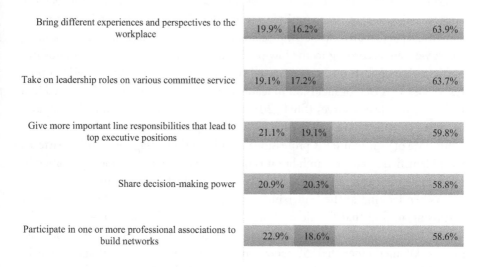

Figure 5.4. Leadership participation opportunities as observed by respondents (in percentages)

sufficient leadership participative opportunities in organizations' initiatives. Quite surprisingly, a substantial percentage of female professionals don't think their organization helps "women like me" participate in one or more professional associations to build networks (41.5%). If networking through professional associations provides invaluable information, visibility and support, such functions could create opportunities for women and increase their leadership participation horizontally within the circles of the networks.

In terms of leadership participation by organizational type, our results showed that female professionals working in public relations and communication agencies share the highest level of agreement in getting the participative opportunities in important line responsibilities (66.1%) and sharing decision making (66.1%). Professionals in private organizations practice more leadership roles via team projects or committee service (66.5%). Professionals in public corporations are getting more leadership opportunities through their networks via the in-circle groups at various professional associations (63.2%). At the same time, professionals in public corporations are not getting sufficient shared decision-making power (58.5%).

Female professionals in the sector of nonprofits, governmental, educational and political organizations do not have sufficient participative opportunities in leadership. The areas that suffer the most include sharing decision making and getting important line responsibilities. However, they reported a high percentage of agreement about the opportunity to bring different perspectives to the workplace (65.8%). The public service sector also offers female professionals more opportunities to lead on committee service (63.9%). The statistics in Figure 5.5 show that participative leadership seems to have a poor implementation among Black women, according to the low percentages of agreement on four out of five participative opportunities as reported by our surveyed African American professionals. This lack of inclusion in leadership participation also is evidenced in a most recent industry survey (Shah, 2018), which found that 87% of white employees agree that they have a clear path for leadership advancement in the near future while 53% of non-white PR professionals indicate they disagree. Similar patterns were identified in our research but it is promising to see other minority women in our sample indicating they have had various participative opportunities.

When looking at the leadership participation opportunities by age, it is not surprising to find that female professionals in the age bracket 31–40 report the lowest level of participation if compared with female colleagues in other age groups. Women older than 50 report much higher percentages of agreement in several leadership participation opportunities, including bringing different experiences and perspectives to the workplace, getting more line responsibilities and leading on team projects and committee service. Women younger than 30 also

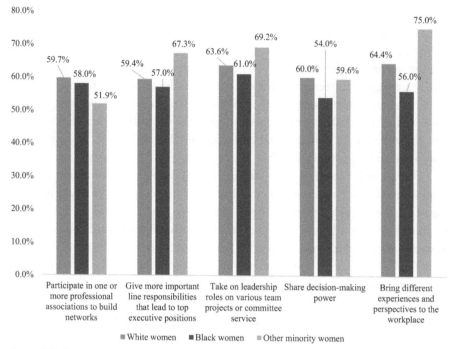

Figure 5.5. Leadership participation opportunities by race (agreement in percentages)

report relatively high participative opportunities. Such findings echoed similar patterns found in leadership development resources. It is noticeable that women in the age group 31–40 are the most vulnerable ones who don't get enough developmental resources and participative opportunities but in a great need and desire for more equal opportunities in both leadership development and participation in leading to the next level of promotion and leadership advancement.

Review on Past Efforts and Projection for Future Improvement

As part of the consequences of leadership development and participation, we asked respondents to evaluate whether women's leadership advancement opportunities in their organization were improved over the past three years. Their overall rating was just slightly above the neutral (M = 4.87 on a seven-point Likert scale, $S.D.$ = 1.41). A little less than 70% of surveyed female professionals agreed their organization has put forward efforts in improving women's leadership advancement opportunities (66.8%). However, two out of ten professionals disagreed.

At the same time, we also asked respondents to predict whether women's leadership advancement opportunities in their current organization will be improved in next three years. The rating shows a projection of small but positive change in the near future (M = 5.03 on a seven-point Likert scale; *S.D.* = 1.33). The percentage of agreement increased to 70.9%. Seven out of ten female professionals believed that women's opportunities for leadership advancement will be improved within their current organization in the next three years. The statistics still show there is 15% of surveyed professionals who don't expect any significant improvement will happen shortly.

Overall, it is encouraging to see female professionals feel confident that the improvement will happen in the near future. However, the slow changing pace based on their projection still reflects the reality that it is difficult for women to move both laterally into strategic areas of communication functions and then upwards through the central leadership pathways to top executive positions in the next three years. The pace of change and improvement is still far too slow given the large number of qualified women in the profession today.

Statistics also provide strong evidence from women with different ethnic backgrounds. As illustrated in Figure 5.6, it is promising to find out African

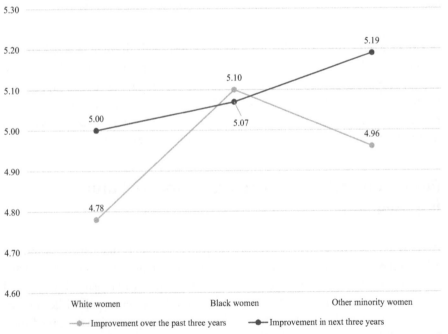

Figure 5.6. Organizations' efforts in supporting women's leadership advancement: in the past and in the future (mean scores as rated by different ethnic groups)

American women rated organizations' leadership development efforts over the past three years the highest. However, their projection of future improvement goes toward the opposite direction, decreasing from 5.10 to 5.07 on a seven-point Likert scale. White women rated organizations' past efforts the lowest but remained positive toward future improvement. Women in other minority groups showed the highest confidence in future improvement of organizations' efforts in supporting women's leadership advancement.

Top Communication Executives and Leadership Performance

Increasingly, senior communication executives become members of the dominant coalition and join the strategic decision-making process in the organization. Such empowerment has enabled senior communication executives to reposition their significant roles in the organizational transformation process. Based on Meng and Berger's (2013b) research on executive leadership and corporate reputation, senior communication executives ideally have the abilities to articulate a vision and demonstrate their consistency by walking the talk. Such consistency at the performance level is crucial as it indicates a high level of involvement and creates a positive culture for communication regarding core values. Thus, top communication executives' leadership performance is fundamental in many ways, including but not limited to modeling ethical behaviors, articulating and sharing vision, motivating followers to be engaged, and leading the communication team and the organization to go through change management (Meng & Berger, 2013a).

Meng and Berger (2013a) defined public relations leadership as "a dynamic process that encompasses a complex mix of individual skills and personal attributes, values, and behaviors that consistently produce ethical and effective communication practice" (p. 143). By identifying six crucial dimensions (i.e. self-dynamics, ethical orientation, team collaboration, relationship building, strategic decision-making capabilities, and communication knowledge management capabilities) and one critical institutional environment (i.e. supportive organizational structure and culture), Meng and associates (2013a, 2013b, 2014) proposed and tested an integrated model of excellent leadership in public relations. They further expanded public relations leadership research into a global context to investigate the supporting role of excellent public relations leadership in issues management and leadership development to prepare the next generation of communication leaders (Berger & Meng, 2014). Their integrated model of excellent leadership in public relations has been adapted and tested in the series of PR

Leadership Report Card studies conducted by The Plank Center for Leadership in Public Relations since 2015 (Meng, et al., 2019).

As part of efforts in supporting women's leadership development and participation, top communication leaders' performance and effectiveness will also affect female individuals' aspirations and motivation in leadership advancement. Therefore, we asked our respondents to evaluate their top communication executives' leadership performance on key dimensions of public relations leadership as developed by Meng and Berger (2013a). We used the similar approach to adapt the original multiple-item measures of leadership dimensions into a single statement of a composite indicator to measure each leadership dimension in public relations. The final measures for the six dimensions of public relations leadership are listed in Table 5.1.

Based on the results of the entire sample, female professionals gave their top communication executives satisfactory scores on most leadership dimensions, ranging from 4.99 to 5.11. The dimension of ethical orientation as part of the important assessment of public relations leadership received the highest score (5.11/7.0) but the dimension of team collaboration is the one least satisfied by surveyed female professionals (4.99/7.0). Our percentage analysis also shows similar patterns. A substantial percentage of disagreement exists in almost every dimension of leadership performance as illustrated in Figure 5.7. Meanwhile female professionals' overall evaluation of the top communication leader's performance also

Table 5.1. Performance of top communication executives: evaluations on key dimensions

Leadership dimensions	Measurement item	Mean	S.D.
Self-dynamics	*Provides a compelling vision for how communication can help the organization*	5.02	1.68
Ethical orientation	*Demonstrates a strong ethical orientation and set of professional values to guide actions*	5.11	1.70
Team collaboration	*Leads work teams to successfully resolve issues*	4.99	1.69
Relationship building	*Develops productive relationships and coalitions to deal with issues*	5.01	1.74
Strategic decision-making capabilities	*Makes valuable contributions in organization's strategic decision-making processes*	5.03	1.68
Communication knowledge management capabilities	*Develops effective communication strategies, plans, messages, and measurements*	5.02	1.67
Overall assessment	*Is an excellent leader in communication*	4.98	1.71

Note: Items for leadership dimensions were measured by the original seven-point Likert-type scale with "1 = strongly disagree and 7 = strongly agree."

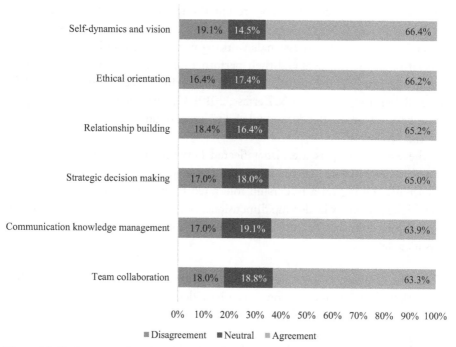

Figure 5.7. Performance of top communication leaders: evaluations on key dimensions (in percentages)

barely reached the satisfactory line (4.98/7.0). Lack of strong performance in leadership behaviors is documented in female professionals' assessment. Such findings echo the results from the 2019 PR Leadership Report Card that public relations leaders received passing grades for their performance (Meng, et al., 2019).

When looking at leadership performance evaluation by different types of organizations, we found that top communication leaders in the category of nonprofit, governmental, educational and political organizations have received the highest satisfactory scores on most leadership dimensions, if compared with their peers working at other types of organizations. Top communication leaders in this category lead in the dimensions of strategic decision-making capabilities (5.27/7.0), ethical orientation (5.23/7.0) and self-dynamics (5.10/7.0). Top communication executives in the corporate setting received the second highest scores when evaluated by female professionals at different levels of leadership reporting line. They showed advantages in the dimensions of ethical orientation (5.20/7.0), communication knowledge management capabilities (5.08/7.0), and team collaboration (5.02/7.0).

Quite surprisingly, top communication leaders in public relations and communication agencies received the lowest performance scores on leadership dimensions. According to the most recent PR Leadership Report Card report and the 2018–2019 North American Communication Monitor, across various types of organizations, professionals working in the category of communication agencies rated their leaders and their performance highest, despite some significant gender gaps on the quality of leadership performance (Meng, et al., 2019; Meng, Reber, Berger, Gower & Zerfass, 2019). On the other hand, the group of nonprofit, governmental, educational and political organizations rated leadership performance lowest.

The evaluation gaps are also reflected between professionals who have a defined leadership role and functions and those who do not. Professionals who are currently taking on a leadership role rated their top communication leader much higher on *all* six leadership dimensions. In addition, they rated three out of the six dimensions significantly higher than those non-leaders did. These dimensions include:

1. The dimension of communication knowledge management capabilities: Top communication executives develop effective communication strategies, plans, messages and measurements (5.20 vs. 4.80, t-value = 2.69, $p < .01$).
2. The dimension of ethical orientation: Top communication executives demonstrate a strong ethical orientation and set of professional values to guide actions (5.24 vs. 4.93, t-value = 2.09, $p < .05$).
3. The dimension of self-dynamics: Top communication executives provide a compelling vision for how communication can help the organization (5.15 vs. 4.85, t-value = 2.03, $p < .05$).

As part of the final assessment, the leader group also rated their top communication leader's overall performance much higher than the non-leader group did (5.05 vs. 4.87, t-value = 1.19, $p = .24$).

When comparing the assessment scores along the hierarchical line of reporting levels, we found similar evaluation gaps between professionals at a higher level of reporting relationships and those at lower levels (e.g. one reporting level and two or more reporting levels). Top communication leaders with zero reporting level rated their own leadership performance the highest on all six dimensions, scores ranging from 5.12 to 5.60. They rated their own communication knowledge management capabilities (5.60/7.0) significantly higher than the other two groups (5.05 and 4.91, respectively) (F-value = 3.07, $p < .05$). Not surprisingly, the group of top leaders also rated their overall leadership performance (5.31/7.0) much higher than the other two groups who reside at lower levels of reporting relationships (5.01 and 4.90, respectively).

According to the general findings from employee cynicism research, perceptual gaps like what we found are to be expected in performance evaluation. The existence of employee cynicism in any given type of organization affects the perceived integrity of organizational leaders to some extent (e.g. Dean et al., 1998). In addition, Trevino et al. (2000) point out employees at the lower reporting level in the organization only know communication leaders from a distance and "any information they receive about executives gets filtered through multiple layers in the organization, with employees learning only about bare-bones decisions and outcomes, not the personal characteristics of the people behind them" (p. 129).

Based on our data analysis, it seems that top communication executives receive a much higher evaluation score on leadership performance from women of color. Our analysis indicates that women in other minority groups rated their top communication leaders the highest in all six leadership dimensions and the overall leadership performance, with significantly higher scores on the dimension of strategic decision making and communication knowledge management. On the other hand, white women rated their top communication leaders the lowest with a particularly low score on the dimension of team collaboration as illustrated in Figure 5.8.

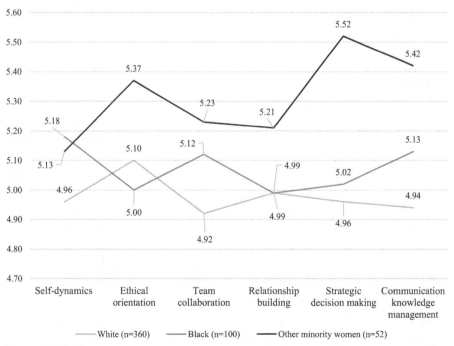

Figure 5.8. Evaluation on top communication executives' leadership performance as reported by different ethnic groups

Years of professional experience also play a role when evaluating top communication executives' leadership performance. The group of female professionals having more than ten years of experience rated all six leadership performance dimensions much higher than junior professionals with less years of experience (i.e. the group with less than five years of experience and the group with six to ten years of experience). They rated the dimensions of strategic decision-making capabilities (5.32/7.0) and ethical orientation (5.34/7.0) particularly high. However, such an evaluation gap disappeared when it is time to evaluate their top communication executive's overall leadership performance: all three groups of female professionals with various years of experience gave their top leader a passing satisfactory score (i.e. 5.04, 4.90 and 4.97, respectively).

Based on statistics, we see variances in leadership dimensions as perceived by female professionals when some key demographic features such as organizational type, race, leadership status, reporting level, and years of professional experience were considered. Such variances further validate the argument made by Meng and Berger (2013a) that public relations leadership represents a complex and multifaceted phenomenon. The perceptions of leadership effectiveness are largely influenced and shaped by situational and environmental factors such as the overloaded information, the digital revolution of digital and social media, fast-changing industry, and the changing dynamics among stakeholders who anticipate and demand more in transparency and shared decision making (Meng, et al., 2019).

Conclusion

As addressed earlier in this chapter, leadership development and participation efforts shall go hand-in-hand as part of the organization's strategic planning efforts in helping female professionals pursue leadership advancement. It is promising to see reported progress on female professionals' leadership advancement in the past three years, although the progress is slow. It also gives us a warning that such confidence in continued progress and advancement dropped for the next three years among our surveyed female professionals. If it is the top communication executives' job to demonstrate the consistency in quality leadership performance in order to pave the path for women who have the desire and the ability to reach the top, the reflective scores on those leadership dimensions we have evaluated present some challenging tasks for top communication executives to catch up. As Meng and Berger (2013b) argued, what they (top communication executives) say and what they do present a strong impact on communication effectiveness as well as on organizational reputation in change management.

Results presented in this chapter provide solid evidence in making a strong argument that organizations shall dedicate efforts and develop initiatives and programs to give female communication professionals opportunities to develop their leadership knowledge and skills, especially for those women who have the desire and have actively reached out for more opportunities, both internally and externally. Based on what surveyed female professionals have shared with us, organizations shall dedicate efforts to build in more on-the-job training programs for them to increase competency while offering them the opportunities to engage in internal and external leadership training and development programs.

It is also critical for organizations to encourage and support female professionals to participate in one or more professional associations to build their networks beyond the workplace so they can establish their in-circle influence. Providing support for women by championing a more inclusive work environment and by developing a more diverse leadership team to undertake actions will drive real change, both in leadership development and participation.

Such support in leadership development shall be further validated by increased leadership participation at all levels and in a continued and sustainable way that demonstrates the ecosystem of organizational structure and system refinements. Results reported in this chapter cite a variety of actions and responsibilities that facilitate participation and advancement. It is important to communicate with women the importance of networking and team building.

Meanwhile, it is more critical to give them more important high-visibility, high-impact line responsibilities so they can practice leadership, even with some possible failures along the road, to prepare them for top executive positions eventually. The high-visibility approach will help eliminate the stereotypes that women are incapable or unwilling to lead (Catalyst, 2003). It will also help remove one of the situational barriers we have examined in Chapter Three: Lack of sufficient numbers of women as role models in high-level decision-making positions.

The North American Communication Monitor 2018–2019 (Meng, et al., 2019) finds significant gender gaps as related to job satisfaction. Female communication professionals are unhappy about several aspects of their job, including they feel their tasks are less interesting and challenging, their job does not have a high status, they don't think their salary is adequate, and particularly they feel their career opportunities are less promising (Meng, et al., 2019, p. 77). We would argue that those unhappy aspects of job status are indirectly related to leadership participation. Limited leadership participation opportunities may be a major reason to cause the negative perceptions among female professionals that their job is not challenging nor promising from the perspective of long-term career development. Top communication executives should lead the way to embrace such support in both leadership development and participation. The role modeling function and expectations of top leaders will create a positive climate and demonstrate their commitment to inclusion by actions.

References

Avolio, B. J. (2010). Pursuing authentic leadership development. In Nitin Nohria & Rakesh Khurana (Eds.), *Handbook of leadership theory and practice* (pp. 739–768). Boston, MA: Harvard Business Press.

Bennis, W. G. (2009). *On becoming leader* (4th Ed.). Philadelphia: Basic Books.

Berger, B. K., & Meng, J. (2014). *Public relations leaders as sensemakers: A global study of leadership in public relations and communication management.* New York: Routledge.

Catalyst. (2003). *Women in U.S. corporate leadership.* New York, NY: Catalyst.

Chatman, J. A., & Kennedy, J. A. (2010). Psychological perspectives on leadership. In Nitin Nohria & Rakesh Khurana (Eds.), *Handbook of leadership theory and practice* (pp. 159–182). Boston, MA: Harvard Business Press.

Conger, J. A. (1992). *Learning to lead.* San Francisco, CA: Jossey-Bass.

Conger, J. A. (2010). Leadership development interventions: Ensuring a return on the investment. In N. Nohria & R. Khurana (Eds.), *Handbook of leadership theory and practice* (pp. 709–738). Boston, MA: Harvard Business Press.

Conger, J. A., & Fulmer, R. M. (2003). Developing your leadership pipeline. *Harvard Business Review, 81*(12), 76–84.

Day, D. V. (2000). Leadership development: A review in context. *Leadership Quarterly, 11,* 581–613.

Day, D. V., & Harrison, M. M. (2007). A multilevel, identity-based approach to leadership development. *Human Resource Management Review, 17,* 360–373.

Dean, J. W., Brandes, P., & Dharwadkar, R. (1998). Organizational cynicism. *Academy of Management Review, 23,* 341–352.

Dotlich, D. L., & Noel, J. L. (1998). *Action learning.* San Francisco, CA: Jossey-Bass.

Ely, R. J., & Rhode, D. L. (2010). Women and leadership. In Nitin Nohria & Rakesh Khurana (Eds.), *Handbook of leadership theory and practice* (pp. 377–410). Boston, MA: Harvard Business Press.

Fulmer, R. M., & Goldsmith, M. (2001). *The leadership investment: How the world's best organizations gain strategic advantage through leadership development.* New York: AMA.

Hernez-Broome, G., & Hughes, R. L. (2004). Leadership development: Past, present, and future. *Human Resource Planning, 27,* 24–32.

House, R. J. (1971). A path-goal theory of leader effectiveness. *Administrative Science Quarterly, 16*(3), 321–328.

House, R. J. (1996). Path-goal theory of leadership: Lessons, legacy, and a reformulated theory. *Leadership Quarterly, 7*(3), 323–352.

Ibarra, H., Snook, S., & Guillén Ramo, L. (2010). Identity-based leader development. In Nitin Nohria & Rakesh Khurana (Eds.), *Handbook of leadership theory and practice* (pp. 657–678). Boston, MA: Harvard Business Press.

Kegan, R., & Lahey, L. (2010). Adult development and organizational leadership. In Nitin Nohria & Rakesh Khurana (Eds.), *Handbook of leadership theory and practice* (pp. 769–787). Boston, MA: Harvard Business Press.

McCall, M. W. Jr. (2010). The experience conundrum. In Nitin Nohria & Rakesh Khurana (Eds.), *Handbook of leadership theory and practice* (pp. 679–708). Boston, MA: Harvard Business Press.

McCauley, C., Ruderman, M., Ohlott, P., & Morrow, J. (1994). Assessing the developmental components of managerial jobs. *Journal of Applied Psychology, 79*, 544–560.

Meng, J. (2014). Unpacking the relationship between organizational culture and excellent leadership in public relations: An empirical investigation. *Journal of Communication Management, 18*(4), 363–385.

Meng, J., & Berger, B. K. (2013a). An integrated model of excellent leadership in public relations: Dimensions, measurement, and validation. *Journal of Public Relations Research, 25*(2), 141–167.

Meng, J., & Berger, B. K. (2013b). What they say and what they do: Executives affect organizational reputation through effective communication. In Craig E. Carroll (Ed.), *The handbook of communication and corporate reputation* (pp. 306–317). Malden, MA: John Wiley & Sons, Inc.

Meng, J., Berger, B. K., Heyman, W. C., & Reber, B. H. (2019). *Public relations leaders earn a "C+" in The Plank Center's Report Card 2019: Is improving leadership even on the radar screen in the profession?* Tuscaloosa, AL: The Plank Center for Leadership in Public Relations.

Meng, J., Reber, B. H., Berger, B. K., Gower, K. K., & Zerfass, A. (2019). *North American Communication Monitor 2018–2019. Tracking trends in fake news, issues management, leadership performance, work stress, social media skills, job satisfaction and work environment.* Tuscaloosa, AL: The Plank Center for Leadership in Public Relations.

Mumford, M. D., Zaccaro, S. J., Connelly, M., & Marks, M. A. (2000). Leadership skills: Conclusions and future directions. *Leadership Quarterly, 11*, 155–170.

Riggio, R. Murphy, S., & Pirozzolo, F. (Eds.) (2001). *Multiple intelligences and leadership.* Mahwah, NJ: Laurence Erlbaum.

Servaes, J. (2012). Soft power and public diplomacy: The new frontier for public relations and international communication between the US and China. *Public Relations Review, 38*, 643–651.

Shah, A. (Jan. 18, 2018). *Why the PR industry's diversity initiatives fail?* PRovoke Media, retrieved from https://www.provokemedia.com/long-reads/article/why-the-pr-industry's-diversity-initiatives-fail. Access date: September 20, 2019.

Trevino, L. K., Hartman, L., & Brown, M. (2000). Moral person and moral manager: How executives develop a reputation for ethical leadership. *California Management Review, 42*(4), 128–142.

Van Velsor, E., McCauley, C. D. (Eds.) (2004). *The center for creative leadership handbook of leadership development* (2nd Ed.). San Francisco, CA: Jossey-Bass.

Wirth, L. (2001). *Breaking through the glass ceiling: Women in management.* Geneva: International Labour Organization.

CHAPTER SIX

Balancing Professional and Family Responsibilities

The Roles of Instrumental Support and Mentoring

Women's social movement has brought changes in social acceptance and changing perceptions of gender equality in the workplace in the past decades (Koch, Luft & Kruse, 2005). With the achievement of educational parity and changes in social attitudes towards men's and women's roles, we have seen continuous labor force participation driven by women (Jones, 2005). Women's increasing participation in the labor force has become a primary dynamic to witness the rise of dual-earner couples in reality and women's earnings have become an essential part of household income. Such change in the U.S. workforce also brings rapid changes to family life and structure. In a most recent Pew Research Center report (2015), two-parent households with one stay-home mother have grown much less common since 1970. As more women have entered the workforce, the share of two-parent households in which both parents are working full time made up 46% of the households in the United States (Patten, 2015).

With the rise of dual-earner couples, the challenges to balance professional and family responsibilities are more intense. According to a recent featured report in *Harvard Business Review*, partners in dual-career couples are highly educated and both of them work full-time in demanding professional or managerial jobs. They also have a strong desire to "see themselves on an upward path in their roles" (Petriglieri, 2019, p. 45). For partners in a dual-career situation, work and professional achievement are major sources for self-identity and self-redefinition, as well as their primary channel for ambition (Petrieglieri, 2019). Consequently, the increased economic freedom based on the dual earnings also increases the satisfaction level of the relationship as evidenced in sociological research (as cited by Petrieglieri, 2019, p. 45).

However, research done by Petrieglieri (2019) also shows, when couples with children place their careers and professional development on equal footing, it brings intense and unique challenges to balance the demands and responsibilities from both ends. According to the Pew Research Center's analysis of Current Population Survey data conducted in the third quarter of 2015, in dual-earning households with two full-time working parents, most parents admit they share responsibility and workload evenly on things such as doing activities with children, disciplining children, and taking care of chores. However, when it comes to certain activities such as managing children's schedules/activities and taking care of children when they are sick, mom still takes the lead (Patten, 2015). Although men have assumed taking an equal share of household responsibilities in the dual-earning situation, women are more likely to say they take on the larger role in many of domestic tasks and family responsibilities (Patten, 2015).

A gender gap among leaders in public relations has been widely acknowledged when women make up 70–75% of those employed in the public relations industry but occupy only 20% of the senior leadership positions (FitzPatrick, 2013; Place & Vardeman-Winter, 2018). The 2018–2019 North American Communication Monitor (Meng et al., 2019) and the 2019 PR Leadership Report Card (Meng et al., 2019) also found consistent and significant gender gaps on most critical aspects as related to public relations leadership: Women rated their top communication leader much lower in terms of the quality of leadership performance. Women in public relations remained less engaged, less satisfied with their jobs, less confident in their work cultures and less trusting of their organizations when compared to men. Based on these findings and facts, this chapter further investigates the challenges of balancing professional and family responsibilities women in public relations are facing. Three related topics on balancing professional and family responsibilities are included in this chapter: 1) women's perceptions of work-family conflict in public relations; 2) coping strategies for women to reconcile work and family; and 3) the role of mentoring for extra support in finding solutions.

Work-Family Conflict

To find out female professionals' perceptions on work-life conflict, we used the construct and measures of work-life conflict developed by Netemeyer, Boles and

McMurrian (1996). According to Netemeyer and associates (1996), the perceptions of "*work–life conflict*" are different from those of "*life–work conflict*" as work-life conflict is a form of inter-role conflict in which the general demands of time devoted to and strain created by the job interfere with performing family-related responsibilities (p. 401). Conversely, family-work conflict is a form of inter-role conflict in which the general demands of, time devoted to, and strain created by the family interfere with performing work-related responsibilities. The assumption made by Netemeyer and associates is that *work-family conflict* and *family-work conflict* are distinct but also deeply intertwined in interrelated forms of inter-role conflict.

Traditional social attitudes have allocated the majority of family-related responsibilities to women in areas such as caring for children, the elderly or sick relatives, which logically implies that women usually have less time to devote to their work and career development. Such social attitudes can be particularly discouraging for women aspiring to and capable of holding senior leadership roles or managerial positions. However, when women in public relations have demanding careers and they have taken work as major sources for self-identification and professional achievement, it is important to discover how they perceive the impact of work-life conflict and how they would overcome their challenges.

According to our survey, in general, women in public relations feel the work-life conflict does cause tension and brings challenges to their working lives and family lives as these two are deeply intertwined. The impact is reflected from different perspectives and to various extents. One of the biggest challenges reflected in their answers is the fact that women have to make changes to their family activities to fulfill work-related duties or accommodate their work needs (54.9% in agreement of high impact). Female professionals feel they don't get things done at home because of their job demands (53.1% in agreement of high impact). They also agree the demands of their work constantly interfere with their home and family life (51.2% in agreement of high impact). The amount of working hours (48.6%) and working strain (45.1%) also affect their home and family life but are less intense if compared to other responsibilities. As illustrated in Figure 6.1, among the five measures as related to the impact of work-family conflict, most women in public relations indicated that changing their plans for family activities is very common in order to accommodate their work schedule as well as demonstrate their performance.

The impact of work-life conflict changes significantly as the age of female professionals changes. As showed in Figure 6.2, two groups of female professionals rated the impact of work demands and time conflict on their family life and responsibilities the highest: women in the age brackets 31–40 and younger than 30. Women in these two age groups admitted that the demands of their work

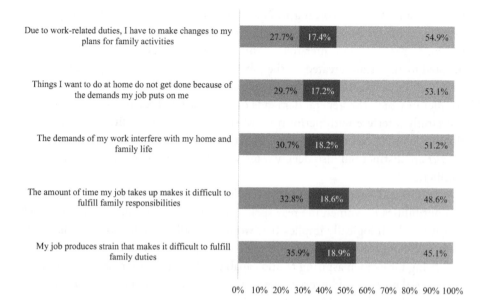

Figure 6.1. The impact of work-life conflict as perceived by female professionals (in percentages)

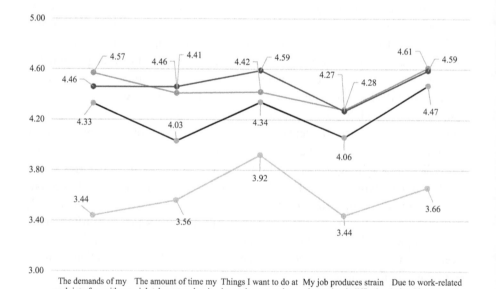

Figure 6.2. The impact of work-life conflict as perceived by different age groups

interfere with their home and family life. Such demands make them find it difficult to fulfill family responsibilities and they have to make changes to their plans
for family activities. For women in these two age brackets, they are fully occupied
by the demands of planning the timing for training and job assignments to gain
professional experience, as well as working towards promotions and competing
alongside men for managerial and leadership positions. At the same time, they are
busy with starting a family. Trade research indicates small children have a marked
effect on women's participation in the labor force. Nonetheless, the more qualified
women are, the more they will keep working throughout their childbearing years
(Wirth, 2001).

Our percentage analysis showed that almost six out of ten female professionals who are less than 30 years old (the youngest age group in our sample) indicated
their work demands generate a high impact on their home and family life (57.9%
in agreement of high impact). Such an intense situation is also reflected among
women in the age bracket 31–40. Half of them agreed that work demands interfere with home and family life.

However, as women grow older, such intensity decreases. Half of women
who are older than 50 don't think work demands would create interference with
their family life. Both groups (i.e. age brackets 31–40 and younger than 30) also
expressed the long working hours have caused a challenge for them to fulfill family responsibilities, if compared to the other two older groups (i.e. age brackets
41–50 and older than 50). Almost six out of ten female professionals in those two
age brackets admitted that they have to make changes to planned family activities
due to the demands of work-related duties.

Just as Ely and Rhode (2010) noted in their research on women and leadership,
junior women are scrambling to build careers while raising children. Excessive
workloads have limited their time for other informal socializing and mentoring
that would promote professional development. The inequality in the hours spent
by men and women on house responsibilities seems to be more pronounced in
industrialized countries than in developing countries (Wirth, 2001). For example, such pattern was evidenced in research on women managers in Switzerland
confirming that a certain proportion of women in leadership and/or managerial
positions reconcile their family and career by delaying having children until they
are well established in their careers (as cited in Wirth, 2001, p. 19).

Our results showed that the conflict caused by work demands and family
responsibilities affects African American women the least, scores ranging from
3.65 to 4.34, and white women the most, scores ranging from 4.26 to 4.55. The
perceptions reported from other minority women stay in the middle as illustrated
in Figure 6.3. Such racial gap in perceptions related to work-family conflict is

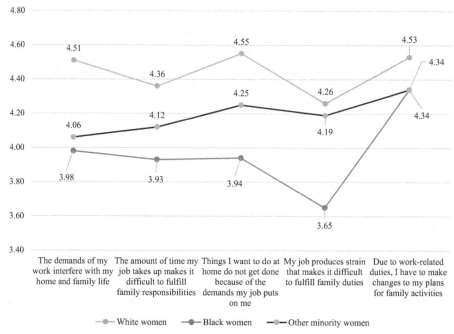

Figure 6.3. The impact of work-life conflict as perceived by different ethnic groups

also evidenced in Pew Research Center's report (Patten, 2015). According to the report (Pew Research Center, 2015), white parents are more likely than those who are non-white to say it is difficult for them to balance work and family. In addition, 65% of white working moms say it is difficult for them to balance the responsibilities of their job with their family-related responsibilities. The percentage of non-white working mothers who said the same drops to 52%. Although the report does not further specify the details of non-white mothers by race, the overall pattern is similar to what we found among our surveyed professionals. More insight on this issue based on our qualitative research is provided in Chapter Nine.

Statistics showed that female professionals who have an officially defined leadership role and perform some leadership functions reported a significantly higher level of impact of work demands on their family life, if compared with other female professionals who do not perform a leadership role and leadership functions as illustrated in Figure 6.4. Such a pattern was also identified when we compare female professionals' responses by looking at their status along the hierarchical reporting line. Women residing at the zero reporting level (i.e. the group of "I am the top leader in communication") expressed a much higher level of interference from their work-related duties to their home and family life.

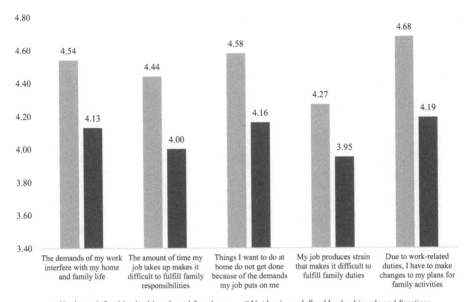

Figure 6.4. The impact of work-life conflict compared by leadership status

Such a finding raises some challenging questions for women who are committed and aspired to reaching top leadership roles: Will taking on leadership roles and functions present a negative impact on home and family life to women in public relations? If this is the reality as experienced and reported by our surveyed female professionals, will that force female professionals to make a decision on one side or the other? What supportive resources are available for women to find the balance between work demands and family life? What kinds of coping strategies would work to prevent women in public relations to face the situation of forced selection between work and family?

When breaking down our analysis of work-life conflict by different types of organizations, female professionals working in public relations or communication agencies reported the highest level of stress due to conflict between work demands and family responsibilities. They have consistently rated four out of the five conflicting situations higher with a particularly high score on the fact that they have to make changes to planned family activities (5.16/7.0). On the other hand, female professionals working in the group of nonprofit, governmental, educational and political organizations reported a relatively low level of interference from work duties to family life. Figure 6.5 shows the details and the patterns.

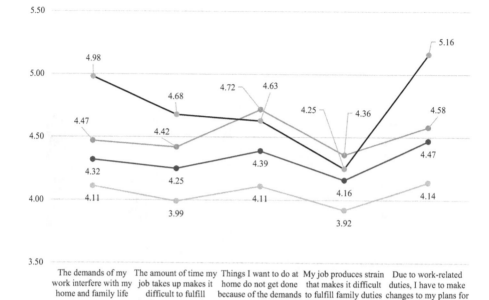

Figure 6.5. The impact of work-life conflict compared by organizational type

Coping Strategies to Manage Work-Family Conflict

Coping research has been deeply rooted in personality psychology and spans widely from sociology, clinical research, anthropology, management, to consumer research (Duhacheck, 2005). In contrast, coping research in public relations has largely focused on publics' crisis coping strategies from the perspective of crisis communication with four types of coping strategies that have been frequently used by publics in crisis (i.e. relational thinking, emotional venting, instrumental support, and action) (Jin & Hong, 2010). When linking a coping situation to work-life conflict as perceived by public relations professionals, only a handful of publications in public relations research can be located (e.g. Aldoory et al., 2008; Jiang & Shen, 2015; Jin, et al., 2014; Sha & Toth, 2005; Shen, et al., 2015). Thus, there is still potential for studying coping and coping strategies, particularly in the literature of women and leadership.

Catalyst research (2003, 2004 & 2005) on women in U.S. corporate leadership has consistently found significant trade-offs, such as postponing marriage or having children, as coping strategies some women in executive leadership have used to achieve balance between work and personal life. In its longitudinal comparison between women in 1996 and women in 2003, Catalyst research reveals women in corporate leadership actually used similar coping strategies over the years to manage work-life conflict. These same strategies include employing outside services for domestic help, sharing responsibilities with a spouse or partner, and curtailing personal interests in order to achieve work-life balance (Catalyst, 2003, 2004). Through the years, the availability of informal work arrangement or formal flexible work programs as part of the work/family policies established by an organization also plays important roles in helping women solve conflict and achieve work-life balance (Catalyst, 2003).

However, research also found although organizations may offer reduced or flexible work arrangements, few women in top managerial and professional positions take advantage of such programs with the fear that any limitation in hours or availability would jeopardize their career prospects (Rhode & Williams, 2007). Similar results are identified in Catalyst research, although women in corporate leadership want options, few of them actually use formal flexible work programs such as compressed work weeks, reduced hours, and leave and sabbaticals (Catalyst, 2003). The fear of jeopardizing their careers has become a hidden reason embedded in workplace cultures, as well as in the reward-and-promotion structure.

According to original psychological research on consumers' situational coping in a stressful transaction, coping is a pervasive and complex psychological process that integrates cognitive, attitudinal, and behavioral reaction and action (Carver & Scheier, 1994; Lazarus & Folkman, 1984). Duhachek (2005) argues that such complexity shall be reflected in the multitude of coping strategies people enact. Such a coping situation can be extended into a professional development scenario. In reality, women do use a wide variety of strategies, rather than just one, to solve work-life conflict and facilitate balance (Catalyst, 2003, 2004).

In our study, we adapted Duhachek's (2005) conceptualization of coping in consumer research by further refining it to fit the coping situation of work-life conflict faced by female professionals in the field. Therefore, we define coping as the set of cognitive and behavioral processes initiated by female professionals in response to stress caused by the work-life conflict and aimed at bringing forth more desirable actions and reduced levels of stress. By asking female professionals to rate a list of potential coping strategies adapted from Duhachek's coping research (2005) as well as Catalyst research on women in corporate leadership (2003), we hope to explore solution-based strategies as related to the coping situation in work-life conflict to inspire practice.

When looking at the coping strategies female professionals in public relations tend to use in helping them manage the work-family conflict, three groups of strategies and/or solutions appear as illustrated in Figure 6.6. The first group (and the highly rated group) of strategies indicate the positive thinking and actions female professionals are using to cope with conflicting work-family situations. Female professionals in the field tend to take a more positive and proactive attitude and approach to handle the situation when the work-family conflict arises. The top-rated coping strategy is to concentrate on ways the conflict could be solved (5.11/7.0), followed by the strategy of thinking about potential solutions to solve the conflict (4.97/7.0).

The second group of strategies are those solutions receiving the rating scores ranging from 4.30 to 4.80. This group of strategies reveal female professionals' intention of using instrumental support to help manage work-family conflict. Duhachek (2005) described instrumental support as "attempts to marshal social resources to take action towards ameliorating a stressor, coping that involves

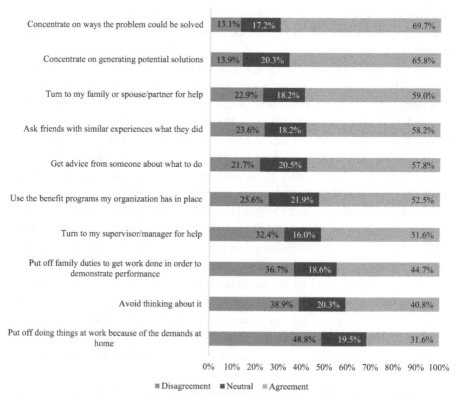

Figure 6.6. Coping strategies to manage work-family conflict, from most preferred to least preferred (in percentages)

co-opting the assistance of others with the intent of ameliorating the stress situation directly" (p. 46). These solution-based strategies include:

1. Turn to my family or spouse/partner for help (4.72/7.0),
2. Get advice from someone about what to do (4.61/7.0),
3. Ask friends with similar experiences what they did (4.58/7.0),
4. Use the benefit programs my organization has in place (4.53/7.0), and
5. Turn to my supervisor/manager for help (4.32/7.0).

Based on the rating scores, it is surprising to see female professionals do not take some instrumental support such as using the benefit programs the organization has in place and seeking help from a supervisor or manager as their top choices. Such findings echo what we reviewed earlier that few women actually take advantage of reduced or flex-time arrangements with the reinforced assumption that such action would jeopardize their career prospects, even though it has become part of the workplace policies or benefit programs.

The third group of least used strategies reflect the fact that female professionals prefer not using any passive actions or avoidance thinking when dealing with the work-family conflicting situation. They prefer not to put off doing things at work (3.54/7.0) nor put off family duties to get work done (4.05/7.0). They also think an avoidance-based approach (3.95/7.0) would not help in such a coping situation. Figure 6.6 illustrates female professionals' preferences in using coping strategies to facilitate the work-family conflict coping situation.

When we look at how female professionals use different coping strategies to deal with work-family conflict across different age groups, some interesting patterns are identified. For example, women across all age groups tend to have positive thinking and take proactive action by focusing on solutions when managing conflict caused by work duties and family responsibilities. In addition, when it comes to use of some instrumental support, women at various ages tend to seek help from family or spouse/partner first.

The biggest differences exist between the youngest group (i.e. younger than 30) and the oldest group (i.e. older than 50) on two coping strategies. The youngest group prefer to ask friends with similar experiences what they did (4.95 vs. 3.61, F-value = 11.33, $p < .01$) or they will try to get advice from someone about what to do next (4.99 vs. 3.83, F-value = 12.76, $p < .01$). Seeking advice and support from reliable sources and experienced people seems particularly important for the youngest group. Such a tendency indicates the importance of having mentorship, either formally or informally, to provide suggestions and solutions when young professionals face work-life conflict but lack the experience to deal with it.

On the other hand, women older than 50 rated those avoidance-related coping strategies the lowest.

When comparing the usage of different coping strategies between female professionals who are already in a leadership position with a defined leadership role and functions and those who are not, the ratings are similar. However, we found that women having a defined leadership role tend to ask for help from her next-level supervisor or manager more often than those who don't have a leadership role (4.55 vs. 4.01, $t = 3.39$, $p < .01$). They also tend to use benefit programs offered by their organization more often than those who don't serve in a leadership role (4.73 v. 4.28, $t = 2.86$, $p < .01$).

We also found that women who are currently in a leadership role tend to put off family duties to get work done in order to demonstrate her performance, if compared with those female professionals who are not in a leadership role yet (4.23 vs. 3.82, $t = 2.49$, $p < .01$). In addition, female professionals who are in a leadership role rated coping strategies reflecting positive attitudes and action much higher than non-leaders did. They expressed that they will concentrate on ways the problem could be solved (5.21 vs. 4.96) and finding potential solutions (5.05 vs. 4.86).

When comparing the usage of coping strategies by hierarchical reporting level, we found that the tendency of using coping strategies reflecting positive thinking and action increases as the reporting level builds up. For example, female professionals who reside at two or more reporting levels along the hierarchical leadership line have a much higher tendency to concentrate on finding alternative solutions to fix the problem instead of seeking help from a supervisor to manage the conflict, if compared to those residing as top leaders in communication. Does such finding simply imply less support for junior-level professionals, less likelihood for them to receive resources to manage conflict, and ignorance of junior professionals' concerns and stress when they struggle with balancing career and personal life?

Similarly, we also found that the tendency of getting instrumental support from the organization decreases as the reporting level builds up. Top leaders in communication tend to turn to next-level supervisor for help or use the benefit programs offered by their organization, if compared to women who are at the lowest level along the hierarchy line. This pattern is consistent with the results we found when comparing leaders and non-leaders in using coping strategies.

If leaders use benefit programs offered by the organization more often than non-leaders, does this imply the inadequate communication and insufficient efforts on the organization side in informing general employees (especially those at lower levels of the reporting line) regarding the availability of related instrumental support? How might organizations develop, explain and offer internal initiatives to better support women when they are in need of instrumental support to cope with work-family conflict? Addressing more systematic and effective communication as related to work/family policies in place should be a priority.

When analyzing coping strategies by comparing different ethnic groups, we found that other minority women rated almost all coping strategies higher than white and Black women did, especially in instrumental support such as turning to family or spouse/partner for help and using the benefit programs their organization has to offer. It is also interesting to find that female professionals working in a public relations or communication agency tend to use instrumental support more in coping with work-family conflict when compared to professionals in the category of nonprofit, governmental, educational and political organizations. For example, women working in an agency tend to seek help from their supervisor or manager more often (4.50 vs. 4.00, F-value = 3.04, $p < .05$).

Coping with work-family conflict never gets easier as the demands on both ends keep climbing. Only when supportive workplace policies and shared family responsibilities are in place, the solutions to manage challenges and conflicts could finally come into play for women (and for men) in this dual-career situation. We also believe that women's networks for support and sharing information on strategies and solutions are also critical for women to learn how to manage conflicts by taking a proactive approach and without sacrificing one or the other.

The Role of Mentoring

Turning to a mentor for advice and support is critical in career development. Mentorship does not only help provide career advice but also contributes to individuals' efforts in building networks. Mentoring involves the pairing, both informal and formal, of younger individuals demonstrating potential with older, experienced and more senior individuals who can provide coaching, support, advice and visibility (Wirth, 2001). As explained in the previous section on applying coping strategies to manage work-family conflict, we found that a widely used coping strategy at the level of instrumental support is to get advice from someone about what to do. If that "someone" can be brought in as a mentor or part of a broader career planning system, it will provide a platform for dialogue to take place between higher levels of leadership and individuals in lower levels of the organization who have the potential and capacity for leadership. Therefore, mentorship is not just about having a meeting with an influential senior colleague, but more importantly, it is about learning from someone's experience to reflect on current situations and strategies. Such mentor-mentee interaction and communication will also lead to mutual learning and listening regarding different approaches to facilitate self-reflection, self-exploration and self-reinvention.

In our survey, we designed four questions particularly related to mentors and mentorship. We first asked our surveyed female professionals to share the number of mentors they have in their professional career. The results showed three out of ten female professionals admitted they do not have any mentors. About one-third said they only have one mentor and another one-third indicated they have about two to five mentors in their professional career. Only about 6.4% of surveyed women reported they have more than five mentors as illustrated in Figure 6.7.

When looking at the responses by race, we found that more Black women reported not having a mentor (35.0%), if compared to white women (28.6%) and other minority women (28.8%). Not surprisingly, fewer Black women reported they have two to five mentors (29.0%) or more than five mentors (3.0%), if compared to white women and other minority women.

Since the main theme of this book is about how women in public relations get over the leadership hurdle, when discussing mentorship, we are particularly interested in whether the gender of the mentor matters to our surveyed female professionals if they indicate they have mentors in their professional career. Statistics showed that three out of ten female professionals indicated their mentors are

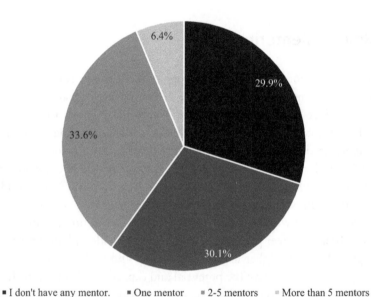

■ I don't have any mentor.   ■ One mentor   ■ 2-5 mentors   ■ More than 5 mentors

Figure 6.7. Numbers of mentors in professional career reported by female professionals (in percentages)

exclusively women (32.3%). More than half have both female and male mentors (54.6%). A small percentage of surveyed professionals indicated that their mentors are exclusively men (13.1%). Professionals who indicated they do not have any mentors were excluded in the analysis.

It is also interesting to observe that the dynamics of mentors' gender changes when female professionals reported they have more mentors in their professional career. Figure 6.8 illustrates the changes in percentages as the number of mentors goes up. For example, when female professionals reported they only have one mentor, almost half of them indicated their mentor is a woman (46.8%). The male-mentor-exclusive situation decreases significantly when female professionals reported they have more than one mentor. In this situation, they tend to have a combination of both female and male mentors.

Sources to Find Mentors

We found that, among female professionals who indicated they have mentors, 32.4% of them are working in the same department and same organization with their mentors. About one-third of them indicated that their mentors are from the

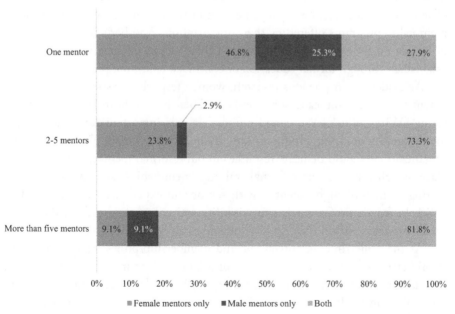

Figure 6.8. The dynamics of mentors' gender changes as the number of mentors increases (in percentages)

same organization but working in different departments (29.7%). A small percentage (15.2%) indicated that their mentors are not in their current organization. Such a finding could help broaden female professionals' view of mentor-mentee relationships by encouraging them to go beyond their in-circle group to find mentors that could help them expand their networks, provide career advice, and offer different perspectives on how the organization works and how to manage challenges and conflicts.

When asking female professionals about the sources through which they established their current mentor-mentee relationships, the top three venues ranked by our respondents include:

1. Through on-the-job communications and experiences (n = 152; 29.7%),
2. Through personal connections and various networking opportunities (n = 124; 24.2%), and
3. Through professional associations (n = 91; 17.8%).

Our analysis also showed similar proportions of female professionals found their mentors via informal conversations with influential colleagues and/or clients (n = 79; 15.4%) or through leadership training and coaching programs (n = 77; 15.0%). At the same time, it is sad to find out organizations have inadequate efforts in developing and enacting successful mentoring programs. We only had one out of ten respondents (11.5%) saying they found their mentors by participating in mentorship programs offered by their organization. Another smaller percentage of female professionals (10.2%) indicated their mentor-mentee relationship was established through formal education or continued education programs.

As evidenced in previous research, women (esp. those aspired ones of high potential in taking on leadership roles) could benefit significantly from the mentoring (Wirth, 2001). We would argue that it is important for organizations to integrate mentoring programs into their broader career planning system. Organizations should dedicate resources to build formal mentoring programs in place, which can offer more formal training, mentorships, and sponsorships by pairing women of high potential with senior and experienced executives. This will help female professionals gain visibility and enlist support from the senior leadership team within the organization and establish an inclusive culture.

At the same time, organizations and membership/professional associations should strive to make mentoring part of a larger talent management program, both laterally and horizontally. According to PRSA's "Mentor Match" program, the profession holds a strong belief that mentoring initiatives are important as they contribute to the development of leadership capacity and offer tailored career advice by demonstrating the joint responsibilities from both mentor and mentee. However, in our research, we still found three out of ten female professionals in today's public relations profession are in a condition without any mentorship, both formally and informally.

Similarly, Catalyst research (2004) found less than a quarter of surveyed female managers in business and professional jobs have expressed satisfaction with the availability of mentoring in the workplace. In our research, only 10% of surveyed female professionals indicated they found their mentors through the mentoring programs offered by their organization. While we focus on analyzing workplace barriers in leadership advancement for female professionals in the field, findings like these urge us to raise some critical questions to challenge the development of mentoring initiatives at the level of availability and the level of quality: Does this simply imply that most workplaces do not have mentoring initiatives in place? Or does it mean the quality of mentoring programs is questionable that fewer successful mentor-mentee cases grow out it? The success of mentoring programs only works if fully integrated into the talent management system to develop sustainable strategies to retain, develop and advance women in their professional career. We hope these critical questions along with our research findings could help organizations move their mentorship initiatives forward, with a goal of exploring diverse approaches in enhancing the joint responsibilities of mentors and mentees to support continuous professional learning and development.

Conclusion

In this chapter, we shift our focus to the topic of work-family conflict and the challenges it creates for women's leadership advancement in the public relations industry. Responses from our surveyed female professionals confirmed that they have to make changes to their plans for family activities when there is a conflict due to work-related duties. Such impact is particularly intense for younger professionals (i.e. younger than 30 or in the age bracket 31–40). White women also reported a much higher level of impact of work demands on their family life. Women who are currently residing in a defined leadership role and performing leadership functions are particularly stressed by the work-family conflict with limited support.

When it comes to using a wide variety of coping strategies to manage the work-family conflict, female professionals tend to hold positive thinking and take positive action to identify and create potential solutions. Family or spouse/partner is their rated No. 1 source to get help when managing work-family conflict. They also value getting advice from someone who may offer coaching and mentoring support. Fewer women actually take advantage of benefit programs in place or turn to their supervisor for help.

This implies organizations should give current work/family policies a systematic review to gather sufficient data about why female professionals are not using them as a solution for solving work-family conflict. Organizations should also strive to educate women about the formal work/family policies by clearly communicating the top-down support to them. If benefit programs are less accessible nor inadequate in practice, it may cause the anxiety among women that opting for flexible or reduced working schedules may jeopardize their career development opportunities.

Similarly, mentoring initiatives require more attention and adequate practice to ensure effectiveness. It is important to help female professionals to build effective mentor-mentee networks by having a combination of male and female mentors in order to gain and learn from diverse perspectives. It is also critical to help female professionals to grow their mentor-mentee networks beyond their workplace to expand their influence and establish their leadership credibility. These external mentoring relationships are valuable for the organization as mentors can provide novel solutions to issues based on their past experiences. It will be valuable if we can gain insights about the significance of women's networks developed via mentoring initiatives offered by their organization and/or professional associations. Information and measurement like this will benefit the profession by knowing the effectiveness of these strategies in supporting female professionals' leadership advancement.

References

Aldoory, L., Jiang, H., Toth, E. L., & Sha, B. L. (2008). Is it still just a women's issue? A study of work-life balance among men and women in public relations. *Public Relations Journal, 2*(4), 1–20.

Carver, C. S., & Scheier, M. F. (1994). Situational coping and coping dispositions in a stressful transaction. *Journal of Personality and Social Psychology, 66*(1), 184.

Catalyst. (2003). *Women in U.S. corporate leadership.* New York: Catalyst.

Catalyst. (2004). *Women and men in the U.S. corporate leadership: Same workplace, different realities?* New York: Catalyst.

Catalyst. (2005). *Women take care, men take charge: Stereotyping of business leaders exposed.* New York: Catalyst.

Duhachek, A. (2005). Coping: A multidimensional, hierarchical framework of responses to stressful consumption episodes. *Journal of Consumer Research, 32*(1), 41–53.

Ely, R. J., & Rhode, D. L. (2010). Women and leadership. In Nitin Nohria & Rakesh Khurana (Eds.), *Handbook of leadership theory and practice* (pp. 377–410). Boston, MA: Harvard Business Press.

FitzPatrick, M. (2013, February 01). A strong case for female inclusion at the top level. *PRWeek*, retrieved from https://www.prweek.com/article/1276818/strong-case-female-inclusion-top-level on September 15, 2019.

Jiang, H., & Shen, H. (2015). Conflict? What work–life conflict? A national study of future public relations practitioners. *Public Relations Review, 41*(1), 132–134.

Jin, Y., & Hong, S. Y. (2010). Explicating crisis coping in crisis communication. *Public Relations Review, 36*(4), 352–360.

Jin, Y., Sha, B. L., Shen, H., & Jiang, H. (2014). Tuning in to the rhythm: The role of coping in strategic management of work-life conflicts in the public relations profession. *Public Relations Review, 40*(1), 69–78.

Jones, J. (2005, August 2). *Gender differences in views of job opportunity: Fifty-three percent of Americans believe opportunities are equal.* Gallup News. Retrieved from https://news.gallup.com/poll/17614/gender-differences-views-job-opportunity.aspx.

Koch, S., Luft, R., & Kruse, L. (2005). Women and leadership—20 years later: A semantic connotation study. *Social Sciences Information, 44*(1), 9–39.

Lazarus, R. S., & Folkman, S. (1984). *Stress, appraisal, and coping.* New York: Springer.

Meng, J., Berger, B. K., Heyman, W. C., & Reber, B. H. (2019). *Public relations leaders earn a "C+" in The Plank Center's Report Card 2019: Is improving leadership even on the radar screen in the profession?* Tuscaloosa, AL: The Plank Center for Leadership in Public Relations.

Meng, J., Reber, B. H., Berger, B. K., Gower, K. K., & Zerfass, A. (2019). *North American Communication Monitor 2018–2019. Tracking trends in fake news, issues management, leadership performance, work stress, social media skills, job satisfaction and work environment.* Tuscaloosa, AL: The Plank Center for Leadership in Public Relations.

Netemeyer, R. G., Boles, J. S., & McMurrian, R. (1996). Development and validation of work–family conflict and family–work conflict scales. *Journal of Applied Psychology, 81*(4), 400.

Patten, E. (2015, November 4). *How American parents balance work and family life when both work.* Pew Research Center. Retrieved from https://www.pewresearch.org/fact-tank/2015/11/04/how-american-parents-balance-work-and-family-life-when-both-work/ on Oct. 01, 2019.

Petriglieri, J. (2019). How dual-career couples make it work. *Harvard Business Review, 97*(5), 43–52.

Pew Research Center (2015, November 4). *Raising kids and running a household: How working parents share the load.* Retrieved from https://www.pewsocialtrends.org/2015/11/04/raising-kids-and-running-a-household-how-working-parents-share-the-load/ on Oct. 1, 2019.

Place, K. R., & Vardeman-Winter, J. (2018). Where are the women? An examination of research on women and leadership in public relations. *Public Relations Review, 44*(1), 165–173.

Rhode, D., & Williams, J. (2007). Legal perspectives on employment discrimination. In F. Crosby, M. Stockdale, & A. Ropp (Eds.), *Sex discrimination in the workplace: Multidisciplinary perspectives* (pp. 235–270). Santa Cruz, CA: University of California.

Sha, B. L., & Toth, E. L. (2005). Future professionals' perceptions of work, life, and gender issues in public relations. *Public Relations Review, 31*, 93–99.

Shen, H., Jiang, H., Jin, Y., & Sha, B. L. (2015). Practitioners' work-life conflict: A PRSA survey. *Public Relations Review, 41*(4), 415–421.

Wirth, L. (2001). *Breaking through the glass ceiling: Women in management.* Geneva: International Labour Organization.

Deep Conversations

Insights and Lessons from Current Women Leaders in PR

This section is composed of three chapters based on our deep conservations with current women leaders in the field. The chapters focus on three key topics: 1) the deeper meaning of leadership and influence as interpreted by current senior female leaders in public relations and communication, 2) how they define and enact the role of an ethics counselor; and 3) the identification, recruitment and role of mentors in their leadership development. Results are based on in-depth interviews with 51 mid- to senior-level female public relations executives serving in diverse organizational settings. Consistent with the goals of qualitative research, chapters in this section address the meaning and essence of leadership based on actual experiences with specific examples provided to illustrate our findings.

CHAPTER SEVEN

How Women in PR Define and Achieve Influence

In recognition of the reality that leadership is about more than holding a specific title or position, we began our in-depth interviews by asking current female leaders in the field how they would define influence. Some of the most common descriptions included being a trusted adviser, practicing thought leadership, being a subject matter expert, exerting a voice that executives listen to, and gaining the respect of other leaders. Others described influence as "being able to persuade people to your point of view" or demonstrating the competency of identifying and cultivating talented young professionals. Some of the descriptions also recognized public relations' role as a boundary spanner who raises the concerns on behalf of various stakeholders, both internally and externally. For example, a former chief communications officer for a *Global 500* company said:

> They are the ombudsman to management on behalf of employees and on behalf of customers and constituents and stakeholders. So, the influencers are the ones facilitating dialogue, and discussion, and empathy and action. And action that makes a difference. I think influence is the leader that can look across the entire organization and bring along his and her peer group to be able to affect positive outcomes and action and leadership and problem solving.

This is consistent with previous research findings which suggest two roles for boundary spanners in public relations: information processing and external representation (Aldrich & Herker, 1977). Through the information processing role, public relations managers gather information through environmental scanning first. Then they choose to act on pertinent information, store, interpret and share information in their communication with senior leaders (Aldrich & Herker, 1977). The second role, external representation, involves providing information from the organization to key publics to maintain the organization's reputation (Aldrich & Herker, 1977). In addition, as internal boundary spanners, public relations professionals should gather "intelligence across the company's various business units" and then connect the dots "to identify strategic decisions that may be inconsistent or not in the company's best interest" (Neill, 2014, p. 600). Through their role as boundary spanners, public relations professionals provide an essential service to senior leadership by helping reduce uncertainty in decision making, which provides them an opportunity to be influential (Hickson, Hinings, Lee, Schneck & Pennings, 1971).

Other women leaders described influence as being a moral compass or conscience. In the context of influence, some of the women discussed their obligation to be an ethical role model. As emphasized by a director of advancement for a college:

> Leading by example is key ... it's very important to me as a leader to bring other people along. I think that is probably the priority for me to show and demonstrate to those coming along what integrity is, what is ethical, what is the right way. I don't own this position; it is keeping the seat warm for the next person that comes along. And hopefully, I'll be able to impact people so that when they do move on and up, they will hold the same level of integrity.

Consistent with the boundary spanning role in public relations, our interviewees mentioned another ethical obligation of an influential leader, which is to make "leadership aware of where the organization may have an obligation or an interest in influencing issues."

With a few distinctions, these descriptions are consistent with prior research focused on influence in public relations. Aldoory et al. (2008) found that both men and women tended to define influence as having a seat at the decision-making table and a voice in making decisions. However, men tended to describe influence in the context of being persuasive and "winning" while women focused more on having access and being heard (p. 740). However, an executive director of marketing and communications for a university did not including winning in her description of influence. Instead, she focused on the importance of being heard as illustrated below:

In all the jobs that I've had in public affairs, I've told folks in the interview process that "What matters to me is to be heard. I don't have to win the day, and win every argument, but it's important to me that my viewpoint is respected and heard." And so what I try to do is [to] let people know that based on my experience and what I know, this is what I think, but recognizing that I might not always – especially if you're talking with the CEO, or a politician who is a mayor and a senator, you can accept or reject my advice, but this is what it is … But at the same time, owning what I know and not being afraid to say, "This is what I know. This is what I'm good at. This is what I've done."

Achieving Influence

Our second group of questions asked how women in public relations can achieve influence. The women leaders emphasized that the path to influence ideally should not be any different for female public relations executives when compared to their male counterparts. However, some women did perceive the path to be more difficult for them and mentioned a range of challenges. Based on our interviews, women of color reported they experienced even more obstacles along their journey.

Some of the common paths to achieve influence included building credibility over time through success with public relations initiatives, establishing trusting relationships with colleagues, and enhancing their business acumen. Relationships or social capital is core to achieving influence. As addressed by the president of a public relations agency:

Very much as one would think about how do you build – how do you start saving for retirement early? Putting into your 401K early. You should be putting the same investment into your career in these areas where you should be building a network, getting out into the industry, being observant, being a catalytic learner in terms of reading, not only what's happening in public relations, the industry itself, but certainly within business today.

According to the social capital theory, social capital refers to "the sum of the actual and potential resources embedded within, available through, and derived from the network of relationships possessed by an individual or social unit" (Nahapiet & Ghoshal, 1998, p. 243). Social capital provides three significant benefits: (1) access to information, (2) timeliness, which allows one to receive information sooner than others, and (3) referrals provided by personal contacts who bring up a colleague's name at the right time and place, so that additional opportunities arise (Burt, 1992). Consistent with the social capital theory, public relations executives need a network of "contacts (a) established in places where useful bits of information are likely to air and (b) providing a reliable flow of information to and from those places" (Burt, 1992, p. 15). Dodd (2012) suggested that public relations should be well positioned in the organization to access social resources embedded "in upper and lower levels of the hierarchy" (p. 48).

A former vice president of marketing and communications in a nonprofit organization said she is deliberate about building internal relationships:

> If they don't know you, they're not going to listen to you; they're not going to spend time with you. So one of the first things I did when I joined the organization was spend a few weeks really getting to know them, going out to lunch, going to meetings, just getting to know them and sit in their office and talk with them, so that trust and that rapport was being nurtured and built. Because yes, they had hired me to do a job, but that doesn't mean that there's trust. That needs to be built.

Others stressed the importance of understanding business, not just public relations. As a senior executive working in a financial institution said:

> I believe the way you do that is you first prioritize knowledge of the business over [the] knowledge of your practice as a public relations professional. And by that I don't mean that understanding your practice isn't important, I just consider that table stakes when we're thinking about influence. And I think the way that we earn the right to share our expertise as public relations professionals is by demonstrating a deep understanding of the business we hope to impact with those skills. And I think that's one of the biggest gaps I sometimes see is that I see public relations professionals who like to "stand apart," and they define themselves by their public relations expertise, and I don't find that is as beneficial for them in having people hear what they have to say and follow their recommendations internally when they can't have a rigorous conversation about the business itself.

Others emphasized the importance of doing your homework prior to providing counsel to senior leaders. As an executive director for a nonprofit organization said:

> Study up on whatever the topic is, research, investigate, and do your due diligence, so that when you do come to the table for your opinion – to share your opinion or to share input, you have facts backing you up. That it's not just gut instinct. Everybody's got gut instincts. Some better than others. But it's always important to be prepared, to do your homework, before you're put in a position to share your opinion. Because if it's all going to be conjecture and opinion, that's not always going to be helpful to your CEO. You have to have some strategy behind it.

At the same time, interviewed female executives provided some cautionary advice. For example, a vice president of global communications for a professional services firm said:

If you don't believe in yourself, no one will believe in you, right? And so part of influence is charisma and presence and confidence. Some people call it executive presence. But I think for women, sometimes there's a challenge if how you come across is a stereotype. Either you're apologizing for being in the room because you don't believe yourself you have permission, and that's coming across in your posture, how you handle yourself, how you set yourself. Or you feel like you have to over-compensate, and then you become the stereotype of the hyper aggressive, kind of bully, if you will. Some people, if you had to choose between those two, very stark stereotypes, you see many women in leadership who are influential, have reputations for coming across as the latter. They have influence many times because they're projecting a persona that admits fear or intimidation or requires some type of respect, like, "Stand up. You must listen. And because of my status and my title, and the people I know, if you don't listen, danger awaits."

She contrasted this hyper aggressive personality with a different type of influence:

There's another more nuanced way to influence, and I think when you think about women that you admire or leaders that you admire, when you think about influencing through grace and influencing through credibility and influencing through results ... But I think influence through grace, credibility, work ethic and through character are ultimately the influencing that I aspire towards.

These descriptions regarding paths to influence are consistent with previous research (e.g. Bowen, 2009). Based on Bowen's (2009) research, public relations' successes are documented in multiple ways, including established credibility over time, recognized leadership abilities along with managing crisis situations, and dealing with issues high in media attention. Similarly, Moss, Warnaby and Newman (2000) found that public relations executives' access to senior leadership depends on the personal credibility and the standing of the individual professional, including others' perceptions of that executive's "competence, expertise and business knowledge" (p. 303).

Influence in Practice

We also asked current female leaders about the types of approaches they prefer to use when providing strategic counsel. To further elaborate on some real-world scenarios, we asked them to provide specific examples of times when they were successful in providing strategic counsel as well as times when they were not so successful. Not surprisingly, many of the examples focused on counsel related to media relations and crisis communication, which have been considered as core areas associated with public relations expertise. In order to generate more practical implications, we asked them to provide lessons based on those experiences.

Regarding their preferred approach, inviting and engaging in dialogue was the number one, followed by recruiting allies (see Table 7.1). Engaging in dialogue and recruiting allies would be considered relational influence resources (Berger & Reber, 2006). As Berger and Reber (2006) suggested, influence is "all about developing relationships with others inside the organization to get ahead, gain access to information and resources, play a role in strategic decision making, and help the organization to do the right thing" (p. 89). Other than engaging in dialogue and recruiting allies, the approaches of conducting research and sharing case studies are also preferred influence strategies as mentioned by our interviewees. These two approaches are considered to be informational resources, which is another critical source of power and influence (Berger & Reber, 2006).

The president and CEO of a consultancy said that she prefers to ask questions and engage in dialogue to help senior executives accept the best solution. As she said, "While you have to speak truth to a person of power, you don't have to hit them over the head with it. You have to get them to see it and understand it."

This approach can be referred to as mutual problem solving or negotiation (Moberg & Seabright, 2000) and ideally should involve both sides listening to each other's perspectives and incorporating those considerations into the final decision (Conger, 1998). A senior public affairs office in the U.S. military described how she engages in such dialogue to provide constructive feedback:

> So, the way I approach it is I come in, and first off, I start complimenting or just emphasizing all the really good things about the way things are already going. Like, "This is working so well. This organization is doing such a great job doing this. Now, what I could say, is maybe we could inch forward and do just a little better by maybe approaching it this way." Rather than just being confrontational right away, which I've never seen work, and I've seen people try it, and then they come back frustrated as to why they couldn't make any headway. But I think about how I work, and I'm

Table 7.1. Preferred influence strategies

Influence Strategies	# who preferred
Engaging in Dialogue	36
Recruiting Allies	30
Conducting Research	26
Sharing Case Studies	17
Sharing Personal Experiences	4
Using Scenarios	3
Raising the concerns of stakeholders	1
Appealing to senior leader's values	1

like, "I don't like someone coming in and just saying everything I'm doing is messed up." So there's so many good things. Why not talk about that? But then, talk about ways to make those good things even better. And if something is really going in the wrong direction, then sort of bring that up within that context of things. And say, "Hey, and we could really turn this around and here's why this will benefit you." And then give them that benefit at the end.

In previous studies, scholars found that rational persuasion or informational resources (e.g. use of data, case studies and laws) was the most common influence approach public relations professionals reported using, followed by building coalitions, then exerting pressure or assertiveness (Berger & Reber, 2006; O'Neil, 2003). However, through interviews with women in senior leadership roles regarding their preferred approaches in the context of ethics counsel, Neill and Barnes (2018) found they tended to equally prefer rational approaches such as making legitimacy appeals and relational approaches such as recruiting allies. The authors suggested that the reason women may be recruiting allies is because they are often outnumbered by men in the board room (Neill & Barnes, 2018). Consistent with this concern, several of the women we interviewed mentioned the importance of recruiting male colleagues as allies. As a vice president said, "You have to recruit the males, because the guys listen to the guys."

A former chief communications office for a *Global 500* company also discussed the importance of recruiting allies and gaining their support for recommendations:

> Oftentimes, I would meet one-on-one, again across the C-suite with the men and women who populated different functions, to talk through ideas, recommendations, challenges, issues. And to build consensus in a one-on-one environment where you can settle on, 1+1 isn't two, it's 12. So that when you come to the table, you have reflected already on their inputs, their thoughts, their concerns, their cares, and you're addressing those and sitting on them and still going forward with whatever it is that is the right recommendation, the right plan, the right discussion. At the end of the day, people want to be heard, whether it's a customer or your CEO. And they want to know you have considered their point of view.

It is important to note that several women relied on more than one influence strategy, and some of the women said they adjust their strategy depending on the communication preferences of the leader they are attempting to influence. As the founder of an independent consultancy said:

> So you have to understand what makes that person tick you know what they get annoyed about, what they get excited about. You have to know that person in terms of the best way to approach them. So is it with facts and logic? Or is through a narrative and storytelling? Is it over coffee in the morning or is it over a glass of wine in the evening? I mean you need to know. And so I would say a strategy is to absolutely

understand the personality of the executive that you are trying to help. And then package and tailor your approach accordingly.

One unique approach involved appealing to the senior leader's own values. A chief communications officer described using this approach when providing counseling to the president of the company about being transparent with employees regarding pending layoffs:

> In this particular case, what has been most successful has been to go to particularly our president and say this is who you are. This type of approach resonates with what you value. You value people, you value communication, you value respect for others, and this is the way that aligns most closely with your personal profile and values. And that has been one of the more effective tools I have used is to appeal to the individual's sense of who they are and what they stand for and what the company stands for.

This approach is consistent with making legitimacy appeals, which are arguments based on what is legal or ethical, and calling attention to the organization's own core values (Berger & Reber, 2006; Neill & Barnes, 2018).

One of the more instructive examples about successfully providing strategic counsel was provided by a senior executive from a global public relations firm. She made the mistake of trying to push a change initiative forward without first getting buy-in from the agency employees. As she explained:

> So coming into it, I had the senior team and there were – let's say at least three or four major strategic imperatives, issue oriented that we needed to fix. And I've already told you I'm a very - I'm kind of impatient and I want it to be done and done quickly. And so I had the answers. And I get them together and I'm like here are the answers for the three really scary things we have to overcome and seize the day. And that went over like a lead balloon … So I just - I went headlong into I have the answers and you will follow me, and that was not going to be effective … So I had to really step back and think about why that didn't work, why we were being so slow to change, and why with a few people following yes, but a few people just really digging their heels in and so I really had to step back. So then the second part, so that was sort of the failure, which again I didn't listen. I was rushing headlong into the answers and wasn't driving consensus building.

With the fact that initially the meeting finished with a strong resistance, this senior executive had to change her strategy by engaging in dialogue with her employees to build consensus. Ultimately the action was successful as described by her:

> Then fast forward to sort of recalibrating, which is spending time, digging in, listening, getting people to follow in a way, because I'm asking if they will help and

asking for their ideas and having them be the ones to also implement the change. So delivering on some of their ideas. We all want – this whole team wanted the office to succeed. It's not like anybody said well, we don't want to win. So we all actually had the same goal. It was just how to go about it in a way that making it their idea.

Moberg and Seabright (2000) referred to this approach as "tell and listen," which requires executives to consider others' views and possibly refine the original recommendation. Sometimes it may be necessary to reach a compromise with colleagues in leading change. As addressed by Goodstein (2000), "as individuals are exposed to an array of varying perspectives and multiple values, one's own certainty about the interpretation or application of a principle may lessen, opening up the possibility of accepting alternative perspectives" (p. 811).

One of the more unusual examples of providing strategic counsel involved creating a mock-up for a multicultural campaign that the client favored, but the Latina executive perceived as insulting to her culture based on her description:

> I'm directing a project. Everybody's insulted, but let's do it as an exercise, because we're going to prove them wrong. When we showed the concepts, literally my clients were both like, "Oh my gosh. This is awful ..." Then I proposed, "OK, good. That doesn't work either, but I'm going to go ahead and provide another concept, from scratch, something new, and we'll begin again." That was an award-winning campaign that the client loved, everybody approved it down-to-up, and they were super happy with the end result.

An example of a time that a senior executive was not successful in her attempt to provide counsel generated some valuable lessons. She made the mistake of asking the supervisor to simply sign-off on the proposed plan without getting him involved in the plan development. It turns out that the supervisor actually wanted to be involved in the decision making. Therefore, a good lesson was learned as described by the chief communications officer:

> What I failed to realize about that person was that they liked to get dirty a little bit. So in that regard, what I should have done was brought in options. I should have brought in three options and said, here's the pros and cons of each option and then gotten feedback, and then perhaps moved to a recommendation, because the final thought might have been actually been some sort of mashup of any of those options. And instead I went in and basically spoon-fed the executive. I've done all the homework for you. Here's the proposal. You need to say yes. And that did not go over well ... I learned that understanding that person's thought process a little bit better helped me adapt, so that the next time I went in I knew to go with options. I knew to go with pros and cons.

When analyzing the various examples of times when senior public relations executives were not successful in providing strategic counsel, the cause often could be attributed to not having a trusting relationship with their supervisor, colleagues or client. A chief communications officer for a *Fortune 500* company explained:

> I've been in situations before like that where you didn't have, either because of time or personalities, credibility built up in an organization to be able to effectively maneuver in a situation like that. The outcomes are not as good. That's where I carry that, "You need to put coin in the bank before it's needed"... Sometimes you'll hear communicators say that through a crises or an issues management situation, you find either a CCO or a particular group of executives you're working with "find religion." What we mean by that is, if they haven't been battle-hardened by an issue or a crisis, it hasn't kicked them in the ass, so to speak, they don't appreciate sometimes the counsel that they're receiving from their communications colleagues. Once they have been through a war or two, or they have been misquoted or they have been burned by the media, or they have gone after by an NGO, or gone through a lawsuit or whatever it might be, they "find religion," and they find the value of that partnership of having a good strategic counsel with them along the way to help them.

Other reasons female executives gave for not being successful included the executive's ego, poor timing of the proposal, not asking enough questions, lack of thorough understanding regarding the history of an issue, personality clashes, or just the reality that the boss is the final decision maker. As a vice president for diversity, inclusion and engagement at a public relations firm said:

> Your role is to be there to counsel and that involves giving your best advice coming from that often a transparent, credible place. But it also involves understanding that ultimately it is their decision, and then the second piece being flexible enough to think of, even if they're going a different direction than you might have suggested, how do you work with that, how do you make sure you are still giving them your best thought process, the best you have to give and then the final thing being trust. They've got to trust that you're on their side and that you're there to help them look good.

Challenges as a Female Executive in Public Relations

On the surface, the expectations for women in leadership in public relations appear to be gender neutral. The women in our study were able to identify a checklist of core competencies that are necessary for advancement to leadership positions. The list included oral and written communication skills, business and financial acumen, critical thinking and problem-solving skills, emotional intelligence, listening, confidence, integrity, the ability to build and maintain relationships, strategic planning as well as the ability to develop and manage employees. This list is comparable with the one developed by Meng, Berger, Gower and Heyman (2012) in their study on excellent leadership in public relations, which included strategic decision-making, problem solving, communication expertise, relationship building and trustworthy/ethical among the most critical competencies.

At the same time, the women executives we interviewed perceived some different leadership characteristics compared to male executives. They cautioned that women should not be too direct or assertive. As explained by an executive vice president at a public relations firm:

> If there's a woman who is more take charge, she's seen as more aggressive, versus a man, he's seen as a bold leader. We've seen the whole "lean in" movement and all of these other things that sort of describe, "Hey, you have to do these things in order to make your voice heard." But then you do that, and then you're labeled as "too bossy," or what have you. I think there is a level of nurturing because we are women and females in general are nurturing creatures. I believe that there's an expectation in our industry in particular for women to be more nurturing than their male counterparts. If you don't show that side, or if it doesn't preclude all the other skills that males typically show, you're seen again as a stoic, colder person, because you're not displaying those feelings or that type of behavior.

In addition, our interviewees expressed they have perceived the stereotypical expectation to remain calm and to keep her emotions in check as a woman while male colleagues can exhibit passion for their recommendations. As a public affairs officer in the U.S. military explained:

> I believe senior female leaders are expected to have a certain temperament. Calmer, or we're expected to kind of stand back, be able to provide even-keeled conversation as we're speaking with senior leaders. I don't necessarily see that as a requirement for our male counterparts. For example, I think at the same level, if we're working a contentious issue or a crisis communication plan, something where leadership is trying to make a decision, there's a real difference in the – there's a real passion for what that decision is going to be. I think there's an expectation that a woman is going to be more congenial or calmer when she presents that, and that the male is going to come in and be forceful, "Here's what we need to do. Here's why we need to do it." Just that difference in temperament sometimes gives the impression that our male counterpart is more committed to his recommendation. I don't think that's necessarily the case. The downside of that is – there's still some perception that if the female leader comes in with that much passion, so to speak, for her cause, that it can actually be a distraction.

Current female leaders also stressed the fact that they are expected to continue to do tactical work on top of their strategic responsibilities. Although such findings have been revealed in previous research two decades ago (Toth & Grunig, 1993), not much change in perception has been evidenced. As a chief communications officer for a *Fortune 500* corporation said:

> Here's what my experience is – is that women in this field must show capacity to provide - to operate at the 30,000-foot level and then also be on the ground and in all the details. My experience is that same expectation does not exist for men in this field. That the men in this field get the luxury of operating at the 30,000-foot level and then get to "leave the details to others below them."

One of the biggest frustrations for women leaders is not being acknowledged in board meetings where they are often outnumbered by men. Seven of the women interviewed without any prompting told a similar story. As a vice president in a public relations consultancy said:

> You'd be in a meeting, I'd say something, it was a suggestion, a point, whatever, and I would finish. A man would say the exact same thing I said, and it would become, "That's such a good idea!" It just floored me. I'm sitting there going, "I'm sorry, but am I invisible? Or are you all deaf?"

The practice is so common that some women are not letting it go unchecked. As a CEO of a nonprofit organization said:

> And so this happened to me in a meeting and I said something and then the person next to me said it. And ... I said, "oh, you mean the idea I just said." And everyone started laughing. But I think like calling people out, because that happens all the time. And I did have a meeting, another meeting where that happened to me, and I didn't speak out. But I made eye contact with someone across the room who was laughing. But we didn't call it out. And I think that's a mistake. So I think calling that out is important as well when you're shorted in that situation as a female.

A few interviewees also felt that they had to provide more support for their recommendations than their male counterparts as described by a director of external communications for a corporation:

> I think a man's word is taken at face value a little more quickly and easily. Whereas I – now you're making me think, am I just imagining this? Or is it true? – That I have to build out a plan that's in much more detail and data-driven to prove the point. I'm questioning whether that's an expectation of myself, or do I really believe that is required. It's a bit of both.

When it came to advancement opportunities, several interviewees acknowledged their reluctance to apply for the positions if they don't feel they have met all the listed qualifications in the job description. A vice president of communications in a corporation reflected on a presentation she recently heard:

Something that she said was women need to feel … they're 95% sure that they can do the job and that they know how to do the job. So they have to be able to do the job before they apply for any position. Whereas men, they have the potential to do the job. In other words, they might not be doing the job, they may not know how to do the job, but they think they can do the job. You know that was one of the things that really struck me … And I thought wow, you know so true, because whenever I have gone for a position, myself, I have reviewed the position description and I've often kind of like check, check, check mental checks in my head of yes I can do this, yes I have done that, yes I know how to do this, versus oh, I could learn how to do this because I have the potential.

When discussing career advancement, a vice president of diversity, inclusion and engagement at a technology company identified three essential factors: visibility, opportunity and advocacy and offered insights based on her life experience:

So, by visibility I mean do other people in the organization know who you are – in essence what's your personal brand. So when your name is said, when they see your name on the invitation to a meeting, a meeting invite, I always scan to see who else is in the meeting, when I see your name, what do I think? So how visible are you? Do they know you're working? You've got your head down, you're working really really hard, you're doing good things, and you're expecting other people to know about it. That's not necessarily a realistic expectation. So one of the issues that may be holding you back might be visibility. Linked to the visibility is the opportunity. So if I'm more senior in the organization and I have no visibility of what you're doing, then it's going to be hard for me to reach down or to suggest that you be given an opportunity to do x, y, z whether it's a cross-training assignment, or a stretch of time that I'm putting you on a special task force, etc. Those kinds of opportunities to show that you can work at a higher level or on a broader scope or with more responsibility, those things are tied to the visibility of the perception that is had by you of others in the position to make that decision. And that's tied to the third piece, which is advocacy. You can't be, especially the larger the organization is, you can't be the one kind of running around necessarily tooting your own horn. You need those who are in, who are higher than you, or who are sitting in different parts of the organization to be your advocate. So in rooms where you will not be, to be the one to say "Hey, you know what, I know her and she's really good." I saw the x, y, z that she did, and it made a real difference. You've got to have advocates. So, this visibility, opportunity, and advocacy are things that all employees need, and they tend to be things that women and people of color are less likely to have at various stages in their careers than others.

While there is much wisdom in that statement, it also raises several questions such as how do female leaders become more visible and how do they find an advocate who is willing to advocate for them at the right moment? One way to become more visible is to volunteer for additional assignments as recommended by an assistant vice president of internal communications at a university:

Be willing to be courageous in terms of raising your hand, to take on additional responsibilities, to sit on different committees, to be on the different affinity groups, to volunteer for leadership roles … just be direct. You have to be able to articulate what it is you want, right? One of the things that I learned along the way, is that if a man wants another position, he will walk in the door and say, "I want to do this." And you have to have that confidence that you can and that you should. And if you look around, the person who has the role, it's not that they're at 100 percent in terms of executing the role, because if that were the case, they shouldn't be in the role. So you have to kind of have confidence in yourself to say, "I may not have all the skills, but I have enough to be able to do it," and so therefore I'm going to voice this interest to someone else so that they know that I have passion around this and it's something I want to do.

At the same time, visibility also requires self-advocacy, which could be something that may be a little uncomfortable at first. A senior vice president at a global public relations firm provided advice on how to do so in an appropriate manner:

I actually think just being really candid about the discomfort of it is a good way to go. So I was fortunate to have some really great managers where I said, "This is really uncomfortable for me, I feel like I'm bragging on myself, but I feel like this is important. Would you agree that this is something I need to be doing?" And any manager that I've ever had has said, "Yes! I want to hear those things." And now that I'm on the other side of it, that's one of my favorite things throughout the day, is when I get to see some of the really great work that my team members are doing, or some praise that they've gotten or some great results that I might not have even otherwise seen, and it never comes across as arrogant or overly self-promotional. So, I think if you just say "Hey, this makes me feel a little uncomfortable, but here's why I'm doing it." It sort of gives yourself that grace to feel comfortable doing it because you can get on the same page with your manager. Because I would be really surprised if any manager said no, I don't want you to do that. And then it's like, OK, this is what my manager wants from me, as opposed to every single time being like, Oh gosh, how are they going to respond to my forwarding this on.

It is important to recognize the self-advocacy can be contrary to cultural norms. A managing director at a public relations firm confronted this reality when mentoring a Latina employee:

I basically was talking to her about sort of naming and claiming and being a little bit bolder and being more aggressive. And she said, "It's just – it's interesting because in my culture for the women that I'm around, and my family members … we're a culture of keep your head down and hopefully someone will notice your hard work. That we can work longer and harder." She said speaking in generalities, we can work longer and harder than our colleagues. We keep our head down … it's seen as brown nosing to be sort of more aggressive or look at me. I'm ready to take this next step or whatever. And so being less aggressive and being more passive. And that's something that's followed her her whole career, because that's cultural. And so she's trying to find the balance and the footing of how to name and claim it and saying, no I will have that seat at the table. And here's what I can deliver when you put me at that seat at the table. And so ... that's really just not in congruence with ... how she was reared.

With the fact that dual-earner couples are on the rise, several interviewees mentioned that their spouses actually coached them on advocating for a promotion or raise. A senior executive at a public relations firm described a defining moment when she was up for a promotion and her competition was a male colleague. As she recounted:

> And I was talking with my husband about it and how interesting that it's my husband, a male, he said, "[her name], name it, claim it. Like any other guy – I guarantee you your guy counterpart is saying this. And you need to be more aggressive." And I'm pretty aggressive in my role. But I was sitting back sort of playing nice you know. And I flew to [headquarters]. I said I'm coming. My boss was like what – you're coming? I think yeah, I'll be there in the morning 9 o'clock. I need to talk to you. And I met with him at 9 o'clock and I said, "I'm either your guy - interesting language, right – I'm either your guy or I'm not your guy. And either way that's your decision to make. Here's why I know that I'm your guy. But if I'm not your guy, I'd like to know it now, because there's someone else, somewhere that will make me their guy. So this isn't the career path that I intended if I'm not your guy. But I can handle it."

She did get the promotion and believes that extra initiative was necessary as it appeared the plan was for the two executives to share the role.

The U.S. Census Bureau (2019) reports that men earn an average salary of $77,953 for careers in management/business/sciences/arts compared to $56,754 for women, meaning women earn approximately 73 cents per dollar compared to men. A study on agency compensation in public relations found that men earn an average of $6,072 more than women when controlling for other factors (Muehlbauer & Rockland, 2017) such as years of experience. In comparison, ethnic minorities earned $9,302 less than whites working at public relations agencies (Muehlbauer & Rockland, 2017). A chief communications officer at a *Fortune 500* company once had a frank discussion with her boss on fair and equitable compensation.

> I said, "Why did you think for one minute that I would have any less expectations for me, my husband, my children, my home, the cars I drive, the colleges they go to school – why would you think I would have any less expectation than you have? Why would I want less for my family than you want for your family?" And that was

shocking to him. I think he looked at me like, "Oh my god, for the first time, there isn't and shouldn't be a difference between if you're male or female. I'm male, so therefore my aspirations are higher or my expectations for my compensation package and what I do with it will vary."

Barriers to Influence—Race

Cultural diversity remains a challenge in the public relations workforce, and most notably in the management ranks (Pompper, 2004, 2007; Qui & Muturi, 2016; Vardeman-Winter & Place, 2017). According to the U.S. Bureau of Labor Statistics (2019), 71.4% of the public relations and fundraising managers are women, 89.8% are whites, 1.4% are Latinos/Hispanics, 8% are African Americans, and 0.4% are Asians. The participants in our study included 27 women of color, specifically 15 African American women, 7 Hispanic/Latina women and 5 Asian Americans. While women representing these various ethnic groups faced unique challenges, there also were a few common obstacles they faced as women of color. First of all, several women expressed that they felt invisible or "hidden in plain sight." An African American independent consultant explained it this way:

> I do hear often once I am connected with someone – not often, but on occasion – where the comment is, "Oh my gosh, where have you been all this time?" The idea that I'm hiding in plain sight, of course, gives me pause and an opportunity to educate that individual.

An African American female working as a director of advancement communications in higher education had a similar perception. She said:

> Years ago, I was working at [organization name] in public relations and development, and our president brought in the leader of – president of a very large ad agency, who was … being called to task for not hiring people of color in his firm. And I had no idea why she called me in her office, but I walked in, she kind of ran my resume down, and he looked at me and he said, "Where did you come from?" And I said, "I've been here all the time. He just hasn't been looking"… As I referred back to the president of the agency, when he asked where have I been. We're overlooked. It's like the invisible man. I can be in a meeting and really be invisible to people in the meeting.

It may sound surprising at first, but some of our interviewees expressed that other colleagues sometimes have low expectations for women of color. The same African American female working as a director of advancement communications in higher education explained:

People don't think you've got the skill set that you have. When you walk in the door, it's automatically assumed you don't know, or maybe you were promoted because of Affirmative Action. And sometimes it's really comical to see the surprise on their faces or when you hear someone say, "They're so articulate." Well, why the hell not? I've got a college degree. Why wouldn't I sound like this?" It's a preconceived notion that people of color are not-as-good-as.

These experiences are consistent with the findings of Cose (1993) who interviewed African American professionals and discovered similar issues such as low expectations and presumption of failure (Grunig et al., 2008). Several women of color said they often experience an element of surprise when others realize they are in management roles. As an African American female working as an executive director of marketing and communications at a university said:

People don't expect me, as a female, but they definitely don't expect me as an African American female, to be the person who is in charge of public relations, the person who is the spokesperson, and I think that there's some skepticism and I've had some people challenge my ability to handle a situation because they don't think that I'm a true professional. I mean I've had people actually say to me, "How did you get this job?"... Or people when I walk into the meeting, or go out to meet them in the office and I bring them into the conference room, I know for a fact they're sitting there waiting for the actual boss to come in. And I sit down and I say, OK, and they're like, "You're [name]?" Yes, that's me.

Even when these women advance to management roles, they sometimes feel like their input is not as valued as it should be unless it is a diversity issue. As an African American female working as an independent consultant said:

I definitely felt that in the agency world where it's like you speak up and people really only listen when it's pertaining to your ethnicity. So if you're a Latino and there's a Latino issue, they want to hear what you have to say, because now all of the sudden you're the spokesperson for the entire Latino community. Otherwise, on a day-to-day basis, they kind of downplay what you say, because it's perceived as not as useful or not as insightful or not as brilliant.

Adding to the perception that their counsel is less valued are client expectations and perceptions. As a Latina independent consultant explained:

I've had clients that have asked whether or not we had different billable rates, because of the fact that we represented the multicultural team and that was a very senior client at [name of company] said, "Wait a minute. Does that mean I have to pay less, I get to pay less for multicultural services versus general market?" How is that possible? The same community basically, a U.S. based community, but who speak different languages and we can do their job and our job. But somehow you think that should come at a discount.

In addition, Latina women felt that their passion is often misunderstood when providing counsel. As a Latina executive working as a strategic communication manager for a technology company explained:

> I definitely know for Hispanic women that when you have a lot of energy, and I tend to talk with my hands, and I talk loud, I'm told that, "Oh my god, you're overbearing, you're aggressive." So that passion comes across very differently than let's say when a man does it … I have noticed that we get pigeon-holed. Instead of saying, "Wow! You have great passion! I love your animation!" You don't get that at all. It's the complete opposite. That's natural – even my husband will say when I'm on the phone with my family and I'm speaking in Spanish, my volume automatically goes up. He's like, "You're having a fight! What's going on?" And I'm like, "I'm not fighting? What are you talking about?" He's like, "Your voice, and your movement in your body, and everything about you changes when you're speaking to family or in Spanish with a friend versus when you're just talking in English on the phone." I have a feeling I'm the same way in meetings.

Several women expressed frustration that they were pigeonholed into only working on multicultural accounts, despite an interest and expertise in other areas such as crisis communication or media relations. For example, a Latina female who previously worked as a vice president of marketing and communications for a nonprofit organization shared her experience:

> And many times, I've been put on projects that were focused on just Latina. Like, they wanted someone to be on a project that had to do with outreach to the Hispanic market, and so they immediately tapped on me to lead that project. Mind you, I have never specialized in that … so I've never put myself in that niche. But they put me there because again I speak Spanish, and they see me as a Latina who would understand the market. So I think that perception that just because you're Latina, or just because you're Asian, or just because you're black, would automatically mean that you need to be on those projects? I don't think so. So that was something I encountered early on in my career. I think it wasn't until I spoke up and said, "You know, I appreciate this, and I'm happy to help here and there, but my specialty is not this. I'm actually a bit more broad/generalist, and I can help in other areas too." I think we needed to speak up and have that confidence to help educate them also and let them know. Because I think if we don't speak up, those perceptions continue.

Regarding the issue of pigeonholing, scholars have referred to two roles assumed by practitioners of color: cultural interpretation and race representation (Grunig et al., 2008; Mallette, 1993). Cultural interpretation involves translating one's own culture to outsiders and similarly race representatives are expected to represent the diverse perspectives of their ethnic group (Grunig et al., 2008;

Mallette, 1993). In previous research, Pompper (2007) found some Latinas embraced their role as an "ethnic insider" and took advantage of the marketability associated with being bilingual. Len-Rios (1998) pointed out that "although practitioners of color may be able to identify with publics of their same race, there are other important factors such as educational level, cultural background, and socioeconomic status that can affect the practitioner's ability to identify with a particular audience" (p. 545).

One frustration associated with being assigned to multicultural campaigns is that practitioners of color are often reduced to tactical roles. One direct impact would be their diverse voices are sometimes not brought into the discussion at the strategic planning phase as described by a Latina independent consultant:

> I think the not having your voice heard when there's a general market project, for instance, and they want to incorporate Hispanic outreach in that project. One of our concerns is we should be at the table at the beginning when that project is being discussed before the plan is set. A lot of times Hispanic, and this plays into African American too, those multicultural teams are not brought into the discussion until the plan has been developed. So that means we're just adding in with little measly budgets something to kind of make the client happy that they're doing multicultural outreach when what would be more effective, and again this goes into the team leaders and senior leadership not thinking broadly about how we can really blow this campaign up. They should bring in these multicultural teams at the time that they're having those preliminary conversations with the clients to make it really cohesive and make sense, not just a translated version of something that was decided by a group that is not diverse.

Another Latina female working as a strategic communication manager for a technology company expanded on why being assigned to multicultural campaigns can be a barrier to advancement:

> The other problem here, and I know I experienced that was at my previous employer, I was one of maybe five people that was bilingual that understood the market, that knew how to do campaigns in that market. If you don't want to be that person, that's fine, but what ends up happening is then there's nobody doing that. And so then you feel this guilt or, "god, it's my job to represent the community that I'm part of. And if I stop doing it, no one else will do it." And so then you feel this sense of obligation, and it's not our fault, but at the same time, it's the fault of, we're not hiring enough diverse candidates, we don't have slates of enough diverse candidates, so we're not even filling the junior ranks with diverse candidates. So that I could move away from that role, I would need someone junior to move into it, right? Well, the pipeline isn't filling up. So if I step away, then the pipeline is empty. And so I think that's why a lot of women feel pigeon-holed to that, not women in general but ethnic minorities, because they may be the only one that does that.

A Latina executive who previously worked as a vice president of marketing and communications at a nonprofit organization provided insight into why she thinks there continues to be a pipeline issue in diversity recruitment and advancement:

> My own reasons around that might be because a) not many Latinas in PR to begin with. It doesn't seem to be a natural decision to go into that. Second of all, I don't how many Latinas even know what PR is or what it consists of, so that lack of awareness of what the field is. And then thirdly, to be a leader in PR, why would they not pursue it or why haven't they pursued it? A lot of it could be, they don't know how - they don't know how to go about it. They don't understand the path. The path is not clear to them how to elevate - how to go up. Some women may be in roles that need certain skill sets that they don't have ... maybe the business acumen is missing or maybe the strategic counsel acumen is missing. So how do we give them those skill sets? How do we pair them up with mentors in the executive suite that could be those champions to guide them and prepare them and almost like a succession plan and prepare them for those roles? ... From another perspective, Latinas also may not want these roles. They may think, "Well, it's going to take way too much time from my family life? Family is very important in Hispanic culture. Raising a family is very important also ... Another one could also be they don't have the education. So it goes back to education, because a lot of our roles, leadership roles, require a higher level of education. As you probably know, Latinos in general, it's low statistics in terms of passing high school, and going onto college and so forth.

In addition to this real barrier to advancement (i.e. pipeline issue), the lack of women of color in leadership positions indirectly communicates to employees that there is less opportunity to advance. As an African American female working as a director of media and public relations at a university lamented:

> It's like you have black people at this institution who've been here 10 or 15 years, some of them have doctorates, and nobody's in a leadership position. Nobody is higher than a director. Some people have been here almost 20 years. And I'm like, "No one can be in an executive level?" To me, that's just ridiculous. Why does this glass ceiling exist, seemingly for black people? There's not even a black male, so you can't even say it's men who get all the opportunities. Well, it's white men and now white women who have those opportunities of leadership at the executive level. And we have no one.

This perceived barrier led to the conclusion that she would need to leave the university to advance. Pompper (2004, 2007) found a similar mindset when interviewing Latina and African American women about their advancement potential and referred to the practice as "outspiraling career moves" (Bell & Nkomo, 2001, p. 161; Pompper, 2007, p. 306). And indeed, eight of the women of color who participated in our study were working as independent consultants either due to lack of advancement or a desire for more flexible work hours. In fact, two of the women reported losing their jobs due to being too outspoken regarding multicultural issues. A Latina executive discussed what she perceived to be her mistake:

> I think I fought too hard. And I didn't go straight to the top with a solution and I talked to my manager. And I probably frustrated the hell out of him, and eventually that's what led to my firing. And the reasons were after 10 years of building a successful and possible practice, working with every agency in the U.S. to extend the competency to their teams, I fought too hard for my team and I didn't seem happy. So they were going to let me go. And had I known, I would have done it differently.

When asked what she would have done differently, the Latina executive said:

> I would have socialized the opportunity so that it wasn't just me. I would have gotten buy-in from other leaders that were not in my – I would have gone straight to corporate or public affairs for help and I would say listen I want to do some sort of an exchange, an employee exchange program, so that my team continues to grow and evolve based on their interests, not just based on them being multicultural and so they get sent to me .... So I would have socialized it differently. I wouldn't have taken on as my fight. I would have socialized it as a firm opportunity.

Some of the interviewees described instances of overt and subtle discrimination they had faced during their careers. One Asian American was mistaken as Latina and someone questioned her ability to speak English. A Latina woman who sought a leadership position was told "You're gonna have a real hard time getting that position. You're going to have an uphill battle, because you're a Latina and Latinas have a lot of work to do when it comes to perception of intelligence." And she received anonymous voicemails left on her phone with messages such as "go back to do landscaping." An African American woman faced one of the most overt cases of discrimination early in her career. As she described:

> So I sent in my resume for a job actually with a PR agency, and it was a small agency. And I walked in the door and the receptionist said, "Can I help you?" And when I told her who I was there to see, she kind of in retrospective gave me an odd look and said Ok. And so I sat down and then this whole thing is kind of seared in my head because I can remember hearing the woman walk up and then the look on her face when she saw that I was the candidate there for the interview, and her words to me were, "but you looked so good on paper." And so she was stunned that I was black with my credentials. Needless to say, and we were still out in the reception area at this point. She knew it, the receptionist knew it, and I knew that there was no way in heck this woman was going to hire me. And that's what happened. I sat through this painful interview - she really didn't even interview me ... and I left that

interview and I was devastated and I was too young and naïve to know what had -
how illegal what she just done was, but I purposed in my heart that I didn't want
any other person to have to go through something like that. So one of the reasons
why I have been active throughout my career in counseling, mentoring informally
or sometimes formally people, to try to help equip them because the only thing that
changes ... people like that is results.

It is appropriate to mention that this executive has 35 years of experience in
public relations, so this experience would have occurred in the mid-1980s. At
the same time, it helps explain why some African American "pioneers" in public
relations are so willing to give back and lift up others as they climb the corporate
ladder (Bell & Nkomo, 2001; Pompper, 2004).

For some African American women, their hairstyle has been a subject of
office conversation. What other colleagues may not realize is that those comments
communicate what is acceptable or not regarding their physical appearance. As an
African American female working as a director of media and public relations in
higher education explained:

> I get a lot of micro-aggressions about my hair. Anytime I change my hairstyle –
> and I made the comment once, because someone said in leadership, "Oh I like your
> hair like this." I went to my boss and I said, "Well that implies, if I wear it" – you
> know, it was flat-ironed, and it was straight, it was long – "That implies that this
> is the acceptable look that I'm to have, that this person in leadership likes. So if
> I cut it, and if I go and wear my afro, does that mean that I am less desirable for a
> position? Or have the look that the university wants?" I said, "I don't think that's
> how he intended it, but that's how that could be interpreted." When you see my
> hair, "Hey, I like your hair," versus, "I like it like that. You should wear it like that."
> Because what I hear, is "This straightened hairstyle is flattering on you, but this is
> what we deem to be more acceptable." So you hear those types of things. So every
> time I change my hair I kind of like groan, because I know it is going to be a topic
> of discussion around the water cooler. While it's something that's small, but it
> enforces that you're different.

Physical stature can be a source of insecurity for some Asian Americans and
their confidence, particularly for those who are petite. As a consultant in a public
relations firm said:

> So I'm half Vietnamese, half Chinese ... I think the one thing for me is my own
> personal perception. I'm very petite if anything it's that one thing that I think is
> my Achilles heel perhaps is that I'm 4'10" and a quarter ... I'm very personable, but
> I feel like you know I don't feel like I have presence. I think other people would say
> differently, probably based on what people tell me. But if anything, that's the thing
> that has been an obstacle for me.

The other issue that was raised by Asian Americans in public relations is the difficulty in finding a network of other colleagues. As an independent consultant explained:

> I'm third-generation Japanese American. I don't speak the language. My parents were in the Japanese internment camps. We didn't even speak the language in our house. The people that were of my own culture, trying to put together these segmented groups, like Asian American Journalist Association - it was harder because, I either had to fit a mold of being the right kind of Asian, I don't want to sound - but honestly it's true. If I was more Chinese than I was Japanese, or more Korean or more Vietnamese or Taiwanese, or Filipino, it was kind of like I was the wrong Asian.

A few of the women raised the issue of intersectionality, meaning they were unsure if how they were treated by colleagues was related to being a woman or a person of color or both. The term is attributed to legal scholar Kimberlé Crenshaw (1991), who used the concept to communicate how gender, race, and class work simultaneously to exclude Black women on multiple levels (Nielsen, 2011). Vardeman-Winter, Tindall and Jiang (2013) asserted that we actually have multiple "social identities" or categories to which we are socially recognized as belonging (Owens, 2003). Therefore, neither gender nor race alone tells the entire story of an individual's lived experiences or her access to opportunities (Collins, 1990; Mallette, 1995; Mattis et al., 2008; Weber, 2001). In addition, the salience of those identities may vary in different social situations (Tajfel, 1981). As an African American executive working as a director of external communications in the retail industry explained:

> As an African American female, you're always – I have always struggled a little bit with – "is this an instance of …" particularly when working with someone new, and I can give you an example of this. Is that person's reticent questions, lack of direct engagement with me in a room, where they're directly engaging with some of my peers in a room, is that because that person is having a difficulty working with somebody who's a woman? Is it because they're having a difficulty working with someone who's a black woman? I don't know. I try really hard not to create my own story in my mind and put that story on other people, but there certainly have been instances where things have come to play where you're just kind of shaking your head and going, "My goodness, what is your deal? Is it that I'm a woman? Or is it that you just can't …" I don't know. I'm sure that there has been some of that. I'm sure that I have had instances where I have felt both, that being a woman has been a challenge, and being a black woman might have been a challenge. And so one or the other, more one than the other, I can't say. I think sometimes I have had roles where there was a very clear and defined difficulty with some of the leaders in my organization working with African Americans, and I felt that. Does being a woman come more into play? Perhaps, perhaps not. I don't know.

Despite facing overt and subtle discrimination, women of color tended to cope by maintaining a positive attitude and a desire to work hard to prove others wrong in their low expectations. As an associate vice president for development at a university said:

> I'm not the militant type where I cower or raise my fists at people, or that kind of thing. So what I do is I continue to do my job. I continue to try to have a great attitude and I just have this drive on the inside. And I know that if it didn't work out here, it's going to work out somewhere else, because I just have this great faith that God's got it. And he's going to move me where I need to be ... you gotta have a faith bigger than yourself. To know that somebody else will open that door or somebody else will work on your behalf.

Another means of coping is pursuing advanced degrees. As an Asian female executive working as a strategic communications officer for a college said:

> Some of the skills I would say is I believe for a female, in my experience, we do need to have one, an advanced degree to even push or give some validity to the position that you're in ... For individuals that are getting an advanced education, to back that up, because I feel as a female, you have to have those, you have to cross every "t" and dot every "i," every comma, every exclamation point. You have to almost make yourself the most marketable in the room.

Another form of coping is reaching out to other colleagues of color. Fortunately, African American women in public relations appear to have a strong network of "pioneers" and peers willing to provide counsel and emotional support. A director of advancement communication in higher education described the value of that connection:

> Being faced with a lot of situations where sometimes I just say, "Oh lord, I'm just frustrated," or just ignore some things that go on. Culturally, having a mentor of color, sometimes we don't even have to speak words. It's eye contact. It's a nod. Somebody who has actually been through what I'm going through on a deeper level. That helps out. It's much better. So does it make a difference? I've had all. I've had men, women, white, black, Latino, Asian, inside, outside an organization, different profession, but there is an advantage of having a colleague, a mentor of color.

However, that network is more difficult for Latina and Asian American women in public relations to tap into as their numbers are even smaller (Pompper, 2007; Qui & Muturi, 2016). As a Latina who previously worked as a vice president of marketing and communications in a nonprofit organization described:

> From other women I've spoken to at conferences and just in general at my different companies, they have - they've experienced similar issues where they didn't have a go-to person, they didn't have a mentor, they didn't have someone that they could

look up to. And then that lack of visibility. Another point that they brought up to me was that they felt almost like a fish out of water. They felt like they didn't belong. And that sense of belonging is very powerful, because it can dissuade you from moving forward in this career. It can say, "Well, I'm in the wrong place. I probably need to go somewhere else." I can tell you, actually now that I'm thinking about it, there were many times when I would sit in a meeting, a team meeting, and I was at the table and I would look around and I was the only Latina woman sitting there, and it felt very lonely. I'm definitely not going to lie, but I definitely resonated with some of the ladies that explained that to me that feeling of loneliness and that feeling of not belonging, that sense of maybe not good enough. And again, a lot of these things are probably in our heads, but it helps if we had some kind of camaraderie in the way that we could help ourselves and say, "You know what, we belong here. We do contribute. Just because we may not be the 'majority,' we still have a lot to contribute."

Conclusion

Influence is established by developing trusting relationships with colleagues over time and through success in public relations initiatives. Female public relations professionals do not only need to develop their business literacy and conduct research prior to weighing in on strategic issues but also ask focused questions of colleagues to make sure they fully understand the issues, concerns and motivations of others. Based on our interviews, female professionals who are currently in leadership positions in various organizations also need to recognize the limits to their influence as they are not always the final decision maker. They should be prepared to address issues when their boss doesn't follow their counsel. Our interviews also revealed those long-lasting obstacles in leadership advancement such as limited opportunities in advancing in their careers and inequality in receiving pay and compensations. According to our interviewees and their life experiences, there are some key strategies for women in public relations to use to facilitate leadership advancement in their careers, which include increasing visibility through self-advocacy and sponsors, as well as seeking new opportunities through volunteering for new assignments. Although race and ethnicity can be a limitation to achieving influence, women in public relations are coping by seeking advanced degrees and demonstrating their success in public relations initiatives.

References

Aldoory, L., Reber, B. H., Berger, B. K., & Toth, E. L. (2008). Provocations in public relations: A study of gendered ideologies of power-influence in practice, *Journalism & Mass Communication Quarterly*, 85(4), 735–750.

Aldrich, H., & Herker, D. (1977). Boundary spanning roles and organization structure. *Academy of Management Review, 2*, 217–230.

Bell, E. L. J. E., & Nkomo, S. M. (2001). *Our separate ways: Black & White women and the struggle for professional identity.* Boston: Harvard Business School Press.

Berger, B. K., & Reber, B. H. (2006). *Gaining influence in public relations: The role of resistance in practice.* Mahwah, NJ: Lawrence Erlbaum Associates.

Bowen, S. A. (2009). What communication professionals tell us regarding dominant coalition access and gaining membership. *Journal of Applied Communication Research, 37*(4), 418–443.

Burt, R. S. (1992). *Structural holes: The social structure of competition.* Cambridge, MA: Harvard University Press.

Collins, P. H. (1990). *Black feminist thought: Knowledge, consciousness and the politics of empowerment.* London: Harper Collins.

Conger, J. A. (1998). The necessary art of persuasion. *Harvard Business Review, 113*(3), 84–95.

Cose, E. (1993). *The rage of a privileged class.* New York: HarperCollins.

Crenshaw, K. (1991). Mapping the margins: Intersectionality, identity politics, and violence against women of color. *Stanford Law Review, 43*(6), 1241–1299.

Dodd, M. (2012). A Social Capital Model of Public Relations: Development and Validation of a Social Capital Measure (Doctoral dissertation). Retrieved April 13, 2020, from http://scholarlyrepository.miami.edu/cgi/viewcontent.cgi?article=1829&context=oa_dissertations.

Goodstein, J. D. (2000). Moral compromise and personal integrity: Exploring the ethical issues of deciding together in organizations. *Business Ethics Quarterly, 10*(4), 805–819.

Grunig, L. A., Toth, E. L., & Toth, L. C. (2008). *Women in public relations: How gender influences practice.* New York: Routledge.

Hickson, D. J., Hinings, C. R., Lee, C. A., Schneck, R. E., & Pennings, J. M. (1971). A strategic contingencies' theory of intraorganizational power. *Administrative Science Quarterly, 16*, 216–229.

Len-Rios, M. E. (1998). Minority public relations practitioner perceptions. *Public Relations Review, 24*(4), 535–555.

Mallette, W. A. (1995). *African Americans in public relations: Pigeonholed practitioners or cultural interpreters?* Unpublished master's thesis, University of Maryland, College Park.

Mattis, J. S., Grayman, N. A., Cowie, S. A., Winton, C., Watson, C., & Jackson, D. (2008). Intersectional identities and the politics of altruistic care in a low-income, urban community. *Sex Roles, 59*(5/6), 418–428.

Meng, J., Berger, B., Gower, K., & Heyman, W. (2012). A test of excellent leadership in public relations: Key qualities, valuable sources, and distinctive leadership perceptions. *Journal of Public Relations Research, 24*, 18–36.

Moberg, D. J. & Seabright, M. A. (2000). The development of moral imagination. *Business Ethics Quarterly, 10*(4), 845–884.

Moss, D., Warnaby, G., & Newman, A. J. (2000). Public relations practitioner role enactment at the senior management level within U.K. companies. *Journal of Public Relations Research*, *12*(4), 277–307.

Muehlbauer, K., & Rockland, D. (2017). Examining Agency Compensation. Retrieved July 16, 2020, from: http://apps.prsa.org/Intelligence/Tactics/Articles/view/12120/1151/Examining_Agency_Compensation#.XROOeIJKjIU.

Nahapiet, J., & Ghoshal, S. (1998). Social capital, intellectual capital, and the organizational advantage. *Academy of Management Review*. *23*(2), 242–266.

Neill, M. S. (2014). Building buy-in: The need for internal relationship building and informal coalitions in public relations. *Public Relations Review*, *40*(3), 598–605.

Nielsen, C. (2011). Moving mass communication scholarship beyond binaries: A call for intersectionality as theory and method. *Media Report to Women*, *31*(1), 6–22.

O'Neil, J. (2003). An investigation of the sources of influence of corporate public relations practitioners. *Public Relations Review*, *29*(2), 159–169.

Owens, T. J. (2003). Self and identity. In DeLamater, J. D. (Ed.). *Handbook of social psychology* (pp. 205–232). New York: Kluwer/Plenum.

Pompper, D. (2004). Linking ethnic diversity & two-way symmetry: Modeling female African-American practitioners' roles. *Journal of Public Relations Research*, *16*, 269–299.

Pompper, D. (2007). The gender-ethnicity construct in public relations organizations: Using feminist standpoint theory to discover Latinas' realities. *The Howard Journal of Communications*, *18*, 291–311.

Qui, J., & Mutui, N. (2016). Asian American public relations practitioners' perspectives on diversity. *The Howard Journal of Communications*, *27*(3), 236–249.

Tajfel, H. (1981) *Human groups and social categories: Studies in social psychology*. Cambridge, MA: Cambridge University Press.

Toth, E. L. & Grunig, L. A. (1993). The missing story of women in public relations. *Journal of Public Relations Research*, *5*(3), 153–175.

U.S. Bureau of Labor Statistics (2019). Retrieved July 16, 2020, from: https://www.bls.gov/cps/cpsaat11.htm.

U.S. Census Bureau (2019). Retrieved July 16, 2020, from: https://factfinder.census.gov/faces/tableservices/jsf/pages/productview.xhtml?pid=ACS_17_1YR_S2412&prodType=table.

Vardeman-Winter, J., & Place, K. (2017). Still a lily-white field of women: The state of workforce diversity in public relations practice and research. *Public Relations Review*, *43*, 326–336.

Vardeman-Winter, J., Tindall, N., & Jiang, H. (2013). Intersectionality and publics: How exploring publics' multiple identities questions basic public relations concepts. *Public Relations Inquiry*, *2*(3), 279–304.

Weber, L. (2001) *Understanding race, class, gender, and sexuality: A conceptual framework*. Boston: McGraw-Hill.

CHAPTER EIGHT

How Women in PR Approach Ethics Counsel

Being an ethical person does not equate to being an ethical leader. As Trevino, Hartman and Brown (2000) wrote, "To develop a reputation for ethical leadership with employees, leaders must make ethics and values a salient aspect of their leadership agenda so that the message reaches more distant employees. To do this, they must be moral managers as well as moral persons" (p. 133). Trevino et al. (2000) suggested that being a moral manager involves role modeling through ethical actions, using rewards and discipline effectively to reinforce core values, and communicating to employees about the importance of ethics and values. Consistent with this expectation for leaders, we asked the female leaders how they would define ethical leadership in public relations and what responsibilities this should involve.

First of all, several of interviewed female leaders listed ethics and integrity as core competencies needed for leaders in general and they also listed it as a key characteristic they seek in mentors and role models. As a chief communications officer for a corporation explained:

> They need to be strong but compassionate leaders. They need to be people who are grounded in some or seem to be grounded in some sort of core values so that there's a reason to ask - to understand why they take certain approaches. I like to know why did you do it that way? What got you there? What were the challenging things that you faced and how did you handle them? So, I look first for or I gravitate to people

who have that, who seem very grounded in some set of principles that's consistent and then I try to understand what that is.

The view of leaders as ethical role models is consistent with neo-Aristotelian virtue ethics. Baker (2008) wrote that "inherent to the virtue ethics perspective" is the role of moral exemplars or role models who educate others how to live moral lives (p. 239; also see Pojman, 2005). Through executive leaders' role modeling behaviors, employees learn virtues or admirable character traits (Baker, 2008; Borden, 2019). When applying virtue ethics to public relations, Baker (2008) identified eight desirable virtues such as humility, truth, transparency, respect for others, care, authenticity, equity and social responsibility. On the opposite side of the spectrum, she named vices such as arrogance, deceit, manipulation and disregard for others (Baker, 2008). These virtues provide guidance on how to live. As Hursthouse (1999) explained "not only does each virtue generate a prescription – do what is honest, charitable, generous – but each vice a prohibition – do not do what is dishonest, uncharitable, mean" (p. 36). She also sees a need for ethical role models or moral exemplars. Hursthouse (1999) recommended that if a person is unsure what to do, he or she should seek out people who are kind, honest, just, wiser and ask them what they would do under the same circumstances.

Moberg (2000) identified four conditions that may be necessary for someone to learn ethical behavior from a role model such as focused attention to the behavior of the role model, motivation to learn, retention of the behavior modeled, and reenactment of the behavior. He also listed ideal characteristics of an ethical role model such as demographic similarity, relevance, and attainability (Moberg, 2000). To encourage ethical behavior, Moberg (2000) recommended that organizations identify morally desirable behaviors, then seek out people engaging in those behaviors, and then publicly recognize them and place them in visible roles to serve as teachers and role models.

Consistent with virtue ethics, some ethical leadership qualities our interviewed women leaders advocated included transparency in communication, honesty, respect for others and fairness. A communications director working in a government agency took that responsibility a step further:

> The keys to ethical leadership in public relations really do center around transparency, integrity, free flow of information, access to information, a commitment to telling the truth and seeking out the truth, and not simply curating what other executives would like you to say. So, it requires some work on our part as communications professionals to trust, but verify, basically. A lot of times, I get information and I just quietly fact check it to make sure that we're not going to get in a situation where the information I've been provided is inaccurate and I need to clarify that. So,

it really is a core of your being that is focused on making sure that everything that you convey is truthful and fair.

Lack of accuracy in information can be a threat to the accountability of public relations leaders as addressed by an associate vice president of development at a university:

> I had some issues at a company where people didn't tell me the truth as their PR person or chief communicator. It damaged my reputation for years, because I went out espousing a certain point of view and got caught in it. And I went to them, but I was dispensable. "Well, we just didn't give that to you." And I knew they were lying. So, every time I went out to make a public statement, I would qualify my messaging.

Consistent with the principles advocated by Trevino and associates (2000), a senior female consultant discussed in her interview the importance of a leader's awareness of organizational culture and rewards systems and how they can influence employee behavior:

> I would say that it's really important for the leader to be aware of any cultural shifts that are taking place within the organization. To ask the tough questions relative to an organization's structure, what are we rewarding? Sometimes, there's a lot of case work on different structures and reward systems that created these ethical lapses. And so how do you ensure through your performance measurement and your award processes that you're not creating problems? An ethical leader has principles that they hold that are non-negotiable, and those principles are aligned with the culture and the structure of the organization.

McDonald and Nijhof (1999) recommended that senior leaders consider five factors that can generate an impact on the ethical decision-making processes in an organization. The first factor involves identifying existing norms and values and determining whether those are fostering or discouraging ethical behavior (McDonald & Nijhof, 1999). The other factors include evaluating the work environment, specifically decision-making processes, the availability of necessary resources, and employees' abilities to make ethical decisions (McDonald & Nijhof, 1999). Scholars recommended that leaders should offer a variety of ethics resources for their employees, including ethics training, a code of conduct, reward systems, ethics hotlines, an ombudsperson, routine ethics audits, and decision-making trees (Bowen 2004; McDonald & Nijhof 1999).

Several women executives also discussed ethical leadership in public relations as adhering to the PRSA Code of Ethics and the Page Principles highlighting the strong influence of these ethics resources. As a vice president of global diversity, inclusion and engagement at a technology company recited from memory:

And so, the Page principles, I think are absolutely the model of ethical behavior and the first Page Principle is tell the truth. At the end of the day, it goes back to what I was saying earlier about giving counsel to senior leadership. At the end of the day, ethical communications have to start with the truth. You need to be authentic, the credibility or the truth is the credibility piece. You need to be authentic about … what you're doing, what you're saying, because to me that authenticity is do your actions match your words? So it's one thing to say this is what we believe or this what we're trying to do, but if you say something and then the actions are at odds with what you say, to me that's not being authentic and being transparent to the extent, letting your public know that here's what happened, we take responsibility for it or we take responsibility for helping to fix it. Here's how we are going to fix it, and here's what we are doing to make sure it doesn't happen again. But I think ethical practice really starts with telling the truth and proving it with action, which is the second one, for the whole thing of actions speak louder than words and being transparent.

This statement regarding adherence to consistent values and principles in public relations further confirms the research findings from previous research (Lee & Cheng, 2012). Lee and Cheng (2012) found that 52% of surveyed PRSA members are mostly familiar with the code of ethics and 18.6% were extremely familiar. In addition, the majority of PRSA members (52.8%) also agreed that the code was useful for preventing ethical lapses (Lee & Cheng, 2012).

To understand what virtuous or ethical behavior should work effectively in practice, Borden (2007) recommended that professionals look toward "their mission, the standards embodied in their profession, and their personal sense of identity" for guidance (p. 16). Drawing on the writings of MacIntyre (2007), Borden (2007) pointed out that when someone enters a practice or profession, he or she must follow the standards of that practice and have an appreciation for the history and traditions. It appears that public relations executives are doing that due to their familiarity with the Page Principles and PRSA Code of Ethics. For public relations, that tradition includes agreed upon virtues (e.g. truth, accountability, transparency, loyalty, fairness) and a code of ethics (e.g. PRSA, The Page Principles) that professionals are encouraged to follow. Specific professional associations such as the Arthur W. Page Society and Public Relations Society of America function as a "moral authority" for members of those groups providing guidance on norms of ethical behavior in the public relations profession (Borden, 2007, p. 76).

Ethics have been recognized as an essential competency in public relations by both public relations professionals and educators. The 2017 Commission on Public Relations Education (CPRE) Report on Undergraduate Education found that public relations professionals ranked ethics third behind writing and communication as a necessary proficiency for a successful career in public relations. Ethics have been described as "a systematic attempt to make sense of our individual and social moral experience, to determine the rules that ought to govern human conduct, the values worth pursuing, and the character traits deserving development in life" (DeGeorge, 2009, p. 13).

In public relations, ethical decision-making "involves making rational choices between what is good and bad, between what is morally justifiable action and what is not" (Patterson & Wilkins, 2005, p. 4). In response to the CPRE report, Neill (In Press) conducted a Delphi study to identify the top ten knowledge, skills and/or abilities related to ethics that are *essential* in public relations. The list included: 1) Personal code of conduct/Ethics/Values system, 2) Personal behavior /Integrity/Accountability/ Trustworthiness, 3) Awareness/Knowledge of code of ethics/ Identify ethical issues/Discernment, 4) Critical thinking/ Problem solving, 5) Honesty/ Transparency/Truthfulness/Candor, 6) Courage/ Speak truth to power, 7) Strategic Planning, 8) Judgment, 9) Counseling abilities/ Ability to articulate and provide recommendations/Oral Communication, and 10) Leadership/Team building (Neill, In Press).

Several of these competencies were mentioned by interviewed female executives when discussing the responsibilities that they personally believe are related to ethics such as honesty, integrity, transparency and courage. An independent consultant discussed the steps involved in ethical decision-making:

> You want to have, at the ready, and I do, an ethical decision-making framework where we're looking at the decision and trying to gather as much information as possible. And really looking at how it can impact all the different stakeholders and knowing what the different alternatives are. When I think about ethics, sometimes we don't even realize that we were facing an ethical dilemma until the stuff hits the fan, right? So, in those cases, the only thing you can do is … fall on the sword, make apologies, make the changes necessary and ask for forgiveness. But if there is time, and you do have those conversations, I think it's important to go through that process, do some scenario planning on … the ethical issues that this organization or this leader can face, and what are the temptations to step outside the bounds of ethics … And so that takes some time to … go through a process and then continue to monitor and evaluate how you are doing and if you are actually walking the talk.

Neill (In Press) also identified the top ten knowledge, skills and/or abilities related to ethics that public relations professionals perceive are *lacking* in the profession in general. The list included: 1) Courage/Speaking up/Confidence, 2) Ethical awareness/Moral understanding, 3) Judgment/ Critical thinking/ Problem solving, 4) Leadership, 5) Personal behavior/ Accountability/Integrity, 6)Transparency/Disclosure/Candor, 7) Moral Compass/Values-based decision making 8) Conflicts of interest, 9) Strategic planning/Research/ Measurement, and 10) Respect for others (Neill, In Press).

The CEO of a nonprofit agency agreed that courage is a requirement to be an effective public relations counselor:

> I think that is a very critical component of PR and that means you also have to have courage to speak out. Because what happens in meetings sometimes when you get to that level is you have people who are afraid to speak out and sort of give the time out. And even I've had this experience even in some of the boards I serve on where you'd have to say, "Ok, let's hold on a second. Like I know ... this is a very great program and we're really moving forward, but let's take a step back and look at the potential implications of this and let's look at how this could impact our audiences" ... And that really is the job of the CCO or ... an agency head or SVP or someone who was client management or something along those lines. That really is your role to serve as that ethical conscience of the organization.

While there was considerable agreement on the characteristics associated with ethical leadership in public relations, there was a noticeable disparity when discussing public relations' responsibilities associated with ethics, specifically whether public relations professionals should assume the role of an ethical or corporate conscience. Goodpaster and Matthews (1982) defined a corporate conscience as "a lack of impulsiveness, care in mapping out alternatives and consequences ... and awareness of and concern for the effects of one's decision and policies on others" (p. 134). Previous research by public relations scholars has found mixed support for the role (Bowen, 2008; Neill & Drumwright, 2012; Neill & Barnes, 2018) and even skepticism regarding its feasibility (St. John III & Pearson, 2016). In the context of crisis communication, St. John III and Pearson (2016) rejected the role of an ethical conscience, claiming it was "problematic" and "of negligible use" (p. 18), and recommended instead that public relations practitioners assume a modest role by encouraging organization-wide ethical deliberation among multiple leaders. Consistent with previous research, we found some women executives who embraced this role while others who believed it was the collective responsibility of public relations executives along with other members of the senior leadership.

A director of media and public relations at a university was one of the executives who does not only perceive this as her responsibility, she has actually acted on it:

> The role of the position is imbued with the power to be the conscience of an organization. But the PR side has to own it. They have to own it. They have to be I feel like that moral compass to say, "Well, you could do that, but that's irresponsible or that's unethical." Or if that doesn't work, it's just like "Hey, if they find out about it, it's going to be really bad for you."

She later described a specific example of a time when she stood up to an external consultant when dealing with a high-profile crisis situation:

> There was a particular incident here, where I found my voice. And I was working - it was like my first few days doing crisis, like a major crisis. And I was told by an outside consultant to basically send an email to a reporter that I felt insulting - it was insulting her lack of knowledge ... And I didn't want to send it, but I was like Ok, so I send the email. And this woman, she fires back, and she goes off on me. I was like good for her. I would've done the same thing. It was insulting her credentials and her experience as a reporter, and I'm sure we didn't do that to her male counterparts. I said right then and there, and I told them, "I will never send an email, correspondence, memo, post-it note, about anything that I don't believe." I said, "I'm going to trust my gut." And that's why I tell people in PR. You kind of trust your gut response, and you hone that by making decisions ... And I said, "I'm not doing it. Now you can send it, you can do it, but it won't have my name on it." And so, it was at that point, a switch flipped.

This account is consistent with findings by Place (2019) in a qualitative study that ethical or moral development occurs as public relations practitioners face "trial by fire" experiences, those she characterized as crisis management and time sensitive issues, or what Plaisance (2015) refers to as crucibles of experiences or key turning points in someone's career. Consistent with virtue ethics, these experiences lead to *phronesis* or practical wisdom (Hursthouse, 1999), which is defined as the "hard-won moral expertise that comes from experience and reflection" (Borden, 2019, p. 172).

Those who embrace the role of ethical conscience also tend to see their responsibility in the context of boundary spanning, which involves voicing the concerns of key stakeholders during the decision-making process. A senior vice president of global corporate communications explained:

> I think it's important to have that seat at the table to have that voice where you can be an adviser. And I found myself at different points in my career being the lone voice ... from a contrary position. And I feel like the communications people because we're on the front line with the public have a better view and understanding of the impact that things will have versus others where their whole job is to focus more internally and they view things so much through a bubble, just not reflective of reality. And so, I think it's really important to have that voice and to be able to make sure that people aren't - that there's no missteps that may just be completely unintended, but they're just not looking at things through the right lens.

Consistent with the arguments of St. John III and Pearson (2016), a chief communications officer for a *Fortune 500* company perceived the role of ethical conscience as too big for one person to fulfill:

I have mixed feelings about it to be honest with you. One is it almost sets the CCO apart from the rest of the C-suite on a higher ethical plane, so to speak. And that assumes that there's always a black and white answer, that there is always a single ethical choice to make, and there are multiple unethical choices to make. And I would say very, very rarely, is it that cut-and-dry. Very rarely. So, I'm a little uncomfortable with that terminology, for lack of a better term. Simply because I think that it can be a dangerous precedent to set to think that there is only one entity in the C-Suite that is weighing those responsibilities, because it's kind of like saying that HR is responsible for employee engagement. If HR is the only entity responsible for employee engagement, god help you because you're not going to be very successful at it.

Neill and Barnes (2018) found support for this perspective in their study with senior public relations executives who viewed the ethical conscience role as a collaborative one that involves partnering with allies in other departments, such as finance, legal, and human resources. The allies would then raise their concerns collectively to senior leaders rather than as individual concerns. People prefer to recruit allies or form coalitions when "they do not have the power to change the organization independently or want to avoid the political consequences associated with unilateral action" (Murnighan & Brass 1991, p. 289).

While some embraced the role of ethical conscience either as a responsibility of public relations or a shared responsibility with other senior executives, a few questioned public relations' standing to fulfill this role. As an assistant vice president of internal communications at a university expressed:

Should we be ethics counselors? I think it would be great if people would listen to the guidance. I don't know whether or not they would in some cases if they would feel like in our discipline we'd have the type of authority to do so.

Those who did embrace public relations' role in ethics counseling tied it to boundary spanning and reputation management. As a vice president of integrated marketing communications for a consultancy expressed:

At the end of the day, it's a relationship business and it's also a reputation business. And you're only as good as your reputation, and you're only as strong as your relationships. So, if you are perceived as lacking integrity, or as lying, or as cutting the truth short to do what you want to do, people's memories aren't as short as you think. And it's a lot harder to rebuild your reputation once you've lost that trust than it is to maybe take a small hit for telling the truth. People will remember you for your integrity versus lying.

Another component of ethics counseling and leadership is to communicate with senior leadership regarding why a certain strategy is the right thing to do in a given situation as explained by an executive in an independent consultancy:

There's so many practical arguments for being ethical. It ruins their credibility. If you're not ethical, you're not going to be trusted in the future. Why should I trust you now, if I couldn't trust you on that? But also, it ruins your credibility with your key audiences, so it's also going to affect your profits. It effects your reputation. It effects your profits and you get caught.

One of our interviewees, who is the president of a public relations firm, also agrees that public relations executives should carry the responsibility of being an ethical role model and proactively communicate about values:

I would almost turn that to say, not only should we make sure that we are serving as the corporate conscience, if you will, from an ethical standpoint, but also, I think from a cultural standpoint. Are we as a corporation or as a company living the values of our company? Are we walking the talk in terms of the culture and the values of our company? Are we shining a light on not only where that's happening in a way that is consistent with culture, but also shining a light on where we may see things that are happening inconsistently? I think so that's the internal thing. I think the other place we can serve as a corporate conscience is when a company is thinking about its purpose in the world and its place in the world, are we serving as, and beyond just CSR, corporate social responsibility, I think when we really consider what is the impact we can make in the world, are we weighing in on the decisions? Are we providing counsel? Are we ensuring all of our efforts align to the company's authentic purpose? And when they're not, are we speaking up?

Neill (2016) previously found that public relations professionals help reinforce a company's core values through routine communication. Several interviewed female executives in our study reported using editorial calendars that involve regularly scheduling content in employee newsletters about the company/organization's core values. We also have interviewees who shared that they have routinely reviewed all their communication messages for inclusion of core values. Such actions are consistent with the responsibilities addressed in ethical leadership literature.

Several of the interviewed women executives also shared specific examples of times when they were able to provide ethics counseling to senior leaders in the organization. Similar to previous research, the types of issues they addressed were beyond traditional communication issues such as crises and media relations and included management issues (e.g. unprofessional behavior in the workplace, workplace safety), diversity, equity and inclusion, employee communication, and support for families following fatalities. A former vice president of marketing and communications at a nonprofit organization discussed how she declined a request to participate in a client pitch while working in an agency environment, which she perceived as a case of "bait and switch":

When I was working at an agency and we wanted to go after a new business, they wanted to bring me in to basically present what we were going to do. When I asked them, "Does this mean that I get to work on this account?" They said, "Oh no, you're not going to work on it. We just want you to come in, show your face. You're a Latina. We're trying to win a Hispanic client, and we want them to see that you are with us and you're going to be there." To me, that was a lie. I don't believe in just showing my face and pretending I'm going to be with them and misleading and misguiding the client. Therefore, the client would believe I would be part of that team and I was not going to be part of that team. I had to decline, and then I told my boss why, and I explained to him, "I don't believe this is the best way to win business. If you would like to bring me on this account, I'd love to help you and I would love to provide counsel, but if you're just going to bring me in to present, I don't think that's a wise move."

When asked about the consequences of that decision, she said, "I never got asked by him again, so that could be a repercussion. But no, I wasn't fired or anything." At the same time, this account demonstrates the courage required to be an ethics counselor. Moral courage involves the public relations executives' "fortitude to convert moral intentions into actions despite pressures from either inside or outside of the organization to do otherwise" (May, Chan, Hodges & Avolio, 2003, p. 255). May et al. (2014) proposed that moral courage requires moral efficacy or "confidence in one's abilities" in order to" justify a courageous moral action" and willingness to deal with potential opposition (p. 71; May et al., 2003). An executive director working in higher education explained it this way:

Your job is to be the person that's not afraid to speak up, that's not afraid to address wrongs and in a constructive way, if possible, and not be afraid of the consequences. I've always told folks when I come and speak to the classes ... I always say, "Never be in a position where you do not believe in the person or the organization you're working for. And if you find yourself in that position, have a Plan B or be ready to leave." And I've done that. I've left a position once because I stopped believing in the person I was reporting to. I saw that person make too many calls that I thought were good for that person and not for the organization. And so, I started looking and preparing for my exit strategy, so to speak. And so, I can say with authority that I've done it. It was the best move I ever made. You have to be bold and unafraid. I was fortunate - I always felt like I was a position that if I left, there would be something better out there for me. I wasn't afraid of not being able to find something else.

In addition to fear, real life financial pressures can serve as barriers to providing ethics counsel, which has been defined as "golden handcuffs" (Berger, 2005). For senior executives, these barriers can include substantial salaries, benefits, and power. A chief experience officer at a financial institution described this challenge:

That's one of the biggest risks that I see - people are much more likely to do things that they are uncomfortable with, that are at the borderline or over the borderline of unethical, when they don't know how they're going to make their next rent payment or their next mortgage payment, or they don't know how they're going to not have to lay employees off, if they don't do this thing that this client asked them to do. But whatever those things are. So, have you structured your life or your business in a way that insulates you from that kind of temptation? It can be a fuzzy line and you have to be ready to get fired for the right reason. And I hope that we are all ready to get fired for the right reason.

Despite these risks, many of the women executives have found effective ways to speak truth to power. For example, an executive vice president working in a public relations firm used a strategic approach to provide ethics counsel to a client regarding a product safety issue as illustrated by her:

It was a matter of laying out the different scenarios. Maintaining the course, versus switching up now, versus switching up later, do you know what I mean? When you lay it that way, and especially when you bring in other factors, i.e. money, exposure to litigation, whistle-blowing, etc., you're able to build a case many times to steer folks in the right direction.

Others at times have chosen to remain silent. An executive director working in higher education reflected back on a time earlier in her career when she did not speak up:

The organization was preparing to make a major purchase of some property that would have been a rather significant purchase to take on something that seemed outside of our mission. And I knew that the purchase was being made for personal reasons. The person making the decision was doing it for personal reasons more so than what was best for the organization. And I did not speak up about it, because I knew I would be overruled, and I regret that. So that was a time when I didn't handle it right. That also led me to the point ... where I ended up not respecting that person and changing positions .... And I was like, I can't stand by and defend this purchase of this property knowing what I know because it's a lot of money, it's not within our mission, and I thought it was a bad move.

The women executives also reflected on lessons they learned over their careers regarding how to provide ethics counsel to senior leadership. Some of their preferred techniques and strategies for providing counsel include citing research and case studies, engaging in dialogue, legitimacy appeals, use of scenarios, and recruiting allies, which are the same techniques used for providing strategic counsel in general (see Table 8.1). However, some additions in the context of ethics counsel include assuming the role of devil's advocate and using the headline test or mirror test.

Table 8.1. Preferred influence strategies for ethics counsel

Influence Strategies	# who preferred
Sharing Research/Case Studies	8
Use of Scenarios	4
Legitimacy Appeals	4
Headline Test	3
Devil's Advocate	3
Recruiting Allies	2
Engaging in Dialogue	2
Sharing Personal Experiences	2
Mirror Test	1

Shahinpoor and Matt (2007) pointed out that the person assuming the role of devil's advocate or loyal opposition does not have to disclose his or her personal views, and does not necessarily have to agree with the views of these stakeholders, which makes this a more socially acceptable way to confront senior executives. For example, a chief experience officer working in a financial institution discussed how the role of devil's advocate may play out:

> I think that we have a unique opportunity to advance conversations that are much harder to have directly. So for example, I can go into my C-Suite here and say, "If you plotted our org chart, if you put pictures of our org chart together, the further up our org chart we go, it gets whiter and male-er. How do we feel about that?" Now anybody could say that. I can say it with more impunity, because I can say, "Look. I'm not accusing anybody of anything. I'm not saying that anybody here is discouraging, racist, biased, whatever. All I'm telling you is, it's my job to tell you how the world from the outside sees you. That is one way the world from the outside would see us. How would we respond to a question like, 'Why does it seem like white people get promoted more than other people?' How would you respond to that question?" Because you happen to have that role, you have the ability to ask those questions and be heard and create productive responses that don't reflect on you personally, in a way that other people can't. So, I think our ability to invoke what other people would think, feel or react to, gives us a certain license and it then becomes our obligation to make sure that we are using that wisely and effectively. So, I am a believer in that.

Interviewed female executives also like to use the headline test to point out the potential media consequences of decisions. As a senior vice president of global corporate communications for a public relations firm described:

> So, one of the most powerful tools is to - if you assume that whatever decision is made becomes public at any point in time, how would this story play out? To

the point of I'll write the story. And I will be sitting – I'll write out the headline announcing and whatever I can get my hands on, and I'll write the story and say, "Ok, fine. Whoever, we're going with your decision. Here's the story that's going to run in the LA Times tomorrow." And I'll read it with the headline and everything. "Is that the way you still feel?" And a lot of times, they'll back down.

A vice president of global communication for a corporation tries to bring people down to reality through the use of a mirror test.

I hold a mirror up. "Could you look at yourself in the mirror if you said this or if you did this approach?" Everybody has a different truth. Everybody has a different perception of how events or things play out. I want to make sure that how I guide my teams is to make sure that they can be proud of what they're doing and stand behind it, just as I do that to myself when faced with situations and there've been times when I've had to fire clients because they just weren't ethically sound.

One key piece of advice offered by the senior female executives we interviewed is to keep the confrontation regarding ethical concerns private, not in public settings, which can make colleagues more defensive. As an executive director of marketing and communication at a university explained:

Well first of all, I think you need to do it as much as possible - try to do it one-on-one. Don't do it in the group setting, because you can lose control of it, especially if there's some highly emotional, bang-the-table person in there. So, I try to do it individually, if possible. If I can't meet with them face-to-face, I'll do it on the phone, but I try to talk to each person involved before I'm in the executive committee meeting or whatever. I think that's really important, because you have to talk to each person through their own particular issues with it, without them thinking they have to either grandstand in front of the rest of the group, or whatever it is that makes them push back.

The choice of approach matters. As an associate vice chancellor at a university advised:

I think number one you have to be careful. You can't be super accusatory. I think falling back on research and case studies and good examples of when other companies have handled things from an ethical perspective really well is helpful. And what's I think even more helpful is those examples of organizations who haven't handled things well ethically and what those repercussions have been. And being able to connect the dots between - point out the commonalities between those situations and the situation you're in and give some really concrete examples of what could happen if we don't choose the right kind of ethical path is very helpful.

Having a good relationship with your colleagues is critical to succeed as well. A chief communications officer said she sets up a "rule of three" with her CEO, which she uses sparingly:

The other I would say is setting ground rules with your CEO, related to how much you're going to push back. I have a "rule of three," that if they say they disagree, OK great, I'll come back again. And if I really think something is critical and that we're going down the wrong path on something, I'll come back a third time. Kind of setting those expectations with your CEO or whoever up front is important because then they're expecting it, you know what I mean? They're not thinking that you're just being belligerent. Of course, there's a way to do it, but you can go, "OK, I've got to invoke the 'rule of three' on this one." If you do it all the time, it completely loses its power. It's kind of that flag that says, "I really think this is important."

Relationships also are critical for trust and credibility reasons and to enable public relations professionals to gather the necessary information in order to provide ethics counsel. As Redmond and Trager (1998) wrote, "Doing a good job is not enough. For your career to move forward, you have to be adept at social relationships, building alliances, and building trust among those above and below you in the hierarchy" (p. 154). In their study with senior public relations executives, Neill and Barnes (2018) found internal relationships were crucial for recruiting allies and coalition members when ethical issues arose, and especially when public relations professionals faced resistance. In addition, these internal relationships across the organization were found to be crucial for public relations practitioners in order to gain the trust of their colleagues to seek their counsel when trying to understand financial, legal and other factors prior to making recommendations (Neill & Barnes, 2018). As a vice president of integrated marketing communications at a consulting firm further explained:

I think in order to be effective with that viewpoint, it's important that communicators have a place at the table so that they're taken seriously, so that they're part of conversations that are going on at the highest level, and that they have the confidence of leadership as a member of the leadership team to be able to introduce those conversations when necessary. I think being very aware of what's going on in the company, being in tune with a broad range of departments. Part of that comes from being visible and having conversations and having the ability to have that antenna of both if something might be off.

Conclusion

Women in public relations are embracing their role in practicing ethical leadership, which involves raising ethical issues, particularly the concerns of various stakeholders, as well as communicating and reinforcing the organization's core values. Successful female executives in public relations acknowledged that their ethical decision making in various scenarios have been guided by professional standards developed by PRSA and the Arthur W. Page Society. By practicing those professional standards, they embrace virtues such as honesty, transparency and respect for others. Assuming the role of an ethics counselor requires courage to speak the truth to power. In addition, success in providing ethics counsel requires building strong trusting relationships with senior colleagues and choosing less confrontational approaches such as the use of case studies and the headline and mirror tests when raising concerns.

References

Baker, S. (2008). The model of the principled advocate and the pathological partisan: A virtue ethics construct of opposing archetypes of public relations and advertising practitioners. *Journal of Mass Media Ethics, 23*, 235–253.

Berger, B. K. (2005). Power over, power with, and power to relations: Critical reflections on public relations, the dominant coalition, and activism, *Journal of Public Relations Research, 17*(1), 5–28.

Borden, S. L. (2007). *Journalism as practice: MacIntyre, virtue ethics and the press*. Burlington, VT: Ashgate Publishing.

Borden, S. L. (2019). Virtue ethics & media. In P. L. Plaisance (Ed.) *Communication and media ethics* (pp. 171–190). Boston: MA: Mouton De Gruyter.

Bowen, S. A. (2004). Organizational factors encouraging ethical decision making: An exploration into the case of an exemplar, *Journal of Business Ethics, 52*(4), 311–324.

Bowen, S. A. (2008). A state of neglect: Public relations as 'corporate conscience' or ethics counsel, *Journal of Public Relations Research, 20*, 271–296.

Commission on Public Relations Education Report on Undergraduate Education (2017). Retrieved from: http://www.commissionpred.org/commission-reports/fast-forward-foundations-future-state-educators-practitioners/.

DeGeorge, R. T. (2009). *Business ethics* (7th Ed.). Boston, MA: Prentice Hall.

Goodpaster, K. E., & Matthews, J. B. (1982). Can a corporation have a conscience? *Harvard Business Review, 60*(1), 132–141.

Hursthouse, R. (1999). *On virtue ethics*. Oxford, England: Oxford University Press.

Lee, S., & Cheng, I. (2012). Ethics management in public relations: Practitioner conceptualizations of ethical leadership, knowledge, training and compliance. *Journal of Mass Media Ethics, 27*(2), 80–96.

MacIntyre, A. (2007). *After virtue: A study in moral theory* (3rd Ed.). Notre Dame, IN: University of Notre Dame Press.

May, D. R., Luth, M. T., & Schwoerer, C. E. (2014). The influence of business ethics education on moral efficacy, moral meaningfulness, and moral courage: A quasi-experimental study, *Journal of Business Ethics, 124*, 67–80.

May, D. R., Chan, A. Y. L., Hodges, T. D., & Avolio, B. J. (2003). Developing the moral component of authentic leadership. *Organizational Dynamics, 32*(3), 247–260.

McDonald, G., & Nijhof, A. (1999). Beyond codes of ethics: An integrated framework for stimulating morally responsible behaviour in organizations. *Leadership and Organization Development Journal, 20*(3), 133–147.

Moberg, D. J. (2000). Role models and moral exemplars: How do employees acquire virtues by observing others? *Business Ethics Quarterly, 10*(3), 675–696.

Murnighan, J. K., & Brass, D. J. (1991). Intraorganizational Coalitions. In M. H. Bazerman, R. J. Lewicki, & B. H. Sheppard (Eds.), *Research on Negotiation in Organization* (pp. 283–306). Greenwich, CT: JAI Press.

Neill, M. S. (2016). The influence of employer branding in internal communication. *Research Journal of the Institute for Public Relations, 3*(1). http://www.instituteforpr.org/influence-employer-branding-internal-communication/.

Neill, M. S. (In Press). Public relations professionals identify ethical issues, essential competencies & deficiencies, *Journal of Media Ethics, 36*(1), forthcoming.

Neill, M. S., & Barnes, A. (2018). *Public relations ethics: Senior PR pros tell us how to speak up and keep your job.* New York: Business Expert Press.

Neill, M. S., & Drumwright, M. E. (2012). PR professionals as organizational conscience. *Journal of Mass Media Ethics, 27*(4), 220–234.

Patterson, P., & Wilkins, L. (2005). *Media ethics: Issues and cases.* New York: McGraw-Hill.

Place, K. R. (2019). Moral dilemmas, trials, and gray areas: Exploring on-the-job moral development of public relations professionals. *Public Relations Review, 45*, 24–34.

Plaisance, P. L. (2015). *Virtue in media: The moral psychology of excellence in news and public relations.* New York and London, Routledge.

Pojman, L. P. (2005). *How should we live? An introduction to ethics.* Belmont, CA: Thomson Wadsworth.

Redmond, J., & Trager, R. (1998). *Balancing on the Wire: The art of managing media organizations.* Boulder, CO: Coursewise.

Shahinpoor, N., & Matt, B. F. (2007). The power of one: Dissent and organizational life. *Journal of Business Ethics, 74*, 37–48.

St. John, B., III, & Pearson, Y. E. (2016). Crisis management and ethics: Moving beyond the public-relations-person-as-corporate conscience construct. *Journal of Mass Media Ethics, 31*, 18–34.

Trevino, L., Hartman, L., & Brown, M. (2000). Moral person and moral manager: How executives develop a reputation for ethical leadership. *California Management Review, 42*(4), 128–142.

CHAPTER NINE

Support Network

Work-Family Integration & the Influence of Mentors for Women in PR

When discussing the challenges facing women senior executives in public relations, it becomes apparent very quickly that the 24/7 demands associated with a career in public relations along with family responsibilities require some difficult sacrifices and at times no good resolutions. Social media has heightened the demands for public relations executives. As a vice president of communication for a nonprofit organization explained:

> You're just on call 24/7. My husband had a heart surgery this year, and I took the day off to be with him at this heart surgery, and I mean it was all day long – emails, and phone calls, and "what about this," "what about that," "have you seen this on Facebook?" "Yes. It's not a big deal. I'm in the hospital" … It's very difficult to take off. In fact, I have not been able to use all my time off that I've earned this year. And part of it is because over the weekend, or in the evenings, something happens and then you've got to get on the phone with the media, or on social media, or something else. It's the nature of the communications now.

Working fulltime in a demanding profession such as public relations places unique challenges for women on how to prioritize their careers and divide family commitments. Such a challenge is particularly intense when they are in managerial jobs and see themselves on an upward path in their leadership roles. For example, as described by a vice president of global communications at a professional services firm:

> Even when you're home, sometimes you can't be home because the phone is ringing, there's a media crisis breaking, you're taking conference calls, and your kids are seeing, "Mom's at work even though she's home, the computers up, the laptop's on the nightstand." It does start to encroach on family life; it's a catch 22. Yes, because of my smartphone and my very lightweight laptop, my office is anywhere. But that's a challenge when your office is the bedroom, when your office is the kitchen counter, or when your office is in the car while the Girl Scout troop is taking a hike and you have to quickly jump and take a call. Work is intruding everywhere. You have to be very deliberate to create boundaries so that you can minimize those intrusions.

Working mothers really do feel the pressure to do it all. Consider this day in the life of a CEO of a nonprofit organization. As she described:

> Yesterday was crazy, because we have our big annual event coming up. So I like woke up at 4 a.m. started working, had calls all morning and then an hour before I left, I quickly threw together some cookie dough, and then ... I was on a call - like throwing together cookie dough and I quickly took a shower. Then I met a colleague from New York for lunch. And then I came home, answered emails, baked cookies and then had a dinner ... until 9 p.m. And then around 8:30 p.m. I got home at 9 p.m., my daughter was crying, because she thought I was going to be home at 8:30 and then so I go upstairs, I have to shower, I'm putting her to bed and then she's upset. Then I have to say, alright here's what we're going to do tomorrow, right. Tomorrow night I'm going to be home for dinner. And so you're always – it's always this negotiation.

Adding to that stress are hurtful comments that people make. As a CEO of a nonprofit organization said:

> But people are like gosh – and people, usually it's men. They're like "gosh, I bet your kids never see you." Or I even had someone be like, "You must be the mom of the year." Like who says something like that. Like to me it hurts me to my core to not be around my kids, right. I would much rather, anything I do is to hang out with my kids. And it like hurts me when people say that, because I'm like really? I mean I feel like – I know actually I'm a great mom. I may not be here all the time, but I'm a fantastic mom.

These competing demands can result in work-life conflict (Aldoory, Jiang, Toth & Sha, 2008; Jin, Sha, Shen & Jiang, 2014). This conflict can be due to role overload, which is defined as "the extent to which the various role expectations ... exceed the amount of time and resources available for their accomplishment" (Miles & Perreault 1976, p. 22). As the women discussed their experiences in our interviews, they revealed some of their coping strategies in managing work-life conflict. Some of their approaches included rational actions (Duhachek, 2005) such as adjusting their work schedules, changing jobs, taking a lesser position, and even resigning due to the travel demands. A senior vice president at a major public relations firm presented her concern and potential solution to her supervisor:

> I've had a conversation with my manager where I've said, "You know, things are more than I can fit in right now, so I have made the decision that I'm going to have to take a step back from 'XYZ,'" and typically those are things that are important, but not as crucial day to day ... and again it's about communicating up front. "I plan on taking a step back from XYZ, are you comfortable with that? Because something has to give. Here's the situation, I expect three to four weeks from now that that won't be the case anymore, but can we get aligned that you're OK with this?" I mean I had a conversation like that this spring with my manager, and of course her reaction is "Yes, and let me also do A and B for you to make this situation easier for you." So I think if you have a good boss, that's crucial. But it's also, if you have a track record of being a strong leader and employee, that affords to you to be able to make those sort of requests and have those sort of conversations. You're coming with solutions, you're coming with a recommendation, but you're also being really clear, "Hey, just need you to know, challenging time right now, here's how I'm going to handle it, do I have your support?"

Fortunately, in that situation the supervisor was willing to make short-term accommodations. However, a senior vice president of global corporate communications had difficulty reducing her travel demands due to changes in senior leadership. As she explained:

> That's why I just resigned. I have four teenage daughters and we're in crunch time on college applications, and I was traveling 50 to 75% of the time internationally and I just can't do it. So, I had been raising it for about a year, and I had a deal with the previous CEO that I would not travel so much, maybe at the most 20%. When he retired and the new CEO came in, he didn't honor that contract and wanted me to travel with him. And so, I kept flagging that this is a challenge for me with my personal situation. If this continues, I'm not going to be able to do it. So, I'd been flagging it for about a year and so I don't think it was any surprise at all.

Decisions like these do impact women's career trajectory in public relations. The executive director of a nonprofit organization had to temporarily take a lower position and reduce her work schedule when she was a single mother. Her career progression involved advancing to a director position but then stepping down to a coordinator position. She explained the consequences of that decision:

> For me, it worked out, I ended up coming back and working my way back into a senior position, but it probably took longer than it might have otherwise. I'm probably eight years behind where I might have been otherwise had I not taken a break.

I didn't actually take a break, I just stepped back. I really think that's still going to be the hardest thing for women in achieving 100 percent equity.

Another coping strategy involved instrumental support (Duhacheck, 2005) in the form of seeking advice from women colleagues and neighbors, specifically when looking for logistical solutions and arrangements for childcare. A vice president of global diversity, inclusion and engagement for a technology company shared how advice from a female colleague provided a practical and tangible solution which helped her relieve the stress:

I remember when my daughter was I don't know maybe 6 months old, and I was working for a woman ... and my boss took me to lunch one day, and she said, "You know what you are going to drive yourself crazy trying to get back to pick your daughter up on time with the kind of job we have. Our hours are unpredictable." And she actually recommended someone that she had used for childcare and now that her son was older, she said, "Why don't you go to her and she can, even though she still does some stuff for us, she's not busy, I'm sure she would love to take care of your daughter and have her in a home environment." That was a god send. That enabled us to not worry and to have her in a home environment, and there's nothing wrong with a daycare center, but just given my hours trying to get there in time before the daycare center closed would have been a challenge.

Instrumental support also came in the form of parents taking turns caring for neighborhood children. As the president of an independent consulting firm explained:

This is the wonderful thing about community. Living in a neighborhood where there were other people with children around the same age, so I would watch their kids in the evening, they would watch my child – I just had one child.

Another form of instrumental support comes from the partner, the spouse or extended family members as mentioned by a chief communications officer at a *Fortune 500* company:

My spouse has taken different career choices because of my role. He has taken breaks from his own career at different times. He's moved internationally for my career. He has stopped work altogether at certain times in our life in order to make that work.

Another chief communication officer also working for a *Fortune 500* company described how she and her spouse negotiated and shared family responsibilities and commitments:

You need to know the strength of your partner and what they're good at and what you're good at and just agree that you're each going to take up a piece of the burden. So, for instance, my husband's going to make sure everybody gets fed. I'm going to make sure everybody's birthday presents are bought. He's going to make sure that … everybody's laundry is done and that the oil is changed in all of their cars. And I'm going to make sure that the family vacation is planned and that our social commitments are organized.

While most of the women executives relied on daycares or nannies for childcare, some women of color relied on their mother or mother-in-law to help with childcare. This reliance limited their geographic mobility but was an economic necessity. However, solutions like this are acceptable as it meets the assumptions and cultural expectations in certain cultures. As a Latina strategic communication manager explained:

Culturally it's not common … if I lived in Latin America to have a nanny. That's very common. I think in the U.S., it's more economic strata. They're expensive. I did end up doing that for about a year with my third child. I shared a nanny. There's nanny sharing that you can do now, which didn't exist with my first kids, and so that made it affordable, but that only lasted a year … My mom expected – she moved in with my sisters when they had kids, she moved in with me – it wasn't even like, I didn't have to ask. And so, I think that is more common. I know a lot of Anglo-friends who also lean on their in-laws, maybe they weren't living in, but that means we're pretty much all in the same economic strata. We don't have the luxury.

While childcare can be demanding early in a woman's career, caring for aging parents can be another challenge during the peak years of her career. As an executive director of a nonprofit foundation described:

A lot of women have to put their careers on hold to accommodate family demands, which is either children or aging parents. Different stages of your life – children usually come about the time you're hitting your stride in your career and you really are starting to get some experience behind you and some credibility built up, and then you're forced to make these choices – family life choices, balance choices. And then as you get older, you then have grown children, but you might have aging parents that require your attention. I think women often have to set aside their ambitions and their career track a little bit to accommodate these other things that put demands on them.

Due to all these stresses, emotional support and venting with other female executives is another effective form of coping. It often comes in the form of mentors and peers. As an executive director explained, "My mentors have tended to be female … as a working mother, I have purposely … sought out more advice that was spanning those two worlds and those two roles."

A director of advancement communications in higher education shared her personal experience as she had the added stress of taking custody of her 7-year-old niece while also raising her own 5-year-old son. For her, finding humor in her lack of perfection is one of the approaches she used to cope with the extra stress. As she described:

> If you have support, if you have emotional support and mental support, and then not hold yourself to such high standards when it comes to keeping the house clean, "Keeping up with the Jones'" and all that other kind of crazy stuff, the material things that tend to bog people down. I went to work and didn't realize until 3 o'clock in the afternoon that I had peanut butter on my shirt! Or my pants turned around backwards or something! And just laughing about it and being able to talk to other people who are in the same situation that do not judge you for something.

As mentioned in Chapter Three, African American women did not report as much of an issue with work-family integration. An insight into why that may be the case was provided by an executive director of marketing & communication at a university. When asked "do you think other women with different race/ethnicities face the same challenges?" she responded:

> That's an interesting question. I've often wondered about that. Because of the fact that many African American women have grown up with the representation that their mothers always worked and work is an expectation. And having a profession and pursuing a profession is a goal among many African Americans. And so therefore, you don't really have that pull to say, "OK, I'm a stay-at-home mom to raise my kids." And so I think there is a difference. But I've never lived the other side, so it's difficult for me – I'm just going by what I see is that we African American females, and males, but African American females, we go to college and get advanced degrees and get positions, and it's because we actually have the goal of rising to certain levels and so that means, we're thinking that we're just going to juggle it all and do what it is we need to do. We want to have families, but we also want to have the profession.

Based on her response to the question, it appears that African American women may have accepted the reality that work-life integration is going to be challenging, but they are committed to making the necessary sacrifices to achieve career advancement. This type of coping is consistent with positive thinking (Duhachek, 2005) by trying to make the best of the situation.

Role of Mentors

Many of the women attributed their success in part to the support of mentors who encouraged them, provided counsel, opened up their personal networks, and directed them to career and training opportunities. When discussing types of mentors who have supported their career development, female executives we interviewed shared a list that included variety—such as having internal mentors from the same organization, external ones, mentors of both males and females, and mentors of the same race/ethnicity. The consensus was that a variety of mentors provides the best support from different perspectives, which some of them referred to as a personal cabinet. As an African American executive working as a consultant said:

> I have a cabinet and my cabinet was very diverse. I had ethnic diversity, age diversity. I always keep at least one young person in my cabinet to keep me connected to what the younger generation is thinking and feeling and perceiving. And so I'm going to get a very different response to a question that I might ask a young person as opposed to an older person, a black person as opposed to a Jewish white man. Absolutely. I'm just not an advocate for having one mentor.

Types of Mentors

While it's important to build a diverse cabinet of advisers, some of the women perceived that female mentors can provide more emotional support and counsel about family issues. As an executive director working at a public relations firm explained:

> They've all been female. I think it's also because as a working mother, I have purposely … sought out more advice that was spanning those two worlds and those two roles. And so that's why they've always been women.

However, some of the women said it can sometimes be more difficult to find female mentors. It's especially difficult for women with young children to find the time to offer mentorship support to young professionals who are new to the profession and eager to be involved in professional development. As an executive director working at a public relations firm said:

> I still am very self-protective as it relates to my time, only because I have a big job and I'm trying to get it done mostly in four days and then I'm running off to lead another life. I don't have the luxury of doing the drinks with people or going out to lunch with people. I'm staring at my lunch right now because I haven't eaten yet. It just doesn't happen as frequently as I'd like or that it probably should.

Fortunately, many of the women reported that men were willing and available to serve as mentors for them. That willingness was especially critical for the women pioneers in our study, those who were among the first to arise to senior leadership positions in public relations. A CEO of a consulting firm discussed how that was a necessity early in her career:

What's interesting in mentorship, when I think back on who made a difference in my life and what did I learn from them, they were almost all men. And I don't think that was by design. It may have been during the time that I was developing as a leader, most leaders were men. It may also be that women didn't know how to lead, and so they weren't good at it, so I didn't look to them for admiring qualities. Now there are a couple women that I look at. I like the way she leads; how did she do that?

In the 1990s, Tam, Dozier, Lauzen and Real (1995) found that practitioners under the supervision of female supervisors scored the lowest in managerial role enactment and career advancement if compared to those with male superiors. Such a perception drove the conclusion that young professionals should seek mentors that are influential and powerful in managerial circles and that typically referred to men. While much has been written about the need for men to mentor women for leadership (Grunig, Toth & Hon, 2008), it appears to have been true in the past, based on the accounts of the female executives we interviewed. However, there is still some fear of backlash due to the #MeToo movement and social stigma. As the CEO of a nonprofit organization expressed:

You have to make a deliberate effort if you're a male and males should help mentor women and get them the job. But there's also this whole ... I'm just really curious to see how comfortable are people with going out to dinner with a female colleague that you're mentoring. Would you go get dinner and drinks with a female colleague? It's a no brainer if you're a male. But how frequent is that with male-female colleagues? ... I go to dinner with men all the time. I go to dinner with women all the time. But I think it's pretty important, because those ... sort of relationships that you develop over cocktails or over lunches is pretty critical. But I don't know if that's something that's frequently done with different genders. And it's like women have to make the effort too to go out there and put themselves out there and make sure we're mixing with the genders where we don't feel like ... it's awkward or weird.

For women of color, finding someone who looks like them as a mentor is preferred. However, it sometimes is difficult to find in reality. A director of advancement communications for a college explained the value of those relationships:

Culturally, having a mentor of color, sometimes we don't even have to speak words. It's eye contact. It's a nod. Somebody who has actually been through what I'm going through on a deeper level. That helps out. It's much better. So does it make a difference? I've had all. I've had men, women, white, black, Latino, Asian, inside, outside an organization, different profession, but there is an advantage of having a colleague, a mentor of color.

When it comes to internal mentors versus external ones, interviewed female executives perceived differences in contributions, which further supports the need for a wide variety of mentors. An associate vice chancellor at a university explained the value of having mentors from the same organization:

> Sometimes I think it's good if you are looking at a particular issue within your organization and you need a little bit of help in terms of how to navigate it, what the politics are, what the history is within the organization, then you probably want to find somebody within that you can rely on.

At the same time, a senior vice president of global corporate communication addressed the importance of having internal mentors to help with with personal growthand career development. Such support and help were evidenced in her own professional development:

> I feel like there isn't really much training and preparation, especially as you move up the ladder. And it's up to you to just find your way. So in all of my various jobs, I have sought out either an official or unofficial mentor within the organization and I've typically sought out a man to be the mentor and to help me navigate or get the access to the appropriate information or up to speed on whatever it might be. So, for example, when I worked at [name of previous employer], I approached the head of investor relations and asked him to be my mentor and he agreed. I just wanted to learn more about the business side of things and to really be able to understand the financial aspects of the business and he taught me those. He let me sit in on investor calls and just to learn more about that side of the business. But I had to seek that training and I'm very glad that I did because at my current position I have to write the script for the CEO for earnings calls and help with quite a bit of the earnings communication and that training ... it became really, really valuable.

Another value associated with internal mentors is they also can serve as advocates by recommending protégés for growth and advancement opportunities. A chief communications officer at a *Fortune 500* company described the role of advocate or sponsor:

> I think a mentor inside your company, and I guess maybe I'm confusing this term with a sponsor or somebody who's really trying to help develop your career, inside of a company. I think those are very different roles than maybe a mentor outside of a company. Inside it's really somebody who's looking out for those opportunities, be it projects or actual roles, where they think you would have either a particular talent to lend in the circumstance or they are finding those opportunities or throwing your hat in the ring for an opportunity they know will give you an opportunity to shine and to stretch and to add new skills. So, in order to do that, they've got to be innately at a different level than you are, sometimes very high, where they're seeing those opportunities and situations before anybody else does ... I really would use the term sponsor internally and mentor externally. That's just my preference. The distinction that I make is that internally, you really can't separate the fact that person

has an influence over the ability for your name to be thrown in the ring for particular opportunities. Promotion opportunities or just simply special projects that will help you grow, and/or are high-visibility projects.

A vice president of global diversity, inclusion and engagement at a technology company has assumed the role of being an advocate for others in her organization:

> If I see someone do something really well, I will drop a note to their boss and their boss' boss telling how great this person was in this situation. Because those things matter and I think they help to encourage to help people think of things they may not necessarily have thought of themselves and any kind of what I call third-party attribution, when someone outside of you or your boss weighs in on how good something is, how well it went. I think makes a world of difference.

Sponsors and advocates are resources associated with social capital, which refers to "the sum of the actual and potential resources embedded within, available through, and derived from the network of relationships possessed by an individual or social unit" (Nahapiet & Ghoshal, 1998, p. 243). Previous research confirmed there are three benefits associated with social capital, including having access to information, and having advantages in timing by receiving information sooner than those without access to social capital. The third benefit is referrals by personal contacts who mention a colleague's name at the appropriate time and place. Then new opportunities develop (Burt, 1992). As a vice president of global diversity, inclusion and engagement for a technology company explained:

> I always say to people in general some of the most important conversations about you and your career will happen in rooms where you are not. And what you need in that room is a sponsor or an advocate; that's a sponsor, someone who's powerful enough to be in that room and can speak on your behalf and the other thing that will be speaking on your behalf is your brand and your body of work. Those are the things that are in that room where you are not.

Some key contributions of mentors and sponsors include opening their professional networks to protégés by making introductions and "pointing out image and behavior detractors" (Pompper & Adams, 2006, p. 314). The challenge in finding mentors is that they are sometimes drawn to people who are like themselves. However, a vice president of global communications who is an African American executive also mentioned this can be disadvantageous to women of color from a different perspective:

> I would say definitely. In the corporate world, we talk a lot about mentorship and sponsorship. A lot of times, you'll see males and females, but just thinking about the nature of the study from a gender perspective, when you have a predominant

number of leaders who are male, they often take young people, who remind them of themselves, to let them shadow them, apprentice them, come on a special assignment with them, sit at the table with them. They give them opportunities because they remind them of a younger version of them. And they're doing it in a way that's not even an overt training curriculum, but a natural way of, "Let me groom this individual in my own likeness, because there's just something about them that I feel an affection toward." When you don't have that likeness in gender or race, those secret, somewhat untapped areas of training and development are not accessible to you. So, then you try to go to what's accessible. Try to get signed up for the training programs or try to put training on your own plate and do it after hours, between hours, like all my degrees I earned while working full time. And so you try to tackle and attach on training and skill building for yourself, whereas you're seeing those opportunities be handed to others because they have those relatability characteristics and those likenesses to those who are in power, which is predominantly male and predominantly white male.

As the vice president of global diversity, inclusion and engagement at a technology company suggested, senior executives should adopt a broader perspective of acceptance when evaluating whom they provide mentorship support:

> People tend to trust and know those that are closest to them and those that are most like them, that's human nature. There's the neuroscience of trust and people tend to - we are wired that way, biologically wired that way. So, there's no negative connotation or association with it. It doesn't make you a bad person. What leaders do - what I call inclusive leaders do, however, is push themselves to make sure they are exposed to a broad variety of talent. And it's in that exposure that if ... I'm an older male and I have this really smart younger female who's on a team that I'm managing, and I don't naturally in my circle of influence necessarily know a lot of younger females, but through knowing this young woman, it changes my perception and it opens up – it's almost like the aperture on a camera – it opens up my aperture to the range of talent and prospects that are out there. That's what inclusion is all about.

For example, an African American female executive working as a director of media and public relations at a university said she benefited significantly from her relationships with her mentor who went beyond the traditional mentoring functions by being a strong advocate for her:

> I had a mentor who was not just a mentor. He was an advocate. And the difference is, a mentor gives you tips and advice. They can review your resume; they can guide you with some decisions. An advocate is someone who not only makes sure you have those things, or will review them for you, but they get you in a place where you can get that resume to somebody or they invite you to the table and let you show what you can do, invite you to the meetings that have leadership in there ... My mentor/advocate was a man, and he fought for me. I was on a grant funding, and the grant

funding was ending. He promised me like, "Hey, I'll make sure you find another position before I do." And that's what he did. He literally opened doors. And of course, I had to close the deal, but he got me to the table and got me with an audience where I was able to secure my next job.

A chief communications officer at a *Fortune 500* company recalled the time when she was first being considered for the position. It was so critical to have a female colleague serve as an internal advocate and provide a wake-up call as she described:

And one of the highest position women in [organization name] ... literally got on my calendar, sat across the table from me in a very formal meeting, and said, "What are you doing?" And so, she really brought a two-by-four verbally to me and said, "If you want this, go for it. And by the way, the Women's Leadership Network is 100 percent behind you. We've seen you in action. We know your experience, we know your capability, but we're also observing the lack of total confidence appropriate, professional gusto that is going to be required to land this job"... Huge learning for women in business, I think to understand that you are pushed up and pulled up well beyond the folks within your immediate sphere or your immediate function or department.

Another interviewed female executive who is the director of media and communications at a university described an experience earlier in her career when she was working in city government. The city secretary served as an advocate by informing her regarding pay inequity and the need to advocate for a raise. She recalled:

I remember I'd been working four years, and finally our city secretary was like, "Hey, you should look at the CAFR [Comprehensive Annual Financial Report] for this year, wink wink. Why don't you come back after five? It might be on my desk. Wink wink." So I was like, OK, what is she talking about? So I go over there. She has tabbed the pages. I open up, and I see what my predecessor made. Almost $45,000 more. It might have been – let me think, at the time. Easy $45,000 more a year. And I know I did more than him as far as changing things and the duties that I've taken on, and I remember just being really angry. I remember when they offered me the job, and I had researched the salary. I had friends who had conducted additional research for me to confirm what I had, and they were like, here is the number. When they made the offer, it was lower than that, and I accounted for something like $1,000 dollars more, and even as I said it I thought, god that was so stupid. But I was worried about losing the job. I was young, and I think, had I did it over again, absolutely, I would've came in super high, based upon my research to get that number. Because I know now, that if you chose me as a candidate, I'm your choice. Searches are expensive. They're time consuming. So I could have negotiated from that position of power, and had my case ready as to here's what my justification for why I deserve that salary, in addition to what the market is saying, but here are the specific skills that I have. But I panicked. And so when you come in low at a company, it's very hard to correct. Everything is based on percentages. So when the city secretary showed me that, I was like what do I do? I had a contact who worked in HR in another city, and she was teaching me how you can apply for reclassification. And so I ended up doing that. I got my salary bumped up $8,000. It wasn't exactly what I wanted, but it felt good to advocate for myself.

External mentors also serve a vital role because of their fresh perspective. A chief communications officer at a *Fortune 500* company explained the different benefits between internal and external mentors in terms of what they can offer:

The value externally is you don't have that baggage attached to it. You don't have the "my role depends on this" or "my future at company XYZ might have to do with this." And they ... can bring different perspectives of other organizations and how other organizations have handled it or how they have personally handled it. I personally have found that the mentors outside of the organization really stay with you throughout your career and are a network, if you will. And they're more about best practices as a corp comms leader. And they tend to be in your field, not all the time, but generally. And then inside the company, those mentors, or sponsors, can be in lots of different roles. They don't necessarily have to be in communications.

External mentors also were valued because of their longevity and connections as a vice president of global communications at a professional services firm expressed:

Organizations come and go, and when you have networks outside, it gives you resiliency and the ability to leave and pivot to new opportunities that you wouldn't see if you only were solely focused on having mentors inside your company or inside even your profession.

Race is another consideration when identifying potential mentors. Women of color feel a strong obligation to mentor fellow women of color and are often sought out by young professionals. An African American woman working as vice president of global communication at a professional service firm said:

I have colleagues who come to me because they don't see people who look like them, many of them walking around as far as the same race or gender, and so they come to me and seek me out to mentor them. And then I also seek out opportunities when I see something, I say something in the right way, especially if it's someone who I think could benefit from it. And if I think, "Hey, I wish somebody had said something to me." So that's my approach to it. It's ongoing, it's every day, and constant.

However, finding Latina mentors is especially challenging due to the lack of diversity in public relations and communication management. Such dearth of diverse resources was addressed by a former vice president of marketing and communication for a nonprofit organization who is Latina:

> My challenges have been lack of visibility in terms of finding another Latina in a public relations role. As I mentioned earlier, I didn't have a lot of mentors that looked like me or had experiences like me, and so I felt somewhat alone in my career. I gravitated to male mentors who kind of took me under their wings and were helpful to me and navigated paths for me and became champions and sponsors. But it was hard. And so, I would say being able to have more Latina female mentors I think would've been very helpful, just to have understood what they went through and how I could have avoided some of my own hurdles and challenges. I think I would've benefitted from that as well.

Desired Personal Attributes of Mentors

In our interviews, we also integrated questions asking current female executives to describe what characteristics they admired or sought in potential mentors. As expected, they listed expertise, experience and success as desired career attributes for their role models. In addition, they also mentioned many other qualities that reflect mentors' personal attributes such as integrity, caring, compassionate, kind, honest, candid, and genuine. This aligns with virtue ethics and the role of moral exemplars by seeking out people who model those virtues to develop *phronesis* or practical wisdom (Hursthouse, 1999), which was referred to as the "hard-won moral expertise that comes from experience and reflection" (Borden, 2019, p. 172). For example, a senior vice president at a public relations firm explained:

> As far as characteristics, certainly for me someone that treats others with respect and kindness is really paramount to me. The way that a leader - I love seeing that servant-leader heart, someone that understands to be great, they need to be helping set other people up for greatness. And someone that is honest and fair and that doesn't - and has grace under fire, that isn't going to be rattled. I probably won't go to them for advice on the easy things, so the type of person that has overcome a lot of challenges and has seen a lot of things and doesn't get shaken by that, but can give counsel on how they've dealt with it.

Our interviewees also mentioned the desired mentors are those who make themselves available, are willing to listen, and provide constructive feedback. This list of leadership attributes is similar to previous research findings on mentoring in public relations, which found protégés preferred mentors who are knowledgeable, insightful, good role models, and patient (Pompper & Adams, 2006). A regional director of advocacy and public affairs at a corporation added mission and passion to that list:

So what I really look for is someone who's passionate about what they're doing, and that passion oftentimes reflects back not only in how they execute their job, but also in terms of - when someone is enjoying what they do, I find inherent in that is a mission behind it, as to why it is versus just a paycheck.

Consistent with sponsors or advocates, our interviewees also addressed some other needs they are seeking from mentors, including a willingness to open their personal networks and help the protégé make connections, sharing opportunities, opening doors and even pushing protégés outside their comfort zone. As a director serving in the U.S. military said:

Especially for me it was individuals who recognized some potential and encouraged and challenged me to try some things that I probably wouldn't have done on my own. And they saw where you could succeed, where you really didn't have that foresight, or you didn't see it the same way they did. Training - the good ones in particular would - and accreditation - I wasn't running out the door to do it, let's put it that way. I was trying to delay because I was new on the job, and lots of time. It was "You know you're only here for so long, you need to start sooner than later." And so they really pushed it, but in a good way.

Responsibilities of Protégés

On the other side of the coin, previous researchers found that mentors seek protégés with whom they feel compatible, who are driven, capable, and professionally mature (Pompper & Adams, 2006). The Plank Center for Leadership in Public Relations provides a free mentorship guide online and lists several responsibilities associated with being a good protégé or mentee. Those include being authentic and open, listening, engaging in reflection, delivering on promises, valuing differences, and giving and receiving feedback (The Plank Center for Leadership in Public Relations, 2017). Current women leaders also pointed out that it is important to be respectful of the mentor's time and come prepared with specific questions. The co-founder of a multicultural communication consulting firm provided counsel on how to approach a potential mentor:

And I think mentorship, a lot of times people think of this whole mentorship idea has to be this formal process, and it really doesn't. It could be as simple as there's someone that you really respect, that you can ask them if they have a few minutes to meet with you and you want to do coffee or something. And you explain to them, "Would you be Ok mentoring me?" Just be very open. And they probably would be very flattered ... So, I think it could be that you meet with a few different people before you find the right fit, because it's going to come down to who do you feel more comfortable speaking with. It's that sort of personal relationship. So it can be a very casual thing. It doesn't have to be a formal meeting or anything. It could be meeting for coffee or whatever it is that you want to do. Just to kind of bounce ideas and have a different perspective on the things that you're doing ... That's why it's important to meet them and see are they a good fit ... it also may be they're not a good fit. But it doesn't matter, because you just met them for coffee. And if you don't want to meet them again, you don't have to. You just say thank you very much and you move on.

Once young professionals find a mentor, the next step is to listen and observe as suggested by an executive vice president at a public relations firm:

Listen and learn as much as you can. The brightest of students, especially in this generation as we did, thought we knew everything. And we don't. As much as I paid attention, there were times in hindsight that I can easily say, "I should have just shut up and listened." ... I would've learned lessons a little earlier than I did. So I would say just sit still and listen and take notes. Maybe they apply to you, maybe they don't, but it can only help.

Martinelli and Erzikova (2016) identified four stages in a mentoring relationship through their interdisciplinary review of mentoring literature (Caruso, 1990; Kram, 1983; Roberts, 2000). These stages include:

1. An initiation phase, which reflects the start of the relationship, and during which the mentor *prescriptively* directs the mentee;
2. A cultivation phase, where mentorship functions are better established and maximized, and where the mentor guides/*persuades* the mentee, so they may begin to *collaborate*, with the mentor ultimately *confirming* the mentee's ability through full delegation of tasks;
3. A separation phase, in which organizational and/or psychological changes within one or both mentoring parties decrease the relationship's fruitfulness; and
4. A redefinition phase, where the relationship ceases to exist or evolves into a new form, such as friendship (Martinelli & Erzikova, 2016, p. 4).

This list of mentoring phases proposes that there is a need for new mentors during different seasons of professional development over the course of a communication professional's career.

Identifying Mentors

The majority of the female leaders we interviewed perceived that mentoring is an obligation for leaders, particularly in the context of training and developing their own employees, but they also should be willing and make themselves available to mentor interns and students. As a chief communications officer at a *Fortune 500* company explained:

> No matter what organization I'm at, I try to tell my team that my role there is to develop them as top-tier communications talent, regardless of where they might decide to use those talents. So, my responsibility is to them as professionals, and to develop that, whether it is - I won't say at the expense of the company, but certainly right there alongside it. I like to say that I want people who are there ... because they want to be working on my team, not because their skills are stale, and they can't go anywhere else or they are afraid to go somewhere else. We're both aligned with the same goal in mind, if that goal is to continue to build your talent.

Some of the female leaders said their organizations have established formal mentoring programs and affinity groups for women and employees of color to support such initiatives. As a vice president working in a corporation described:

> The senior women leader's group, that was all about first bonding together supporting each other, and there were only, if you go to the top two salary grades in this organization, there were only like 14 of us in an organization of 5,000 women that rose to that level. So bonding together, but in service of helping the next generation of leaders. So over time, that senior group was intended to get more involved with and bring along people in the general women's group. So that was kind of a multi-layered I guess I would say mentoring venture. I think we made great strides. I was and continue to be surprised by women in the general women's organization who reached out to me as I was leaving and even still to say what an impact I had on them.

Formal mentoring programs have been found to be mutually beneficial for both employees and their employers. Formal mentoring relationships typically involve an employer assigning a more experienced person with a less experienced one, while informal mentoring describes relationships that develop organically through the consent of both parties (Jablin, 2001; Tam et al., 1995). Martinelli and Erzikova (2016) suggested that "within organizations, mentoring might focus on *instrumental* support, such as providing instruction and feedback to assist with career advancement, and/or *psychosocial* support, such as role modeling and encouragement" (p. 4). In the area of *instrumental* support or career development, "mentors provide protection, coaching, challenging assignments, career planning advice, sponsorship in the organization and a network of social connections" (Berger, Meng & Heyman, 2009, p. 14). *Psychosocial* support for the protégé is offered "through a mentor's friendship, counseling, acceptance and confirmation of work, and role modeling of expected values and behaviors" (Berger et al., 2009, p. 15).

Mentors serving as role models are consistent with social learning theory, which suggests that we learn not only from our own experiences, but from observing others' actions and consequences (Bandura, 2001). Scholars proposed that we are more likely to imitate the behavior of those who have visible signs of success such as wealth, power, or status (Cialdini & Trost, 1998). Bandura (2001) referred to this vicarious learning when people are "motivated by the successes of others who are similar to themselves and are discouraged to pursue behavior by others that has led to adverse consequences" (p. 274). A *Harvard Business Review* article reports positive outcomes from mentoring programs: "Research on junior to mid-level professionals shows that [mentorship] programs enable them to advance more quickly, earn higher salaries, and gain more satisfaction in their jobs and lives than people without mentors do. For employers, the benefits are not only higher performance but also greater success in attracting, developing, and retaining talent" (De Janasz & Peiperl, 2015, p. 101).

The president and general manager of a public relations firm provided examples of *psychosocial* support from two different mentors that gave her a fresh perspective toward her work. The advice came both early in her career and more recently. As she described:

> I've had a client mentor when I was really new to the business. And he really encouraged me to leave where I was and to take that next promotion, that next leap out of where I was. And that meant he wasn't going to get ... have me leading his account anymore. And he taught me a lot about- I just said something like, "I can't wait to not be new in this new role anymore. I can't wait to be the expert of everything." And he said, "Oh, no, no, no. You're looking at this the wrong way. Relish the newness, relish the challenges, relish the newness, because once it's not new anymore. Then you're not alive. You're bored. You're not growing"... Our chairman is a great mentor to me. I feel like it's a two-way street. And he asks me for advice all the time, because he's a great listener ... his advice to me was relish the problems that come your way. Because so much of what I do is problem solving. And so relish the problems that come your way, because if they're not coming your way after a period of time, then they're going to someone else and you're not needed to solve them ... so then particularly during a period in my career where I felt like it was whack a mole, like problem, problem, problem. ... it was really beating me down and he gave me that pep talk and so then, even to this day, I say, "oh, that's a problem. That's a problem coming my way. I'm being asked to help solve it." And so, it helped me sort of re-train my brain around being excited to run towards it instead of run away from it.

Neill and Weaver (2017) also found the value mentorship can provide to young professionals when they face ethical challenges in public relations practice but lack experience and need guidance to manage such challenges. According to Neill and Weaver (2017), the majority of the young professionals surveyed

(68.8%) indicated that they have a mentor with whom they could discuss ethical concerns, and that they would be comfortable discussing ethical concerns with a mentor outside of their employer. In addition, young professionals who had a mentor were significantly more likely to report that they felt prepared to offer ethics counsel compared to those who do not have a mentor (Neill & Weaver, 2017).

Many of the women we interviewed participate in mentoring programs through PRSA nationally and their local chapters. Such action further highlights the important role of professional associations as a source for young professionals to identify potential mentors they admire and develop sustainable mentor-mentee relationships. Young professionals also can request informational interviews with professionals they admire that may lead to mentoring relationships. As a director of communication in the U.S. military described:

> For management, go seek out somebody that you really respect as a leader that is a supervisor or that is a manager. You can do it, you don't have to necessarily be in the area, it could be a phone call, it could be an interview … by phone, but you need to be respectful of their time and have good questions, and figure out what it is you want to know from them. If you can, one-on-one, face to face is always better, go for coffee or lunch. Go to their office and have a short meeting. Or ask to shadow for a day or two. I did that, and that was an awesome experience. So after that, I thought, "Wow! Why aren't people doing this more?" And most people said that I suggested it to, "I didn't even think about that!" A few of them have, and that's good, more of them are doing it, but it's intimidating to ask somebody, because you're always afraid to ask. I guess the main thing is, they should not be afraid to ask. Most of the time unless people's schedules just don't allow it, I have not seen anybody turn anyone away or say no. They'll be like, "Send me some questions, and I'll send you something back in writing." Or, "Sure, I can make time for a phone call!" Or, "Ok, let's go for coffee."

Conclusion

Findings of our interviewees confirmed that women executives in public relations constantly face the challenges of addressing and balancing family demands and commitments including childcare and caring for aging parents. To deal with the stresses associated with role overload, they have used various coping strategies such as rational action, instrumental support, emotional support, emotional venting and positive thinking. However, some of their decisions did result in setbacks for their careers such as taking a lower position and reducing their work hours. Fortunately, spouses and extended family function as a support network by sharing some of the responsibilities that allow women in public relations to continue to pursue managerial and leadership roles.

As suggested by our interviewed female executives, finding and developing a personal cabinet of mentors can be crucial for career development and advancement as different mentors can enrich leadership advancement from diverse perspectives, such as providing sound counsel, opening their personal networks to protégés, sharing opportunities, and pushing them to expand beyond their comfort zone. A sponsor or advocate inside the organization is a critical type of mentor as they can advocate for protégés in meetings when the protégés are not present due to various reasons such as hierarchy. They can also recommend the protégés for different growth and career opportunities inside the organization. In addition to formal mentoring programs inside a company, young professionals should consider joining professional associations, which are a great source for networking and finding external mentors. As suggested by our interviewed female leaders, young professionals also can use informational interviews as an effective way to seek additional mentoring and build relationships.

References

Aldoory, L., Jiang, H., Toth, E. L., & Sha, B. L. (2008). Is it still just a women's issue? A study of work-life balance among men and women in public relations. *Public Relations Journal, 2*(4), 1–20.

Bandura, A. (2001). Social cognitive theory of mass communication. *Media Psychology, 3*, 265–299.

Berger, B. K., Meng, J., & Heyman, W. (2009, March 11–14). *Role Modeling in Public Relations: The Influence of Role Models and Mentors on Leadership Beliefs and Qualities* [Conference Presentation]. International Public Relations Research Conference, Miami, FL, United States.

Borden, S. L. (2019). Virtue ethics & media. In P. L. Plaisance (Ed.) *Communication and media ethics* (pp. 171–190). Boston, MA: Mouton De Gruyter.

Burt, R. S. (1992). *Structural holes: The social structure of competition.* Cambridge, MA: Harvard University Press.

Caruso, J. E. (1990). *An examination of organised mentoring: The case of Motorola.* (Unpublished thesis). British Thesis Service, DX 147810.

Cialdini, R. B. & Trost, M. R. (1998). Social influence, social norms, conformity, and compliance. In S. T. Fiske, D. T. Gilbert, & G. Lindzey (Eds.), *The handbook of social psychology*, (Vol. 2, pp. 151–192). New York: Oxford University Press.

De Janasz, S., & Peiperl, M. (2015, April 27). CEOs need mentors too. *Harvard Business Review.* Retrieved from https://hbr.org/2015/04/ceos-need-mentors-too. Access date: October 1, 2019.

Duhachek, A. (2005). Coping: A multidimensional, hierarchical framework of responses to stressful consumption episodes. *Journal of Consumer Research, 32*(1), 41–53.

Grunig, L. A., Toth, E. L., & Hon, L. C. (2008). *Women in public relations: How gender influences practice.* New York: Routledge.

Hursthouse, R. (1999). *On virtue ethics.* Oxford, England: Oxford University Press.

Jablin, F. M. (2001). Organization entry, assimilation, and disengagement/exit. In F. M. Jablin & L. L. Putnam (Eds.), *The new handbook of organizational communication: Advances in theory, research, and methods* (pp. 732–818). Thousand Oaks, CA: Sage Publications.

Jin, Y., Sha, B.-L., Shen, H., Jiang, H. (2014). Tuning in to the rhythm: The role of coping in strategic management of work-life conflicts in the public relations profession. *Public Relations Review, 40,* 69–78.

Kram, K. E. (1983). Phases of the mentor relationship. *Academy of Management, 26*(4), 608–625.

Martinelli, D., & Erzikova, E. (2016). *Mentoring Research and Best Practices White Paper.* Retrieved from: http://plankcenter.ua.edu/wp-content/uploads/2017/07/Mentoring.final_.10.19.16.pdf. Access date: October 1, 2019.

Miles, R. H., & Perreault, Jr., W. D. (1976). Organizational role conflict: Its antecedents and consequences. *Organizational Behavior and Human Performance, 17,* 19–44.

Nahapiet, J., & Ghoshal, S. (1998). Social capital, intellectual capital, and the organizational advantage. *Academy of Management Review, 23*(2), 242–266.

Neill, M. S., & Weaver, N. (2017). Silent & unprepared: Most millennial practitioners have not embraced role as ethical conscience. *Public Relations Review, 43*(2), 337–344.

Plank Center Mentorship Guide (2017). Retrieved from http://plankcenter.ua.edu/wp-content/uploads/2017/08/The-Plank-Center-Mentorship-Guide.pdf on October 1, 2019.

Pompper, D., & Adams, J. (2006). Under the microscope: Gender and mentor-protégé relationships. *Public Relations Review, 32,* 309–315.

Roberts, A. (2000). Mentoring revisited: A phenomenological reading of the literature. *Mentoring and Tutoring, 8*(2), 145–170.

Tam, S. Y., Dozier, D. M., Lauzen M. M., & Real, M. R. (1995). The impact of superior-subordinate gender on the career advancement of public relations practitioners. *Journal of Public Relations Research, 7*(4), 259–272.

Synthesis and Summary

Building a Constructive Path to Drive Change

This section summarizes the research, presents key themes that emerged in the findings, and concludes with what organizations can do to advance women's leadership in public relations to establish an environment of inclusiveness within and beyond the organizations. Ultimately, one of the many important reasons to study leadership is to facilitate the development of future leaders. We wish to reframe the importance of leadership development at both the developmental and participative levels. We argue that the development of leadership capacities shall go hand-in-hand with strong participation in leadership opportunities and performance. We hope scholars, educators and professionals of public relations, both men and women, will benefit from our deep exploration of the topic.

CHAPTER TEN

Building an Ecosystem

A Constructive Path to Leadership for Women in PR

Women's capacity for leadership depends not simply on their individual developmental goals, but more on the societal and organizational contexts and structures within which leadership identity is defined and leadership opportunities arise. According to research done by Catalyst on women in corporate leadership, there has been progress for women gaining leadership positions in the workplace over the past ten years (Catalyst, 2003, 2004). However, the progress is slow and the existence of various situational barriers has been reconfirmed (e.g. lack of role models, lack of significant management or line experience, the challenge of balancing family responsibilities and career advancement, etc.) in holding women back from reaching top leadership roles as evidenced by previous research (e.g. Aldoory & Toth, 2004; Aldoory, Jiang, Toth & Sha, 2008; Catalyst, 2007; Place & Vardeman-Winter, 2018; Vardeman-Winter & Place, 2017) and our current research. There seemed to be only modest change in what we found compared to what previous pioneering scholars found in terms of the gender disparity in the profession.

When looking into the literature, it is not hard to locate longitudinal research that focuses on women in middle management who have worked for *Fortune 500* companies throughout the U.S. (e.g. Wentling, 2003). Based on the longitudinal track of the career development of women in the middle management and leadership (i.e. 1995–2003), the majority of those interviewed mid-level women managers indicated that they have not attained the positions to which they ultimately aspire. The majority of them do not believe they are progressing as rapidly as they think they should or they would (Wentling, 2003). It is likely that the deeply rooted societal biases towards women still wield a substantial impact. We've seen lots of rhetoric but minimal action or follow through to bring about substantial progress and significant improvements.

Research on gender issues in public relations also found similar trends and patterns reflecting the slow progress of the profession. Scholars have raised the compelling case that it is crucial to remove the gender inequalities in leadership practice of the industry and increase women's presence in leadership roles in public relations (e.g. Grunig, Toth & Hon, 2001; Place & Vardeman-Winter, 2018). However, the educational emphasis on career preparedness (Place & Vardeman-Winter, 2018, p. 169) and the scholarly expectation on publishing in prestigious academic journals (Grunig, Toth & Hon, 2001, p. xv) have limited our discussion of women in public relations leadership, their capacities for leadership development, and their real opportunities in leadership participation.

Therefore, we dedicate this book to an analysis and synthesis of research on how women in public relations can break through the ethical and leadership challenges, with an ultimate goal of suggesting an ecosystem that can build a constructive path to prepare women in public relations for leadership. Each chapter of this book has taken its essential role in addressing various aspects related to leadership development and participation for female professionals in the field, including situational barriers, the meaning of having influence as a female leader, ethics counseling, leadership development and participation opportunities, mentorship, and instrumental support in coping with work-life conflict. In addition, we also examined the additional challenges faced by women of color when pursuing leadership and career advancement opportunities.

These findings continue adding some optimism to the sense of progress by revealing a wide set of strategic directions and testable solutions to address the challenges embedded in women's leadership advancement in the public relations profession. We hope each of these chapters encourage multiple entities, from the society, the professional associations, the organizations, the educators, the female professionals, their male counterparts in the field, to students of public relations, to continue exploring and changing the longstanding forms of gender inequalities in leadership practice in the public relations profession.

We have maintained primarily a scholarly focus in this book when exploring this topic in order to advance our understanding of such leadership and ethical obstacles to women's leadership advancement and their effects on the overall progress in the public relations profession. Meanwhile, we also hope that many of the related sub-topics we have analyzed and many of the current female executives' experiences we have shared throughout the book will generate solid practical implications to push the organizations and the profession to think creatively and develop solutions comprehensively in order to provide strong support for women who aspire to top jobs in the field. Understanding the barriers female professionals face in gaining leadership roles helps shed light on how we can unite collaborative efforts with multiple entities by building a constructive path to support women in developing their experiences and identities in leadership roles. To enhance female professionals' capacity to exercise leadership effectively, we believe it is critical to extend the promise by placing it in a developmental and participative leadership context, both within and beyond the organization.

In this final chapter, we first present the key themes that provide a trend map to summarize and synthesize many of the findings revealed by our research project. We have presented detailed findings in each chapter. It is time for us to propose an agenda to link research results to practical implications at both the individual and organizational levels. These key themes have their implications to inform practice and provide solutions for organizations to support female professionals' leadership advancement and participation. These central themes will also set a new research agenda among the academic community to advance research and training on leadership and diversity in public relations.

Five Key Themes Inspired by Findings

1. *Lay the foundation for gender equality throughout all phases of talent management and the leadership pipeline to build an ecosystem for leadership development.*

If women comprise nearly 70–75% of the jobs in today's public relations profession, why does the gender representation for senior leadership still lag far behind in the reality? We asked this critical question before diving into our year-long research journey. This seems to be a paradox and an insoluble question facing the profession for the past few decades since some earlier benchmarking studies of gender issues in public relations (e.g. Grunig, Toth & Hon, 2001; Toth & Cline, 1991). The continuing influx of women (both whites and minorities) has altered the structure of the public relations profession rapidly. However, such rapid change is not reflected equally at the level of senior leadership within the organizational structure. There is evidence that a significant proportion of young females reside at the junior level in the profession after freshly graduated from college. According to our findings, it is promising to see a substantial percentage of women serve as direct supervisors at the lower- and/or middle-levels of leadership positions. At the same time, it is also discouraging to find out when it is time to level the playing field of senior communication leadership, the storyline changes and the big picture of gender-representation flips, as mirrored by the snapshot of the gender representation revealed in our research.

Based on the responses from our surveyed female professionals in the field, we identified three top situational barriers which hold women back from reaching top leadership jobs: 1) workplace structures; 2) double standards in domestic roles and professional demands; and 3) social attitudes towards female professionals. It is disheartening to admit that not much has changed in the past few decades or even longer when it is time to assess workplace structures, policies, family responsibilities, and social attitudes, all of which contribute to shaping people's expectations and experiences associated with women. Although women are just as ambitious and competent as men and desirous of more line responsibilities as men, as found in a most recent study conducted by Zenger and Folkman (2019), a female professional's qualifications for taking a leadership role are still challenged at each level.

This brings up a fundamental question in terms of how the society and the organization can provide support for women by establishing an ecosystem that focuses on long-term leadership development, instead of seeking short-term productivity and evaluating single-task-based performance. An understanding of women's ambition and motivation in leadership achievement shall be integrated into the organization's talent management system and programs. At the organizational level, the leadership team which focuses on the organization's talent management strategies shall make a conscious effort to create an environment of commitment to mainstream gender equality within the organization and along its leadership pipeline.

Research has suggested that a lack of gender diversity in the boardroom could limit an organization's opportunities for learning and innovation (Adams & Ferreira, 2009; Francoeur, Labelle & Sinclair-Desgagné, 2008). Women bring different experiences and perspectives to their workplace because of their engagement in different social relations and social causes. Organizations may fail to tap these different perspectives if they are reluctant to recognize women's career preferences and workplace commitments (Catalyst, 1999, 2007; Ely & Thomas, 2001; Meyerson, Ely & Wernick, 2007). Strategies to promote female professionals' leadership shall be integrated into new and/or existing mechanisms for talent management programming, implementing, representing, monitoring and evaluation in the organization.

2. *Create a mutual learning and sharing platform to integrate authentic leadership advancement experience into leadership development initiatives.*

Our research reveals the sharp gaps between leaders and non-leaders on various aspects of leadership challenges. Female professionals who are currently in certain leadership roles actually reported much stronger opinions on situational barriers to leadership advancement. If the perceptual differences are the true reflections of their leadership advancement journey, such experience shall be shared and communicated to young talented female professionals in their early stage of career development in order to effectively help them develop leadership identity. More importantly, current and past female leaders' opinions and perspectives of leadership advancement should be valued by the organization and used as valuable resources and cases to monitor and re-assess current leadership development efforts. Their experiences will provide valuable insights for employers' organizations to evaluate gender-based policies and programs by finding the blind spots, adding diverse perspectives, and increasing equal opportunities. An organization can improve its leadership development programs by:

1. Defining a clear set of objectives for leadership advancement for talented female professionals at the organizational level;
2. Designing equal opportunity programs around the objectives and coordinating the content;
3. Engaging female professionals who have the desire in leadership advancement in leadership development content;
4. Allowing constant feedback and flexibility within leadership development programs for continued engagement and self-reflection;
5. Making sure to assign clear leadership roles that have genuine leadership participative authority to confirm commitment;
6. Ensuring that all commitments made concerning the DE&I management are consistently kept across the organization;
7. Establishing women and diversity networks or affinity groups to provide mentoring opportunities for younger employees; and
8. Assigning employees with leadership potential to oversee committees or lead short-term projects to develop leadership competencies and cultivate leadership capacity.

3. *Provide mentoring and networking opportunities by celebrating successful female leaders as role models and demonstrating joint responsibilities.*

When we explored issues causing the underrepresentation of female professionals in senior-level positions in public relations, one set of questions concerning female professionals' leadership advancement addressed the lack of a sufficient number of women as role models in high-level decision-making positions. Therefore, it is critical to monitor and evaluate progress on women's representation at all decision-making levels within the organization. It is also important to facilitate the communication between those who are already in leadership positions and those who are on the rise in their career advancement.

At the same time, it is even more important to focus on the mutual learning and joint responsibilities that grow out of the mentor-mentee (or mentor-protégé) relationship. Such action can be developed into a sustainable mentoring program that goes beyond experience sharing and storytelling. Junior female professionals could benefit particularly from mentoring as it can increase their visibility and access to high visible assignments and key senior executives. As mentioned in our findings, visibility, opportunity and advocacy are essential components to career advancement and they are closely tied to mentoring and sponsorship. In an effort to promote women, organizations shall consider pairing talented female professionals with senior-executive mentors (both men and women), within or outside their own organizations. Mentoring is not just a program or a tool to promote better management. More strategically, it shall be used as part of a broader career planning system for women who have the desire to reach top leadership.

As mirrored in our findings presented in Chapter Six, surveyed female professionals value mentorship and they believe mentorship and sponsorship are critical in supporting individuals' leadership advancement. However, we still see a substantial percentage of female professionals (at various levels along the hierarchical reporting line) reporting having no mentor in their career. Organizations should prioritize the conscious efforts in celebrating successful female professionals at all levels and providing mentoring and networking opportunities so that women can learn from each other about leadership participation and success. It is important for female professionals within the organization to not only see role models but also have the opportunity to be connected with senior women regarding career planning, tracking, coaching, training, building influence and balancing work duties and family responsibilities. It also will help junior female professionals further develop their leadership qualifications. Having influential mentors does not only provide a continuation of efforts to support the advancement, but it will also create organizational climates that embrace diversity, equity, and inclusion in the workplace (Powell, 2018). Mentoring also is about cultivating talent for the future viability of an organization. As more senior executives retire, it will help ensure the organization can continue to flourish.

4. *Link influence building to career tracking to develop meaningful evaluations in diversity-and-inclusion management.*

Although diversity-and-inclusion management is a hot topic in the public relations profession today, the inconsistency and uncertainty of practice in implementing diversity, equity and inclusion initiatives is a constant challenge in the reality. Thomas (1990) argues that diversity management shall be valued as a process by which organizations could create an environment that encourages all employees to reach their full potential when aligning organizational objectives and individual career goals. Research has indicated that gender and race are two important focus areas in designing and implementing diversity management strategies, and the failure of effective diversity management affects structures, policies and outcomes within the workplace (Greene & Kirton, 2011; Herdman & McMillan, 2010; Kirton & Greene, 2005). Thus, Mor Barak (2011) suggests that the goal of DE&I management shall focus on creating an inclusively social, legislative, and organizational environment that respects and values individual differences and perspectives.

Individual differences influence the dynamics of diversity management practices. Based on the overall results from our surveyed female professionals, having influence as a female leader in public relations has multiple levels of meaning. The top three characteristics that define influence include being seen as a trusted advisor, having career advancement opportunities, and having a voice that colleagues and co-workers listen to. The interpretation of having influence changes depending on the types of organizations. Women of color define the meaning of having influence with much stronger expression and opinions. For them, having influence means being able to demonstrate expertise and gaining visibility. Therefore, if gender and race are two major considerations in implementing diversity management strategies, the different interpretations on having and building influence will add further complexity to accommodate differences.

In Meng and Berger's (2018) research on talent management focusing on millennial communication professionals, strong evidence is found that five key areas in talent management—recruitment, engagement, development, retention and gaining—are significantly and positively correlated. Such intertwined relationship indicates performance at high (or low) level in one area would predict the same performance (high or low) in other areas. These dynamic relationships are also reflected in DE&I management. That is, organizations that have programs and metrics in one area should also have programs and metrics in other areas in order to provide a broad and consistent support for addressing equity and diversity in leadership advancement. Female professionals who experience these supportive organizational practices that link building influence to career tracking will also acknowledge greater job and career satisfaction. The conscious efforts in supporting DE&I management will also bring higher levels of psychological well-being to female professionals.

One issue of concern raised by our interview participants is that senior executives tend to mentor junior employees who remind them of themselves. If mentoring contributes to an individual's broader career planning journey, this type of unconscious selection or preference will limit the scope of mutual learning and put many other qualified female professionals in a disadvantaged situation. Therefore, to make a mentoring program successful, executives need to be willing to step out of their comfort zone to seek out and mentor promising young women, employees of color, or any employees of potential to ensure they have equal opportunities for leadership development. As addressed in today's DE&I management research, diversity shall be seen to consist of both visible and non-visible differences of employees that include but are not limited to factors such as sex, age, background, race, disability, personality and work style (Kandola & Fullerton, 1994). Similarly, we would argue that a successful mentoring program shall also strive to respond to the different needs, career aspirations, contributions, and lifestyles of mentors and mentees to demonstrate the joint responsibilities and reflect the nature of mutual learning.

5. *Keep balancing professional and family responsibilities a priority with strong top-down communication support.*

The influx of women into the practice of public relations faces the reality that women's working lives and personal lives are deeply intertwined. It makes the solution of balancing professional and family responsibilities an ever-challenging one. According to our research, women in public relations agree that the work-life conflict brings tension and stress at various levels. They need to make constant changes to family activities to fulfill work-related duties. The amount of working hours and working strain affect the quality of their home and family life. This challenge is especially prevalent in public relations due to the expectations around monitoring and responding to social media issues 24/7. Professionals in the younger age bracket or those just starting their families express a much stronger interference. The inequality in hours and workload spent by men and women on household responsibilities also intensify constraints.

Although surveyed female professionals indicated that they have used a wide variety of coping strategies to manage work-life conflict, it is also disheartening to see women do not take some instrumental support provided by their employers such as benefit programs in place, flex-work arrangements, or supervisor's help. They still largely rely on domestic support from their family or spouse/partner. Female professionals at lower levels along the reporting line in the organization are less likely to use formal flexibility programs, if compared to women who are currently in a defined leadership position in their organization. If organizations have established a wide array of initiatives concerning flex time, part time, leave policies, childcare assistance, why are such initiatives often inadequate in practice? If the majority of women in middle management continue to aspire to senior leadership roles and they believe they will attain these positions in the future (Wentling, 2003), why are they still opting out for flexible or reduced schedules? Research indicates female executives clearly question whether they can actually use those flexibility programs in place and remain on an upward career trajectory (Catalyst, 2003).

If this is their biggest concern, organizations shall make sure information about such flex-work programs is delivered to female professionals at all levels and with strong top-down communication in supporting women's choices. Some recent reports have found that organizations have begun rolling out new ways to offer consulting arrangements and career assistance for women who have to temporarily leave the labor force, as well as launching executive programs to help them transition back (McGinn, 2006). Ely and Rhode (2010) also mentioned some nonprofit organizations are developing innovative scheduling and compensation structures to support work-life balance and to ensure women can have a personal life as well as leadership opportunities. Given the significant commitment individuals have to their work and life, work-family policies require more frequent and systematic assessment to reflect needs and highlight support.

Implications for Professional Development and Education

Embedded in the personal stories shared by the women executives are nuggets of wisdom that have been shared throughout this book. Leadership development and participation require leaders to be responsible for continually developing themselves and their successors in the leadership pipeline. Therefore, we asked women executives directly about what advice they would provide to young professionals who are interested in careers in leadership. Their answers addressed several aspects, including what young professionals of potential should be doing now to prepare themselves for career advancement, what mistakes they should avoid, and what training opportunities they should seize. Particularly, a number of strategies have been mentioned.

One of the most common ones was that the young women should consider joining professional associations and volunteer for leadership roles within those organizations. Several of the women discussed experiences serving in leadership roles with organizations such as PRSA chapters and the Junior League. It is also critical for young professionals to volunteer to take on additional responsibilities inside their organizations as a form of professional development. As a Latina female executive who previously worked as a vice president of marketing and communications advised, "Seek out opportunities, being proactive. Don't just wait to get an assignment. Don't just wait to hear back from someone. Pick up the phone. Take someone to lunch. Grab coffee with someone. Be proactive. Be the go-getter."

Other advice focused on working hard and "earning your stripes" by succeeding in public relations initiatives over time. Once young professionals are ready to advance, they need to advocate for themselves and have confidence. Young professionals also should be voracious readers whether it involves self-study to enhance their business literacy or keep up with current events and industry trends. Reading does not only increase their knowledge, but as the women executives pointed out it gives them something intelligent to speak about when networking. Networking has proved effective in helping provide valuable information, visibility and support through the in-circle influence. As suggested by women executives, broadening networking opens up opportunities for young professionals of potential.

Much of the advice regarding mistakes to avoid focused on lack of professionalism including social media posts, workplace etiquette, and sloppy work. They also stressed a few mistakes related to ineffective management of emotional intelligence, including being arrogant or "know it all," being impatient, or pushing too hard too soon. They also suggested that young professionals should be receptive to criticism and feedback and try to learn from mistakes. It's equally important for young professionals to learn to focus on group not just personal success and teamwork. As a communications director working in a government organization explained, "In terms of mistakes, I would say trying to do it on your own is going to be hard ... So is trying to be a singular achiever. You have to build teamwork."

Young women also need to seek out professional development opportunities whether that be training offered through their workplace, webinars and conferences offered by professional associations, and formal education programs such as accreditation (APR) or a master's degree. Mentors and sponsors/advocates can provide counsel on which training opportunities to pursue at various points in a protégé's career development. Budget and time will always be constraints. Regarding time, some women executives report purposely setting aside and protecting time on their calendars for professional development. Regarding budget limitations, some women actually save money to invest it in their own professional development.

As the profession is in a time of rapid change and development, expectations on communication leaders' skill sets, competence and change management are evolving intensively. Conversations with women executives also confirmed that public relations education programs at the university level require more components on leadership learning and experiences. As addressed in Erzikova and Berger's 2012 research on leadership education in public relations curriculum, educators play a critical role in helping students develop leadership awareness and skills by developing critical-thinking skills, focusing on ethical problem solving, and modeling leadership behaviors in their classes. Berger and Meng (2014) also suggested that public relations education could be designed around the vision that "sees every student as a potential leader who requires essential leadership skills" (p. 306). In this way, public relations education could offer support in cultivating leadership learning and preparedness around the leadership dimensions as developed by Meng and Berger (2013): self-dynamics, ethical orientation, team collaboration, relationship building, strategic decision-making capability, and communication knowledge and management capability, with the goal of building a culture for communication leadership within the organization.

Such advice is consistent with the recommendations suggested in the Commission on Public Relations Education 2017 Report (2018), *Fast Forward: Foundations and Future State. Educators and Practitioners.* The report highlights trends and changes in public relations education that emerged between 2006 and 2016 and addresses that the joint efforts from industry and academy, practitioners and educators are needed in order to build a diverse "school-to-workplace pipeline" (p. 144). The report suggests that educators and practitioners shall collaborate to enhance students' extra-curricular and co-curricular involvement "with a particular focus on leadership skills" (Commission on Public Relations Education 2017 Report, 2018, p. 20). Such leadership involvement could be reflected through universities' PRSSA chapters, student-run agencies, internship work, or volunteer work with other campus and community organizations. Educators shall also consider using and integrating rich resources on leadership and ethics available at The Plank Center for Leadership in Public Relations at the University of Alabama and The Arthur W. Page Center for Integrity in Public Communication at Penn State University such as video interviews, research whitepapers, recorded webinars, ethics training models, and other materials to enrich the learning and engagement in many public relations classes.

Future Research Direction

The project of *PR Women with Influence* extends our pioneering scholars' research on gender issues in public relations by providing new perspectives on leadership development, leadership participation and the discussion of ethical leadership to elevate the ethical advocacy functions of public relations professionals. Our research has provided a wide range of information and discussion on situational barriers in female professionals' leadership advancement, strategies used to build and exert influence, female professionals' leadership participation opportunities, their constant battle in balancing work and family, as well as current executives' insights about women's future leadership development journey. We also admit some weaknesses reflected in the study, which can further inform future research to continue enriching our knowledge and advancing practice in this area.

One of the potential areas for future study is to add the global perspective to enrich the multicultural sensitivity in leadership development. We have dedicated our research efforts through this particular project to include national samples in the United States, in both qualitative and quantitative approaches. Despite the rich findings, we fully admit the critical need in the near future to expand our knowledge on women and leadership in the public relations industry from a global perspective. When looking at the bigger picture of women in leadership worldwide, we can locate research in management confirming the disheartening facts such as 1) Women have slowly increased their participation rates in managerial and professional jobs in most countries, 2) Women generally have made progress at lower-management positions but are still underrepresented at senior levels of management; 3) Women in all countries still get paid less than men, even when working in the same jobs; 4) Gender segregation is still prevalent with the fact that more men are working in engineering, construction, and science while more women are working in human resources, marketing, and public relations; and 5) There is still a dearth of statistics and research on certain minority groups (e.g. Black and other minority ethnic groups, disabled women managers, single-parent women managers) within the female management positions (Davidson & Burke, 2016).

The need is strong and the response should be quick in addressing this issue globally. As the Commission and Public Relations Education 2017 Report addresses, "Public relations students entering global society professionally should have developed an acute curiosity antenna, in order to be receptive to and comfortable with the world's many variations of thought, action and effect" (p. 150). Therefore, future research is needed to expand our research to include other cultural perspectives to establish universal support. When diversity and inclusion and multicultural sensitivity are inextricably related, future research shall carry the force to address the challenge and integrate cultural perspectives that emphasize multicultural insights.

One area that merits additional study is the issue of intersectionality faced by women of color who reported that they had difficulty identifying if the barriers they face to career advancement were based on their gender or race or both. While some scholars have explored these issues (e.g. Golombisky, 2015; Vardeman-Winter & Tindall, 2010), more research is merited to identify additional barriers that are specific to women of color. For example, in our study, we learned that Latina women are sometimes held back due to the leadership pipeline issue or the lack of younger women entering the profession who are able to assume tactical responsibilities such as translating communication materials. As advocated by intersectionality scholars (Golombisky, 2015; Vardeman-Winter & Tindall, 2010), public relations functions operate beyond visible differences and should contribute to the understanding of non-visible differences. Therefore, future research could explore barriers faced by women in specific ethnic groups such as African Americans, Latinos, or Asian Americans, as well as other minority groups that represent differences and entail a wide variety of benefits and leadership involvement.

Another area that deserves additional attention is that of sponsors as related to mentorship. Issues that can be explored include what motivates more senior executives to "sponsor" or advocate for young professionals and what can organizations do to encourage more senior executives to identify and advocate for younger employees in their organizations and especially to advocate for women and employees of color who are less likely to benefit from sponsorship.

Last but not least, we call for more research on ethical leadership. It is quite concerning that our research found employees lower in the hierarchy are rating their senior executives low in the area of ethical leadership. The reason why this issue is of concern is from the perspective of role modeling. Moral or ethical managers need to set the tone for ethical behavior by both talking about the importance of ethics and core values and living it out to foster an ethical culture. It appears there are some communication issues as those closest to these executives rate them higher on ethical leadership suggesting that distance from the top is likely the issue rather than actual behaviors. Studies should be conducted with exemplars or organizations where employees rate their senior executives high on ethical leadership to identify best practices that can be implemented to cultivate a healthy and ethical culture.

Conclusion

All of these key themes summarized from and inspired by findings in our research deserve more attention from both the professional and academic communities. The existence of situational barriers and inequalities between men and women in the labor market explains many of the difficulties women in public relations face in pushing against the glass ceiling. Supporting women in public relations in leadership advancement shall be pushed to the forefront of practice and research. We hope our research inspires more scholars and educators in public relations to integrate diversity and leadership into their own research, practice, and teaching. We also hope that the sub-topics we explored and discussed in this book help create a new research agenda to advance the theory of diversity and leadership in public relations. All of these initiatives deserve more attention from the industry and the academy. To make that possible, we need more knowledge about what works in the world. We are at the forefront of teaching and research on diversity, equity, inclusion, and leadership. Supporting women and other minority groups' leadership advancement in the public relations industry and developing leadership participative opportunities for them build the foundation for this research and we hope that our efforts will bring united collaborations from multiple entities to push for real change for the profession, both nationally and globally.

References

Adams, R. B., & Ferreira, D. (2009). Women in the boardroom and their impact on governance and performance. *Journal of Financial Economics, 94*(2), 291–309.

Aldoory, L., & Toth, E. (2004). Leadership and gender in public relations: Perceived effectiveness of transformational and transactional leadership styles. *Journal of Public Relations Research, 16*, 157–183.

Aldoory, L., Jiang, H., Toth, E. L., & Sha, B. L. (2008). Is it still just a women's issue? A study of work-life balance among men and women in public relations. *Public Relations Journal, 2*(4), 1–20.

Berger, B. K., & Meng, J. (2014). *Public relations leaders as sensemakers: A global study of leadership in public relations and communication management.* New York: Routledge.

Catalyst. (1999). *Women of color in corporate management: Opportunities and barriers.* New York: Catalyst.

Catalyst. (2003). *Women in U.S. corporate leadership.* New York: Catalyst.

Catalyst. (2004). *Women and men in the U.S. corporate leadership: Same workplace, different realities?* New York: Catalyst.

Catalyst. (2007). *The double blind dilemma for women in leadership: Damned if you do; doomed if you don't.* New York: Catalyst.

Commission on Public Relations Education 2017 Report. (2018). *Fast forward: Foundations and future state. Educators and Practitioners.* Retrieved from http://www.commissionpred. org/commission-reports/fast-forward-foundations-future-state-educators-practitioners/ on September 17, 2019.

Davidson, M. J., & Burke, R. J. (Eds.). (2016). *Women in management worldwide: Progress and prospects* (2nd Ed.). New York: Routledge.

Ely, R. J., & Rhode, D. L. (2010). Women and leadership. In Nitin Nohria & Rakesh Khurana (Eds.), *Handbook of leadership theory and practice* (pp. 377–410). Boston, MA: Harvard Business Press.

Ely, R. J., & Thomas, D. A. (2001). Cultural diversity at work: The effects of diversity perspectives on work group processes and outcomes. *Administrative Science Quarterly, 46*(2), 229–273.

Erzikova, E., & Berger, B. K. (2012). Leadership education in the public relations curriculum: Reality, opportunities, and benefits. *Public Relations Journal, 6*(3), 1–24.

Francoeur, C., Labelle, R., & Sinclair-Desgagné, B. (2008). Gender diversity in corporate governance and top management. *Journal of Business Ethics, 81*(1), 83–95.

Golombisky, K. (2015). Renewing the commitments of feminist public relations theory from velvet ghetto to social justice. *Journal of Public Relations Research, 27*(5), 389–415.

Greene, A., & Kirton, G. (2011). Diversity management meets downsizing: The case of a government department. *Employee Relations, 33*, 22–39.

Grunig, L. A., Toth, E. L., & Hon, L. C. (2001). *Women in public relations: How gender influences practice.* New York: The Guilford Press.

Herdman, A. O., & McMillan-Capehart, A. (2010). Establishing a diversity program is not enough: Exploring the determinants of diversity climate. *Journal of Business and Psychology, 25*, 39–53.

Kandola, R., & Fullerton, J. (1994). Diversity: More than just an empty slogan. *Personnel Management (London), 26*(4), 46.

Kirton, G., & Greene, A. M. (2005). *The dynamics of managing diversity: A critical approach* (2nd Ed.), Oxford: Elsevier.

McGinn, D. (2006, September 24). Getting back on track. *Newsweek.* Retrieved from https://www.newsweek.com/getting-back-track-109529 on Oct. 2, 2019.

Meng, J., & Berger, B. K. (2013). An integrated model of excellent leadership in public relations: Dimensions, measurement, and validation. *Journal of Public Relations Research, 25*(2), 141–167.

Meng, J., & Berger, B. K. (2018). Maximizing the potential of millennial communication professionals in the workplace: A talent management approach in the field of strategic communication. *International Journal of Strategic Communication, 12*(5), 507–525.

Meyerson, D. E., Ely, R., & Wernick, L. (2007). Disrupting gender, revising leadership. In D. Rhode & B. Kellerman (Eds.), *Women and leadership: The state of play and strategies for change* (pp. 453–473). San Francisco: Jossey-Bass.

Mor Barak, M. E. (2011). *Managing diversity: Toward a globally inclusive workplace* (2nd Ed.), Los Angeles, CA: SAGE.

Place, K. R., & Vardeman-Winter, J. (2018). Where are the women? An examination of research on women and leadership in public relations. *Public Relations Review, 44*(1), 165–173.

Powell, G. N. (2018). *Women and men in management* (5th Ed.), Thousand Oaks, CA: Sage Publications.

Thomas, R. R. (1990). From affirmative action to affirming diversity. *Harvard Business Review, 68*, 107–118.

Toth, E. L., & Cline, C. G. (1991). Public relations practitioner attitudes toward gender issues: A benchmark study. *Public Relations Review, 17*(2), 161–174.

Vardeman-Winter, J., & Place, K. (2017). Still a lily-white field of women: The state of workforce diversity in public relations practice and research. *Public Relations Review, 43*, 326–336.

Vardeman-Winter, J., & Tindall, N. (2010). Toward an intersectional theory of public relations. In R. L. Heath (Ed.), *Handbook of public relations* (2nd ed., pp. 223–235). Thousand Oaks, CA: Sage.

Wentling, M. R. (2003). The career development and aspirations of women in middle management–revisited. *Women in Management Review, 18*(6), 311–324.

Zenger, J., & Folkman, J. (2019, June 25). Research: Women score higher than men in most leadership skills. Blog post. *Harvard Business Review*. Retrieved from https://hbr.org/2019/06/research-women-score-higher-than-men-in-most-leadership-skills on Oct. 3, 2019.

Index

A

advocates 6, 181, 182, 187, 206
Aldoory, L. 14, 130–1
Arthur W. Page Center for Integrity in
    Communication, The 25, 207
Arthur W. Page Society 26, 160, 170
authentic leadership 87, 201
Avolio, B. J. 87

B

Baby Boomers 16
Baker, S. 158
Bandura, A. 63, 190
Barnes, A. 135, 164
Berger, B. K. 9, 13, 64, 97, 98, 102, 134,
    139, 203, 207
Boles, J. S. 108
Borden, S. L. 160
boundary spanning 130, 163, 164

Bowen, S. A. 133
Brown, M. E. 64, 75, 157
building-a-dialogue strategy 70

C

career advancement xv, 65–9, 141,
    178, 180, 189, 197, 198, 202, 203,
    206, 209
career development 5, 18, 103, 109, 119,
    124, 178, 181, 189, 192, 197, 201
Catalyst 43, 45, 114–15, 123, 197
challenges, as female executive in public
    relations 138–44
Chitkara, A. 53
Commission on Public Relations Education
    2017 Report on Undergraduate
    Education (CPRE)
    *Fast Forward: Foundations and Future
        State. Educators and Practitioners* xvii,
        160–1, 207–209

communication 8
  culture for 11
  executives, leadership performance
    of 97–102
  internal 11, 14, 141, 164
  job responsibilities in 32
  knowledge management capabilities 13,
    97, 99–101, 207
  transparency in 158
Conger, J. A. 87
contingency approaches, in public relations
  leadership 11–12
coping strategy 16–18, 39, 108, 113–19,
  123, 152, 153, 174–8, 191, 198
Cose, E. 145
Crenshaw, K. 151
critical-thinking skills 207

D

data analysis 26–7
demographic similarity 158
diversity-and-inclusion management 203–
  4
diversity, equity, and inclusion (DE&I) 10,
  80, 204
Dodd, M. 132
double standards in domestic roles and
  professional demands 47, 200
Dozier, D. M. 10–11, 180
dual-career couples 107–8
Duhachek, A. 115–17

E

ecosystem, building 197–210
education, implications of 205–8
ELS *see* Ethical Leadership Scale (ELS)
Ely, R. J. 111, 205
Erzikova, E. 189, 207
ethical conduct, leadership role and 76–7

ethical conscience 13, 162–4
ethical decision-making 161
ethical leadership 13–14, 63–81
  definition of 64
  demographics of 76–81
  moral manager aspect of 64, 75
  organizational types and 79
  principled behaviors of 73–6
  race and 79–81
  reporting level and 77–9
Ethical Leadership Scale (ELS) 75
ethical orientation 4, 13, 97, 98–100,
  102, 207
ethics counsel
  preferred influence strategies for 168
  women in 157–71
ethics counseling xvi, xvii, 8, 14, 16, 18,
  39, 63–5, 69, 70, 81, 164, 165, 198,
  64, 72–4
ethics, definition of 161
ethnic insider 147
excellence 10–11
  characteristics of 10
external mentors 179–86

F

feminist scholarship, in public relations
  research 5–7, 11, 14
Fitzpatrick, K. 7
flex-work programs 205
Folkman, J. 3–4
future research direction 208–10

G

gender
  diversity 200
  equality 199–201
  gender-related research 15
  inequalities 198

influence on public relations practice 5–6
issues in public relations 5
and leadership styles 14–17
and performativity 7
segregation 208
skewed gender representation, in top
    leadership 42–5
Gen Z 16
Golombisky, K. 7
Goodpaster, K. E. 162
Goodstein, J. D. 137
Gower, K. 139
Grunig, L. A. 5–6

H

Hartman, L. 157
Heyman, W. 139
Hon, L. C. 5–6
Hursthouse, R. 158

I

IABC Excellence Study 10
influence of female PR leader in public
    relations
    achievement 131–3
    barriers to 144–53
    meaning, defined 65–70
    in practice 133–8
    preferred strategies 134
    strategies to build and enact 69–72
    types of organizations 67
    women of color 67–8
    years of experience 69
instrumental support 176
interactive leadership 14
internal communication 11, 14, 141, 164
internal mentors 179–86
intersectionality 151, 209
intersectionality theory 6, 7

interviewed female professionals, sample
    profiles of 29, 30–1
IRB 26

J

Jiang, H. 151
job
    engagement 5, 18
    responsibilities, in communication 32
    satisfaction 5, 79, 103
    stress factors 5
Junior League 206

K

Kegan, R. 87–8
knowledge
    and leadership 9
    management capabilities 13, 97, 99–
        101, 207

L

Lahey, L. 87–8
Lauzen M. M. 180
leader development 86
leadership
    challenges xiv, xv, 7, 17, 18, 35, 198, 201
    competencies 3, 85, 88, 89, 201
    dimensions of 4, 5
    effectiveness 11, 102
    identity 197, 201
    interactive 14
    opportunities 8, 47, 94, 195, 197, 205
    public relations *see* public relations
        leadership
    readiness to provide 72–4
    roles of 35–7, 76–7
    skills 9, 11, 85, 207

styles 14–17
transformational 9, 14, 15
leadership development xv–xvii, 7, 8, 10,
    16–19, 39, 59, 69, 85–104, 127, 195,
    198–201, 204, 205, 208
    "being" dimension of 87
    definition of 86
    "doing" dimension of 87
    future improvement, projection for 95–7
    "knowing" dimension of 86–7
    and participation, relationship
        between 92–5
    resources for 88–92
    review on past efforts 95–7
leadership participation and development,
    relationship between 92–5
Len-Rios, M. E. 147
life–work conflict 109

M

MacIntyre, A. 160
management development 86
Martinelli, D. 189
Matt, B. F. 168
Matthews, J. B. 162
May, D. R. 166
McCall, M. W. Jr. 87
McCauley, C. D. 86
McDonald, G. 159
McMurrian, R. 109
Meng, J. 9, 13, 97, 98, 102, 139, 203, 207
mentoring 89, 119–21, 202–3
    relationship, stages of 188
"Mentor Match" program 122–3
mentors
    desired personal attributes of 186–7
    identification of 188–91
    as role models 190
    role of 178–9
    sources of finding 121–3
    types of 179–86
#MeToo movement 180

Millennials 16
Moberg, D. J. 63, 137, 158
moral courage 166
Moss, D. 133

N

national online survey of
    female professionals, in PR/
    communication 27–9
Neill, M. S. 135, 161–2, 164, 165,
    170, 190–1
neo-Aristotelian virtue ethics 158
Netemeyer, R. G. 108, 109
networking 89, 202–3, 206
Newman, A. J. 133
Nijhof, A. 159
North American Communication Monitor
    2018–2019 103, 108
Nye, J. S. 12

O

on-the-job training 88–90
organizational types
    and ethical leadership 79
    influence of female PR leader in public
        relations 67
    vs. gender of direct supervisor/
        manager 43
    vs. gender of the highest ranked
        communication leader 44

P

Pearson, Y. E. 162, 163–4
Petriglieri, J. 108
Pew Research Center 107, 112
    Current Population Survey analysis 108
    women and leadership survey (2015) 3
phronesis 163, 186

pigeonholing 146
Place, K. R. 15, 163
Plaisance, P. L. 163
Plank Center for Leadership in Public
    Relations, The 25, 41, 207
    Leadership Report Card studies 4,
    5, 98–100
Pompper, D. 147, 148
power relations 12
PR Leadership Report Card (2019) 108
professional and family responsibilities,
    balancing 107–24
    mentoring, role of 119–21
    mentors, sources of finding 121–3
    top-down communication
        support 204–5
    work–family conflict 108–14
        coping strategies to manage 114–19
professional development, implications
    of 205–8
protégés
    career development 207
    responsibilities of 187–8
PRovoke 4
PRSA *see* Public Relations Society of
    America (PRSA)
PR women in leadership 4–8
public relations leadership 8–17
    contingency approaches in 11–12
    definition of 9, 97
    gender-related research in 15
    global implications of 12–13
    as integrated process 12–13
    perspectives of 8–17
    power and 12
    principles of 10
    roles 8–17
    see also leadership
Public Relations Society of America 160
Public Relations Society of America
    (PRSA) 26, 170, 190, 206
    Code of Ethics 81, 159
    International Conference, Boston
        (2017) xv

"Mentor Match" program 122–3
Page Principles 159, 160

R

race
    as barriers to influence 144–53
    and ethical leadership 79–81
    and mentors 185
rational problem-solving process 11
Real, M. R. 180
Reber, B. H. 64, 134
Redmond, J. 170
relationship-building skills 13, 15
reporting level, and ethical leadership 77–9
research design and methods 25–9
    data analysis 26–7
    interviews 26
    national online survey of
        female professionals, in PR/
        communication 27–9
Rhode, D. L. 111, 205
role modeling behaviors 158
role theories 10–11
rule of three 169–70

S

Seabright, M. A. 137
self-dynamics 13, 97, 99, 100, 207
self-identity 87
self-perception 87
Shah, A. 44
Shahinpoor, N. 168
situational barriers to PR women's
    leadership advancement 41–59
    identification of 45–51
    impact of 51–6
    leaders' *vs.* non-leaders' perceptions
        on 48, 49
    projection of improvements in next three
        years 56–8

skewed gender representation, in top
leadership 42–5
situational theory of leadership 12
skewed gender representation, in top
leadership 42–5
social attitudes towards female
professionals 47, 200
social capital 131–2, 182
social justice 7
social learning theory 63
sponsors 69, 153, 181, 182, 187, 192, 206
St. John III, B. 162, 163–4
strategic decision making 9, 13, 97, 99,
101, 102, 134, 139, 207
styles of leadership 14–17
support network 173–92
surveyed female professionals, sample
profiles of 29–37

T

talent management 122, 123, 199–201, 203
Tam, S. Y. 180
team collaboration 13, 97, 98, 99, 101, 207
Thomas, R. R. 203
Tindall, N. 151
Toth, E. L. 5–6, 14
Trager, R. 170
transformational leadership 9, 14, 15
Trevino, L. K. 101, 157, 159
trust in the workplace 5

U

underrepresentation of women, in top
leadership 52–6
United States (U.S.)
Bureau of Labor Statistics 4

Census Bureau 143
history of public relations in 41
U.S. *see* United States (U.S.)

V

Van Velsor, E. 86
Vardeman-Winter, J. 15, 151

W

Warnaby, G. 133
Weaver, N. 190–1
women of color 209
as barrier to influence 152
as barrier to leadership
advancement 47–50
influence with strong opinions 67–8
work–family conflict 108–14
coping strategies to manage 114–19
working mothers 174
work–life conflict 109, 174–5, 204, 205
workplace structures, as barrier to
leadership advancement 45, 200

Y

years of tenure
as barrier to leadership
advancement 50–1
impact on interpretation of influence 69
and leadership performance 102

Z

Zenger, J. 3–4

AEJMC–PETER LANG SCHOLARSOURCING SERIES

Launched in 2014, Scholarsourcing is a joint book publishing venture of the Association for Education in Journalism and Mass Communication (AEJMC) and Peter Lang Publishing that has redefined how scholarly books are proposed, peer-reviewed, and approved for contract. An initiative of 2013–2014 AEJMC President Paula Poindexter, Scholarsourcing is based on the concept of crowdsourcing, with AEJMC members proposing books which are then voted on by the association's membership. Authors of top proposals are invited to write full book proposals that are then reviewed by the Scholarsourcing Series editorial board, with the goal of offering at least one book contract annually.

A very special thanks goes to all who have contributed to the success of Scholarsourcing. These include AEJMC Executive Director Jennifer McGill; Peter Lang Publishing, particularly editor Kathryn Harrison and founding editor Mary Savigar; Founding Series Editor Jane B. Singer; founding editorial board members Carolyn Bronstein, David Perlmutter, Paula Poindexter and Richard Waters; and the hundreds of AEJMC members who have contributed ideas and input, along with a rich supply of wonderful book proposals.

To order books, please contact our Customer Service Department at:

peterlang@presswarehouse.com (within the U.S.)
orders@peterlang.com (outside the U.S.)

Or browse online by series at www.peterlang.com